HER TURN

HER TURN

Why It's Time for Women to Lead in America

Vicki Donlan
with Helen French Graves

Westport, Connecticut
London

Library of Congress Cataloging-in-Publication Data

Donlan, Vicki, 1951–
Her turn : why it's time for women to lead in America / Vicki Donlan with Helen French Graves.

    p. cm.
   Includes bibliographical references and index.
   ISBN 978–0–275–99924–7 (alk. paper)
   1. Leadership in women—United States.   2. Leadership—United States.
3. Women in the professions—United States.   I. Graves, Helen French, 1950–   II. Title.
   HQ1421.D66   2007
   305.43′331710973—dc22   2007026083

British Library Cataloguing in Publication Data is available.

Library of Congress Catalog Card Number: 2007026083
ISBN-13: 978–0–275–99924–7

First published in 2007

Praeger Publishers, 88 Post Road West, Westport, CT 06881
An imprint of Greenwood Publishing Group, Inc.
www.praeger.com

Printed in the United States of America

The paper used in this book complies with the
Permanent Paper Standard issued by the National
Information Standards Organization (Z39.48–1984).

10 9 8 7 6 5 4 3 2

This book is dedicated to all the women and men, girls and boys, who have ever been told that they couldn't do something because_____(you fill in the blank). Regardless of your gender, your race, or a hundred other things that stereotype you, you can do and be everything you want to be. This book is a testament to that dream.

Every one of us is a gift—an individual gift with talents, skills, and abilities like no other. When we, as a society, don't take advantage of every individual's gifts, we lose.

This book is also dedicated to my parents, who gave me everything I needed to believe in myself, and then, most important, to my husband and son, Fran and David, who have been my biggest fans and cheerleaders throughout my business career. I have been blessed with a wonderful family. My parents nurtured me from the day I was born and let me believe that I was a valuable and important human being—someone who could make a positive impact on the world whether it was as a mother, wife, or business leader. My husband and son took pride in my work and joined me in my accomplishments to let me know that they are with me all the way.

Having cheerleaders in our lives, male, female, young, and old, is the most important ingredient any one of us can enjoy. It provides the foundation for self-confidence that is critical for moving us to the next level. These are the blessings of a good life, and I appreciate them every day.

Contents

Chapter 6 Women Entrepreneurs: The BIG Engine That Could and Does   77

The Workplace Revolution   85
Role Models   89
VCs, Angels, and Others   91
Just Imagine   94

Chapter 7 Legally Blonde—and Black, Brown, Red, and Gray   97

In-House Counsel   105
Here Come the Judge   107
A Proactive Restructuring   109
Just Imagine   111

Chapter 8 Women in Healthcare and the Sciences: Prescription for Change   113

The Sciences   119
The Business of Science   122
Women's Health   126
Women's Progress   128
Just Imagine   130

Chapter 9 Bias in Higher Education: The Firestorm   131

Tenure Track or Tenure Off-Track?   133
President Is Gender Neutral, Right?   138
Just Imagine   143

Chapter 10 Women and Nonprofits: Wage and Donation Gaps   145

Women's Contribution   149
The Second Career   151
Negotiating the Nonprofit Way   152
Women-and-Girls Programming   153
Her Part   155
Follow the Leaders   158
Writing the Check   160
Just Imagine   161

Chapter 11 When Women Rule: A Woman in the White House   163

Show Me the Money   167

Acknowledgments

We are grateful to all those who so freely gave of their time and opinions for this book. The future of women's ability to lead is in the hands of the thought leaders who were interviewed and/or who took the time to respond to our surveys and help us in general. Our thanks go alphabetically to the following:

Clinton Allen, Sharon Allen, Mara Aspinall, Suzanne Bates, Corinne Broderick, Candida Brush, Ann W. Caldwell, Jacqueline Cooke, Celia Couture, Nicole Cozier, Martha Crowninshield, Diane Danielson, Gail Deegan, Diana DeGette, Linda Denny, Geri Denterlein, Marsha Evans, Joseph Fanning, Marsha Firestone, Cathy Fleming, Alexandra Friedman, Mary Gegler, Sara Gould, Mary-Laura Greely, Sharon Hadary, Stephanie Hanbury-Brown, Myra Hart, Marian Heard, Swanee Hunt, Susan Ivey, Rosabeth Moss Kanter, Ilene Lang, Barbara Lee, Liz Levin, Margaret Marshall, Ellyn McColgan, Barbara J. McKenna, Evelyn Murphy, Gloria Nemerowicz, Nancy H. Nielsen, Annette O'Connor, Tom Peters, Donna Burns Phillips, Katherine E. Putnam, Lauren Stiller Rikleen, Barbara Rockett, Rhonda Rockett, Bill Samatis, Jeanne Shaheen, Lois Silverman, Diane Sutter, Ruth Sweetser, Marie Wilson, Toni Wolfman, and Ellen Zane.

We also wish to thank the thousands of inspirational women whom we have had the honor to profile in *Women's Business* over the past ten years, and especially those we have included in this book. Those thanks go to: Martha Coakley, Deborah Dunsire, Peg Feodoroff, Trish Karter, Teresa

Heinz Kerry, Janet Kraus, Christina Lampe-Onnerud, Lynn Margherio, Becky Minard, Judith Nitsch, Mary O'Donnell, Katherine O'Hara, Regina Pisa, Jean Qiu, Kathy Sherbrooke, Ruth Simmons, Denise Squillante, Sue Welch, and Valerie Yarashus.

We felt more empowered by every interview. Women are thriving across professions—business, law, medicine and the sciences, higher education, politics, and nonprofit—and are ready for greater challenges ahead. The ideas of where women are in America today from these influencers of tomorrow provide us all with the foundation for the work we need to do for a better country. We thank them all for their participation and words of wisdom.

Introduction

Exclusion from Leadership: When Fact Is Stranger Than Fiction

If you just picked this book up in the science fiction section of your bookstore, please go directly to the manager and shout, "It *Is* Time for Women to Lead in America. Display this book in your window and at the front of the store next to all the nonfiction bestsellers." As the customer, you, of course, are always right and the manager will comply. That "comply" part is the science fiction of my proposal because so few people are thinking about the importance of women's leadership today.

I think about it all of the time.

Every morning I get up, make a cup a coffee, and read two or three newspapers. Yes, I still read newspapers. I have been doing this during my entire business career. I'm looking for leads, looking for ideas, looking for people to reach out to, and, most important, I'm educating myself on what's happening locally and in the world.

What amazes me, thirty years after I started this practice, is that there are still so few women mentioned, profiled, quoted, or in any way visible in the newspaper—and this phenomenon stretches across all professions. What I'd like to see in the media are the role models who provide us the full scope of what we can be or hope to be. Male or female, we are given an opportunity to view the world through our own rose-colored glasses and decide who is relevant to the path we choose to take for our career, family, and overall lifestyle. But for half of the population, the female half, the role models aren't there.

Let me assure you that this book is not a radical feminist exposé or a rant on how women can do it all and men should become extinct. Not at all! Unlike other books on women's leadership, this book is for women *and* men. Why? Because our country needs the talents and skills of all who want to contribute to making sure America remains the world leader through the twenty-first century. For this to happen, both sexes are required to participate in the transformation of a nation that is hovering on crisis because half of the population is not fully represented in top leadership positions.

This book makes the case that America has the greatest power of all industrial nations, able to draw on the education and capabilities of all its inhabitants, and yet it seems stuck in reverse. What's more, women aren't pulling together and wielding their strength. Women must understand what their power is, how to work together to use it, and why it's time to stop the whining and, instead, to take control. We need a change in our corporations, our medical institutions, our universities, our political representation, our social programs, our home environments, and our global relations—and women are ready for the challenge of change.

When I started my newspaper, *Women's Business*, it was to provide visibility for women in business and the professions. I compare the old adage, "If a tree falls in the forest and no one hears it, does it really exist?" to, "If we don't see successful women in business or in the professions in the media, do they really exist?" The answer is *yes*. Absolutely, *yes*; they exist in numbers too big to be ignored. Ten years after our first issue, *Women's Business* has profiled or showcased more than three thousand women in nine states, and we have many, many more stories to tell. But my newspaper is not your typical newspaper. Women need visibility, and they need to see the resolve of the complex issues that thwart their rise to leadership addressed front and center. Leadership is their destination and yet the journey continues.

As a matter of fact, the journey has gotten bumpier in the last few years as what appears to be an array of choices for women has obscured the obstacles that still exist, whether when navigating a path to the corner office, or when raising money to start a business or political campaign, or when simply taking time off for family and losing pace with career and salary opportunities regardless of the sector in which they work. These obstacles have been illusive to men and to the young women just starting their careers, but in time these same barriers will raise their ugly heads—for the young women; that is—unless things change.

Men have had their turn. Now it's women's turn to step up. It's just time. Women are losing ground every year. Financially, according to Evelyn Murphy's book, *Getting Even: Why Women Don't Get Paid Like Men—And What to Do About It*, women are losing from $700,000 to more than $2 million in their lifetime by not taking control over their compensation packages. The wage gap affects men as well as women. As the AFL-CIO declares on its Web site, "Equal pay is about basic justice and fairness and basic family economics. More wives and mothers work for pay than ever before, and they are working more. Their earnings are essential to family support. Pay discrimination costs women a lot but it robs husbands and families, too." I couldn't say it better.

The AFL-CIO's 2004 "Ask a Working Woman Survey" showed that 62 percent of their working women provided half or more of their family's income. Yet, 25 percent of them said they were not earning equal pay. So when I say this should matter to men just as much as to women, the numbers back me up. The men in these families are just as much on the losing end as the women. The AFL-CIO also found that men have another stake in equal pay. Those men in occupations largely held by women, such as clerical and sales work, receive lower pay because of discrimination against women. Equal pay for equal work in these circumstances means a pay raise for men, too.

Two years later, the 2006 survey reported no improvement of concerns, with 97 percent of working women, across age and race lines, worried about the rising costs of healthcare, job exporting, higher education costs, and lack of retirement benefits. The greatest outrage stated was the continued increase of pay and retirement packages for CEOs while workers' compensation was frozen or cut.

At the other end of the spectrum, Catalyst, the women's business research and advisory organization, reports that it will take women forty-seven years to catch up with men in populating the senior executive suite in *Fortune* 500 companies.[1] Who has that kind of time? That's longer than a career's lifespan if sixty-five is the typical retirement age. No wonder women are dropping out of corporate America—the very place where the nation's eyes do follow its leadership, the very place where a CEO's name is recognized coast to coast, the very place where the corner office rarely sees a woman behind this very important desk. And to corporate America's detriment, if she doesn't see a path to the executive suite in her future, she will continue to reach instead for the closest door to map her own course. Human capital, particularly female talent, is a cost factor that corporate America cannot continue to ignore.

Nor can corporate America afford to ignore the boardroom, where the statistics are even worse. Here, women will wait seventy-three years for parity. "So what?" you might ask. This is why I care. The decisions made in the boardroom affect what you and I can buy, and make or break the stock market investments we make.

Here's more to fuel my argument for women at the top of our nation's major corporations. Eighty-five percent of the purchasers of their products and services are women. Shouldn't these boards want to understand their customers' perspective, and pronto? Of course they should and, in their marketing analysis, they do. Yet few realize it's imperative to include the majority of their customers—women—on their boards. If they did, they'd be even more successful. As we note later, there are a number of studies pointing to this very important fact—important, if your compensation is based on your company's profit margin—that the most profitable publicly traded companies are those with female directors.

Business, of course, is not the only guilty party in the gender equation. In politics, women are not encouraged to run as often as they should because the question of "how much money she can raise?" supersedes the importance of her skills. Political data shows, however, that when women do run, they win, particularly when running for local office.[2]

In healthcare and the sciences, while women account for more than half the graduates at U.S. medical schools, they are not yet well-represented in the upper echelons of their profession.

In the legal world, record numbers of women are entering law schools, but the current organizational structure of American law firms creates a significant barrier to becoming a partner. Tenure puts a disproportionate number of women compared to men off-track in higher education, where other obstacles as well contribute to their dwindling numbers on the path to a college or university presidency.

And in the nonprofit world, women are moving from their traditional volunteer activities into paid leadership positions, but their pay does not yet match that of their male counterparts. This same type of pay gap affects not just women's bank balances but also where our philanthropic dollars and resources go.

The challenges for women in attaining leadership across the board are so great, so weighty, so difficult—and yet there are women in every sector every single day overcoming these challenges. Take small business, for example, where women are flexing their leadership muscle, whether they're leaving corporate America or simply are compelled to start and grow their own companies. Women currently start two out of every three new businesses in this country, making them a large part of the small business engine that keeps our economy moving. In fact, the White House designates a week each year to honor small businesses for doing their part, it's that important. What's more, once started, women-owned businesses are more likely to be in business at the crucial make-or-break five-year mark and are less likely to be in debt, according to the Center for Women's Business Research. Walk down any main street of any town in America, and you'll find that half of all businesses are women-owned.

Women's representation in small business is a telling example of the leadership qualities women bring to our country and to the world. It's the same strength women bring to law, to politics, to medicine and the sciences, to higher education, and to the nonprofit world. In each of these professions, there are examples of women who have not been deterred by the history of obstacles standing in their way for success. More and more, they're breaking down barriers to get the education necessary to compete equally in law, medicine, and higher education, and knocking on doors, and asking for support in politics and nonprofit.

Women have a long history for the willingness to tough it out whether or not the structure fits their needs. Even the isolation that comes with being the first does not keep most women from trying and giving it their all. And yet women are still not equally represented in leadership positions. Our country, based on laws, must have the perspective of women at every level in politics to consider adequately all sides of every issue presented, guaranteeing our right to full representation.

And in the sciences and education, women have not been afraid to pursue knowledge at any cost in order to practice their passion for discovery and learning. As volunteers, women were the first in America to nurture and assist with the needs in war and in peacetime and will continue to be part of finding the solutions for those with less.

Don't get the impression, however, that I'm letting women off the hook. Characterized as risk-averse, they're more likely to say, "I have to know more," "I don't know if I can," "I'm not ready yet," whereas men generally tend to jump right in. Look at any woman who is at the top, and you'll see what can happen once women realize they're skilled, capable, and ready.

As a woman who started her own business, I can tell you the risk and reward of breaking out of the mold is well worth it. I have been told that few can keep up with me. My standards are too high. I work too hard. My goals are too lofty. The truth is, I am excited about what I do. I feel passion for my work and will do whatever I can to succeed. I see where I want to go and will move mountains to get there. Do I believe that I am the exception? Absolutely not! I know hundreds of thousands of women who have a picture of a goal in their heads and will do whatever it takes to turn that picture into reality. I have counseled many women over the years on how to get their businesses off the ground. Many of the women I mention in this book have built businesses much larger than my own.

And, as you'll see, the same passion and drive and vision do play in the *Fortune* 500, at the law firm, in Congress, in the teaching hospital, and in the universities that have the first shot at shaping our future leaders. But these women are the exception, not the rule, when there's no reason women can't and shouldn't rule.

The fact is, since women represent half of the country's talent pool, it doesn't have to be this way. What women have not learned is how to work together. There is power in numbers. Women have the numbers not only to compete, but also to lead. If women don't take this opportunity now, they'll keep losing ground because, by taking themselves out of the pipeline, they lose the connections that are necessary for leadership positions in every area in which they seek advancement.

So, if now is not the time for women to take the lead, then, when? There needs to be a sea change. We can't wait forty-seven years or seventy-three years for what can and should happen today. We must make it clear to the next generation of both men and women that by not making equality of the sexes a priority now, America jeopardizes the strength of its position as the leader of the free world.

We need to fill the pipelines with women to reflect proportionally their percentage of the population and then promote them, not just leaving them to languish. If we continue the momentum that has women populating in good number the entry and middle levels of nearly every facet of the economy to the next level—leadership—I firmly believe we'd see a dramatic change in the fortunes of this country. As we discuss throughout this book, with women taking the lead, priorities will change. The next generation in this country and around the world will take on greater meaning and importance. Women will see to it that human rights are a priority at home and abroad.

The facts in this book speak for themselves. My opinions are based on my more than fifty years of living life as a woman, experiencing the ups and downs of being a businesswoman, and interviewing legions of other women from all walks of life. I sent out surveys and interviewed more than seventy people, mostly women, but also some men. The interviews I've included in this book are the opinions of the brave people who held nothing back, knowing that their honesty will help all women take "one small step for (wo)man and one giant leap for (wo)mankind." When you find a quotation without a citation in the book, it came from my personal research. The other quotes came from the pages of newspapers and magazines across the country and around the world. You see, I am not the only one focusing attention on the progress of women's leadership. Yet, I believe this book takes the subject one crucial step further by spotlighting the urgency.

So please, take that step today. Take this book to the bookstore manager and demand that *Her Turn: Why It's Time for Women to Lead in America* join every other important book in the window and on the Must Have shelf. And then take this book home to read. You won't be sorry you did. Instead, you'll be glad that finally there's a call-to-action for women and men in America.

CHAPTER 1

The New "Problem That Has No Name"

"The problem that has no name—which is simply the fact that American women are kept from growing to their full human capacities—is taking a far greater toll on the physical and mental health of our country than any known disease."

—Betty Friedan

It was Betty Friedan in 1963 who shocked the country with her book, *The Feminine Mystique*, by labeling the malaise women were feeling at the time as "the problem that has no name." Now, more than forty years later, it's men with the malaise.

It was while I was talking about the underlying concept of this book that I realized the evolution of this new problem without a name. When explaining to men that I was writing around the questions, "What's holding women back?" "Why has the progress for women in business and the professions and politics been so slow?" and "Are women their own worst enemies?" I'd get a polite nod. But when told that the title of the book was *HER TURN: Why It's Time for Women to Lead in America*, these same men overwhelmingly responded, "What about the children?" Not once did I hear that women aren't ready or women don't have the strength, intelligence, passion, determination, or aptitude needed to lead. No, the only response was, "What about the children?" As a modern workingwoman and mother, I did my best to hold my tongue and my sarcasm and responded instead, "Don't children come from a man and a woman? Why do you believe that children are the responsibility of the woman?" This response immediately evoked a puzzled look. I would then go on to explain that my belief for the need of greater participation by women in leadership positions in no way meant that I thought that the children should be abandoned. It is quite the contrary. We are at a crossroads in our society where men have the opportunity to take a greater part in the nurturing of their children and to share in the joys of parenting. This response again would generally meet with another quizzical expression, and then their question, "Don't you think women are born to be better nurturers than men?" Aha! The problem.

Rosabeth Moss Kanter, the Ernest L. Arbuckle Professor of Business Administration at Harvard Business School and the author of sixteen books, answers the problem with no name and men's worry over who's going to take care of the children this way: "Well, why don't *they*? It's not who's going to take care of the children, really. I think we have just not solved the way family life intersects with work life in the United States, especially compared to the Nordic countries. We don't believe in early childhood education, and, as many political candidates say, we should have after-school, extended school day and not just day care—all of which would be really good for this country and the kids and society and the future—but somehow we don't do it."

You might say there is nothing new in almost all men believing that women are better at raising children. And, you'd have a point. What is important here is that in the last thirty or more years, women have earned their way into the corner office, into the boardroom, into the halls of justice, and are now vying for the people's house—The White House—and more, and yet they have made no progress as being seen less involved in the home.

Let me put it another way. Women have been successful at proving that they can do just about any job a man can do and have often deserved to lead the team in the line of work. What women have not been successful in doing and, perhaps, can even accept some of the blame for, is not finding a way to demonstrate that men have the ability and most likely even the passion for childrearing.

"For women to succeed and be treated equally, the major change that now has to happen is with men and their careers," says Mara Aspinall, president of the $240 million Genetics division at Genzyme. "Men need to be allowed to think about their own family life balance."

Aspinall and her husband are a prime example of this. He took a sabbatical to care for their newborn second son while she returned to work twelve days after giving birth. "It was an ideal time for him to take a sabbatical. While his organization was very supportive, it took a longer time for others to appreciate a dad as the primary caregiver," she says. "My colleagues had a very tough time with my returning so quickly. One woman came into my office, closed the door and asked if the baby was still in the hospital—because she could think of no other explanation of why I would be back in the office so soon. The reality is that there are lots of men who, if it were socially acceptable and financially possible, would prefer to be home with their family."

Aspinall is careful to point out that she returned to work because she wanted to, not because she feared for her job or her position in the company. Her position was secure and the company was generous with its leave policy. The choice was to take advantage of the workplace policies as they should be used—by men and women alike. It's when we turn lip service into spoken reality that we'll have true equity. Don't we all owe dads in this country this opportunity—and without any hesitation? The macho-man routine is old and out-of-date, or it should be. Women are nurturers and men are breadwinners—we see it all the time, and men, not only women, are on the losing end.

We are all well aware of the fateful, and some might say outright foolish, remarks former Harvard University president Lawrence Summers uttered at a conference regarding the lack of women's innate abilities in math and science. A media extravaganza ensued, eventually leading to Summers' resignation. Score some points for the media for underscoring women's value. Yet, night in and night out, television instills the image of Dad as a complete bumbling idiot when it comes to parenting. There is no outrage from men or women on the media's perspective on men's role as guardians. Men can work, lead companies, make money, and father children, yet they are incapable of making a bed, cooking a meal, or changing a diaper. It's interesting to note that in the TV sitcom, women are making it: They lead companies, make money—and juggle the man, who is incompetent when it comes to the household, along with the rest of the family. There are no points for women's value here, however. Every one of these stereotypes plays into why women are being held back. Kanter calls it "the lingering stereotype" and it's hampering progress in equality of the sexes.

"Top positions really require 150 percent of people's time, energy and loyalty, and not everybody wants to give that nor should they," Kanter says. "But the fact of family responsibility still haunts women because there's an assumption made by many people who are looking at candidates that the women will drop out, and that assumption might or might not be true." So, what does it take for a woman to overcome this lingering stereotype? "If you're an ordinary woman, you have to be extraordinary to beat an ordinary man," Kanter says. "It's still based on assumptions, but again, the more women who get up there [to the top], the more things will change."

And what about the single parent or the single person who doesn't have the luxury of a second breadwinner in the family? Shouldn't the system allow for their rise to their best potential regardless of gender? A January 2007 *New York Times* article[1] announced that for the first time in history, 51 percent of women are now living without a spouse. The data came from the 2005 Census, and compares to 35 percent of women living without a spouse in 1950 and 49 percent in 2000. The report dramatically changes the way we *must* model social and workplace procedures. The year 2005 was also the first time in our history when married couples became the minority in American households. Employers and the government *must* respond to this information with new ways of distributing benefits and shaping pathways to independence. Stephanie Coontz, director of Public Education for the Council on Contemporary Families, comments,[2] "This is yet another of the inexorable signs that there is no going back to a world where we can assume that marriage is the main institution that organizes people's lives. Most of these women will marry or have married. But on average, Americans now spend half of their adult lives outside of marriage."

The Census Bureau's 2005 American Community Survey showed that, among the more than 117 million women over the age of fifteen, only sixty-three million are married. The report also showed that the proportion of married people has been waning for decades, particularly among the younger age groups. So, although our culture is still in a marriage mindset, the statistics tell us that the reality is very different. This is neither the place nor the time to address why there are these changes to the institution of marriage. It is, however, the time to accept the change and demand that our society begin to live with the reality of a changing culture. We cannot expect women to take advantage of the education and opportunities available to them in 2007, the same opportunities that have always been available to men, and then tell them the children are their responsibility, too. It just doesn't make sense.

Our beliefs are so grounded in the fact that women are the ones who give birth that we forget to assess logically not only what might be best for the child but also for society. Allow me to provide you something else to think about here. Today, many gay and lesbian couples choose to have a family. In the case of a lesbian couple, a decision can be made as to which individual will bear the child. This very important decision is thoughtfully made for what is best for the family. Can you imagine if this were the opportunity for every couple in the country?

Of course, this choice is not available to most couples. But that does not mean that there is not a choice when it comes to childrearing. Every individual in this country is responsible for the next generation. They are the leaders of tomorrow and they are the reason we work so hard to make our world better. The most visible sign of this, and a moment I hope will remain vivid in our minds, was at the swearing in of our first woman Speaker of the House. At the opening ceremonies of Congress on January 4, 2007, congressmen and congresswomen brought their families to witness the momentous occasion. Nancy Pelosi was escorted into the House chamber by her grandchildren, and all the children were invited to the speaker's chair to touch the gavel. Senator Blanche Lincoln, a Democrat from Arkansas, said it best on *Good Morning America*,[3] "We're here to make this great country better for the next generation. ... [We need] reminders, every now and then, of what it is we're trying to do, and the choices that women make. They have to get results."

Having heard loud and clear that it's men's concern about the children that is holding women back, I decided to ask women for their thoughts. I surveyed 650 women with the following question: "What is holding women back from leading in America? In your profession? In all professions?" Within minutes, I received dozens of responses, all with a similar theme. The following comments speak clearly to what women see as the obstacles.

"I work in a very male dominated industry—particularly at the senior levels. Success often requires senior sponsorship, investment skill as well as growing the business (asset gathering). Often men have greater success due to broader networking opportunities (college/grad school classmates, golf, etc.) particularly as the majority of CIOs, CFOs, and treasurers are men. It is also a demanding field that can require long hours and travel, which means a good support system and understanding spouse. A friend who heads Credit Suisse's global equity team out of London said to me that almost all of the women she knows who have succeeded in this business either are not married, have no children, or have a spouse who is home or in a low-demanding profession—and I think it is the exception that you can have two people in demanding professions and still have a successful marriage/family without the demands taking a toll.

"I have fought at firms to allow flextime (not widely embraced in the investment profession) in order to retain and attract qualified individuals. At my firm, 20 percent of employees are on flextime (male and female), and it is hugely successful for them and the firm, but that is the exception, not the rule. For example, when I was offered a position at BlackRock, a firm at the time that was only sixteen years old, less than 20 percent of the investment professionals were women (although they boasted that they had nearly a fifty-fifty ratio—the women were all in operations, support, and marketing). They told me that they hire a mix of about fifty-fifty for the investment staff each year. When I asked why they couldn't retain them, BlackRock responded that they never asked why they left! Discussions with individuals in the know indicated that working on that team was like spending your days in a locker room—enough said."

> —Barbara J. McKenna, CFA, Principal, Longfellow Investment Management Co.

"Believing they belong at the top and helping each other the way men do."

> —Suzanne Bates, CEO, Bates Communications

"I believe the country is still fighting with the stereotypes of women and their place in the world. It is still difficult for a number of people, including other women, to trust that women are perfectly capable, willing, and courageous enough for the job. I also believe that women are not always given the exposure to leadership opportunities because of where they are in the hierarchy within companies. Thankfully this is changing, but slow to happen. In my case, having spent twenty-five-plus years in corporate America, I was always waiting for the opportunity to prove my value. I was sometimes turned down for promotion because I lacked experience, but when I sought the experience, I was often not given it. I also felt that the company looked out for displaced men more than displaced women. I have several examples of jobs being split in two so that a displaced man would have a place to fall—clearly this was convenience rather than need. I wish I had an equal number of examples when this happened on behalf of women."

> —Celia A. Couture, Founder, CC Consulting

"Women have a collaborative, non-hierarchical mindset. Women function best as peers and don't like following other women. Men are competitive and hierarchical. This means that when women lead, it is most successful when it is collaborative. Men don't usually respect this. A woman who listens to them rather than tells them what to do is their peer, not their boss."

> —Katherine E. Putnam, CEO, Packaging Machinery Company Inc.

"It's hard to pin down one thing, but if you looked at the big picture, I would say that it's a corporate work model that's outdated and needs re-engineering. In the past, when America has had to change the existing culture, it took the government to come in and make sweeping changes like child labor laws, the Nineteenth Amendment, Social Security, minimum wage laws, the GI Bill, and Title IX. Now, we have a conundrum. We are not a world leader when it comes to family policies in the workplace. And now it's America that needs some changing, yet they (current leaders) have neutralized the government from doing so. As long as families are put below the shareholder value and it still takes two incomes to be 'middle class,' it's the women who are going to suffer—because it is the women who do 100 percent of the child-birthing and still remain the vast majority of caretakers. As such, women are going to be forced to make choices between their work and their children and, even if they don't have children, they will be hit with a 'Potential Mommy Penalty.' Without incentives or penalties, why would those at the top of the ladder want to change anything? Believe me, if it were left to them, we'd still have children working forty-hour weeks."

—Diane Danielson, CEO, downtownwomensclub.com

"It takes a long time to reverse a pattern of domination, both culturally and actually, but it is happening slowly in our country. The media continues to play a big role in discouraging young people from seeing the arenas of leadership as wide open to all people. Leadership is not understood as the inclusive process it needs to be, but rather as lodged in one very powerful person. Leadership is often portrayed as an onerous, all-consuming, antagonistic, have-to-know-all-the-answers kind of thing, and many women don't see themselves filling that kind of role. To the extent that society defines leadership as more inclusive and complementary, more people will imagine themselves productively participating. Power and resources are still much intertwined in America, and women and people of color often have less access to resources upon which to build.

"In education, access remains a huge issue for people who are the first in their families to go to college and for lower-income people. In terms of leadership, there are some very visible women leading major educational institutions, but the numbers are still small. This remains true for intellectual leadership as well, where a man's voice, especially when affiliated with a prestigious institution, gets heard before a woman's voice that is saying the same thing."

—Gloria Nemerowicz, President, Pine Manor College

"The major elements holding women back right now from leading in America are the appropriate opportunities to do so. Life is so much about *chances*. Being in the *right* place at the *right* dawning moment. But many women are still not getting those chances. That is why they have not led America more. This is true in all professions, including law. To a lesser extent, there has been one other key element holding women back from such leadership positions, and ironically, this is one which women *do* control: the basic faith in oneself to master the hurdles that will enable the assumption of such leadership roles. Too many women are afraid they won't be able to pull it all together—the travel, the meetings, the dinners, the work—and still have any semblance of a personal life. So they don't even *try*. And it's so shortsighted. I always tell the women I work with, 'Yes, you can make this work. But you don't have to do it alone. Find the right help at home with your kids. Talk with your spouse about how to divide up some of the parenting responsibilities. Figure out how to make this work for you. Don't say that you *cannot* do this. Because you *can*. And you can do it really well! Believe in yourself and the rest will fall into place.' And I noticed some time ago now that the women who never seemed to have this fear of failing everyone and everything, who just grasp the opportunities as they come and figure it out as they go, are the very ones who have succeeded wildly. They never stopped to say: 'I cannot *possibly...*' or 'I don't know *how* to....'"

—Mary-Laura Greely, Member, Mintz Levin

"Confidence and the old boys' network. Let me explain. First, on confidence. Professional women today are harder working and, in many cases, better educated than their male counterparts. Yet, despite women's greater access to higher education, women are slower to find their voice in business and politics. Over and over again, I hear women say: 'It wasn't until I was in my forties that I really developed the skill and ability to throw my hat in the ring for leadership roles.' Women should take advantage of professional development courses, training in public speaking or graduate-level business courses (the high-testosterone kind) to gain the confidence necessary to make sure that they earn their leadership stripes in their thirties, rather than waiting until their forties or fifties. The old boy network may have gone underground (it's more subtle now) but it is not dead. Take a look at the day planner for any male senior executive: Unless he's dining with a female client, business prospect or potential lover, he's not socializing with his female colleagues. In my own profession, there are many women in public relations, but fewer female business owners. Key barriers include access to capital coupled with a reluctance to take risks."

—Geri Denterlein, CEO, Denterlein Worldwide

To sum up the comments from my survey, women are being held back by each other, by their different leadership style, and, most important, by a government that has not kept up with cultural changes and mandated the kinds of family leave programs that allow all available workers to succeed. And, it is also clear that women understand that men are still more comfortable with each other. Regardless of the push to get women into more senior positions, men will always look to fill an opening with one of their own. This is not because they discriminate against women, but because it is the decision with the least effort and potential long-term complications.

We have to be honest here and accept that men think more like other men than they do like women and they certainly believe they understand each other better. There is little comfort for men in trying to picture their second-in-command as a wife, mother, housekeeper, and business decision maker. The visual just doesn't connect for scores of men. I have been told many times over the years that men with stay-at-home wives have the most difficulty in seeing the long-term success potential for the women they employ. Those big-type CEOs who predictably make the little jokes about their wives "who shop 'til they drop" are clueless when it comes to how they should act around career women. Should we scream discrimination with this behavior? Of course not. Eventually these "knuckleheads," the only term I can comfortably use for these gentlemen, will learn that the business world has passed them by and they are seen as dinosaurs by most men and women.

This problem may be greatest on Wall Street. Over the past decade, most of the top brokerage firms have had sex discrimination cases brought against them. Clearly, a lawsuit was less expensive than doing the right thing. A *DiversityInc* 2007 article[4] spotlights the paltry amount of diversity in the pipeline. The lack of opportunity as well as pay inequities cause diverse individuals to leave the industry. And, for women particularly, the highly publicized sex discrimination cases that most of the major brokerage houses have undergone and succumbed to are reason enough to take their talents elsewhere. We shouldn't have to look alike to get ahead.

When looking at sheer demographics, the company that doesn't seriously begin to recruit and retain its women is going to be left in the dust like so many dinosaur bones. The Bureau of Labor Statistics reports that, by 2010, the number of available jobs is projected to increase by more than twenty-two million. The labor force, however, is only projected to increase by seventeen million. Every man and woman, with the capacity to do so, must be able to fill these positions. Retaining talent is not just good business sense, it is crucial for our economy. But back to how this will be possible. America once and for all must address priority Number One—our children and families.

For every step forward, the worry about the children brings women two steps back, or that's the potential unless, as Kanter points out, a woman is so extraordinary that she's able to supersede the prevailing mindset. Here's an example. When interviewed for this book, Diana DeGette, a Colorado Congresswoman who's Chief Deputy Whip and in her sixth term, shared her story of beginning her run for the seat made vacant by Pat Schroeder: "Schroeder was the icon of American politics and she had been there for twenty-four years. She had raised her kids in the job and yet some people said to me, 'Well, I'm not supporting you because we already had a woman,' and I said, 'Well, men have been succeeding each other for generations in Congress and it seemed to work out OK.' Then other people said, 'How will you raise your kids in this job?'" DeGette knew that Schroeder's children were the exactly same age as hers, two and six, when she had been elected to Congress. DeGette continues, "Twenty-four years later and they're still asking me the same questions they asked Pat." Given the success of so many women in politics today, isn't it time we stop asking the same "what about the children?" question in reference to women's leadership? As DeGette points out, her career in law that preceded her career in public service was just as demanding of her time.

I believe the answer is to give more women political power and that question, once and for all, can and will be resolved. Women will make their case: that they are up to the challenge of accomplishing any job a man can do. But we have hardly begun the work toward the emancipation of men. It's time to accept our collective advances and create a level playing field for men. At the moment, we can't be the best in the CEO office and the best at reading bedtime stories at the same time. This is a serious point of order for women if they're to come full circle into creating the life they want. They can't have career, home, and children all to themselves. Clearly, there is no balance in having it all, all by ourselves. Balance comes with being able to depend on the support of all of those around us. Our complex society is in need of a shakeup, something we will discuss at the end of this book in how we get there. But for now, let's agree to the understanding that our first priority is the next generation, without whom we have little reason to achieve grandeur. When all of us are found to be accountable for their success, we will truly be the role models for the world.

CHAPTER 2

Vive La Difference

"My grandfather once told me that there were two kinds of people: those who do the work and those who take the credit. He told me to try to be in the first group. There was much less competition."

—Indira Gandhi

Much has been written on how men and women are different. Much has been written about how men and women are alike. Right brain, left brain—women use one and men use the other. Women are better nurturers, caretakers, multitaskers, and jugglers of all that needs to get done. Men, on the other hand, work best when they focus on one thing at a time. Men are from Mars and women are from Venus, to coin a phrase. Men are hunters and women are gatherers. Men play sports, women play dress-up. Men want fast, sporty cars. Women want safety and comfort in their vehicles. Women are good at language and history and men excel at math and science. Women want a man with money and a good job. Men want a woman who is happy to stay home and cook and clean.

Does this sound right to you? Does it fit the world you live in? Can we stereotype people because of their gender? Race? Economic background? Religion? Physical disability? Accent? Ancestry? Sexual orientation? Size? Or age? When a former president of Harvard University even questions the innate abilities of men and women, his words bring on a firestorm of protests. And, for some, his words brought to memory the long-put-to-rest theory about the innate abilities of whites and people of color.

It might make for good reading, or better yet for good debate, but I've learned you can't judge a book by its cover. I guess that tells you what generation I come from. As much as I would like to assume that any one of the categories listed above could easily describe a person, I have learned that until you really get to know someone, nothing can tell you much about them. And, that is particularly true about men and women. The only thing we can all agree on is that most men and women are biologically different.

Now, this chapter is not meant to amuse you but to enlighten you because the moment you make a preconceived decision about someone because of one of the just-mentioned categories, you have sunk to the lowest form of bigotry and discrimination—stereotyping. Plus, you lose out on the opportunity of discovering for yourself just how wonderful Mother Nature is. People from all walks of life, all sizes, and colors, and religions can teach you something you don't know. Every person has value as a human being and you will be better for learning what that special quality is if you leave your judgmental nature at the door.

A *spring 2005 Q&A*[1] provides a glimpse of what it's like to be a female in a highly visible, typically male-dominated field, that of chief justice of a state supreme court. The female chief justices in Illinois, Massachusetts, Utah, and Wisconsin at that time, Mary Ann McMorrow, Margaret H. Marshall, Christine M. Durham, and Shirley S. Abrahamson respectively, agreed that there are special burdens and advantages to being the rare woman with such high visibility.

First, there's the positive. "You're a celebrity," says Durham. Next, there's the we've-come-a-long-way satisfaction that McMorrow relates. As a young prosecutor, she was asked to argue a case before the Illinois Supreme Court. Thrilled with the opportunity to be the first woman to do so, she worked hard to prepare her brief and argument. Right before the "big day," McMorrow was told that a woman could not argue before the Supreme Court. Of course, she was hugely disappointed. "Now I sit on the very court before which I was not permitted to argue," she says. "When I see so many women arguing and drafting briefs, I cannot help but think what a waste of talent there was so many years ago."

And then there's the pressure of being one of the few of your gender. Durham said of the scrutiny she felt all along: "If I had failed as a trial or an appellate judge, it would have rebounded not just to my detriment but also to that of women lawyers across the board."

So many professions and careers benefiting from differing points of view make a *vive la difference* attitude a strength. It is almost impossible to imagine that women in America didn't have the freedom to express themselves openly in all the ways men have as guaranteed by the Constitution. Whether as a chief justice or in any other role that makes a positive impact in how we live our lives, men and women bring qualities to bear that benefit the society as a whole.

We are fortunate in America for our freedom of speech and ideas and what allows not only individuals but also the media to express themselves. Our media, as flawed as it might be as expressed in this book, sometimes gets it right in giving women the right kind of visibility. When reading the headline for a *Wall Street Journal* interview with the four Sullivan sisters,[2] I immediately recalled the famous story of the five Sullivan brothers, who had enlisted in the Navy in February 1942, with the promise that they would serve together. The ship they served on was attacked and all five brothers died. Their plight inspired a movie and initiated a change to the policy of the U.S. War Department. Had *The Wall Street Journal* picked the Sullivan sisters with an instinct that their story, too, could move a generation?

The Sullivan sisters grew up in Elberon, New Jersey, in the 1960s. Their upbringing, similar to mine and many other women with dads and moms who want their daughters to be independent, was about learning a strong work ethic and the determination to succeed. Their dad, an executive at AT&T, taught them what he knew about launching products, profit margins, teamwork, and competition. And their mom taught them that ambition is a feminine quality and that self-discipline is important. The results of these parents' work in mentoring their daughters to be leaders: Denise Sullivan Morrison is president of Campbell USA; Maggie Sullivan Wilderotter is chair and CEO of Citizens Communications Company; Colleen Sullivan Bastkowski is regional vice president of sales at Expedia Inc.'s Expedia Corporate Travel; and Andrea Sullivan Doelling is a champion horse jumper and a former senior vice president of sales at AT&T Wireless.

The article quotes these sisters as having had "to outperform men, take jobs men didn't want and draw on the perseverance they learned as children." And they "continue to make their own opportunities, another lesson learned from their parents." Yes, the media can, and occasionally does, expose real stories of women who are making it and even gives them credit for it.

The Sullivan sisters' story brings up the importance of being taught confidence at an early age. In my experience, the most confident people are the least judgmental people. Perhaps, I'm stereotyping with this observation, but I don't think so. When you are comfortable in your own skin, you have less reason to question someone else. Diversity is all about bringing more perspectives to the table. Debate is all about having more than one opinion to discuss. If there were only one way to think about things, life would be pretty boring. Nothing is more enriching than to have a different point of view expressed and have a whole new way of looking at a particular issue. I often say to my husband, you don't have to tell me I'm right, just tell me that you understand my point of view. Of course, I then remind him that if we talk long enough, I will be right, so he might as well give in early . . . but I digress.

Seriously, not enough can be written about the importance of bringing people with different views to the table for discussion. Our recent involvement in Iraq is a perfect case in point. Every leader must surround himself/herself with different perspectives. It is the only way of seeing the whole picture and making the best decision. Communication styles are a major component of this discussion. Generally, women are seen as less communicative at work regarding their needs, yet able to speak more openly than men in every other aspect in the rest of their lives. Men speak more directly about what they want at work but seem unable to do the same in other situations.

Could it be that it isn't the gender but the circumstance and the "what-is-expected-of-me syndrome" at play here? Sociologists, psychologists, and academics have spent decades arguing the gender myths. These myths are then transposed into our TV shows, movies, books, and newspaper and magazine articles. We are what the media and others tell us we are. Or are we? *The Economist*[3] reports that the world over, parents still prefer having boys over girls. The premise that boys have a better opportunity for economic success and therefore better prospects for survival is as antiquated as believing women's hormones can drive them to insanity. In other words, these are ideas, or myths, held by a generation long past. Girls today get better grades, earn more degrees, attain higher financial returns in their investments, and, because they tend to do the housework, childrearing, and work outside the home, they outproduce men. The media is obligated to restate the facts of the power and future of girls.

The media's image of girls and women does not reflect the reality of their achievements. Women may be involved in a juggling act at work and at home, but the majority of women are making it work. The working mom understands the need for outside support from family, friends, or structured day care. She coordinates the needs of every member of her family. The stay-at-home mom doesn't have it any easier as she involves herself in her community, at her child's school, and more. But too often the media pits the career mother against the stay-at-home mother. The stay-at-home dad is pitted against the status quo for macho men. Family values are spouted by both political parties but answers for catching up with the progress of the rest of the world, or more specifically with Canada and Europe, are not in the dialogue. The most educated generation in our history is caught in the crossfire of wanting it all, and yes, all at the same time. When the best and the brightest, and I mean the majority of graduate students—women, the supposed weaker sex—are ready to take on the world of work at every level, our culture is set in a tailspin as to how to respond.

A JWT Worldwide survey, released in March 2007, dubs single twenty-something women as "Atalantas" and describes them as "independent, educated, upwardly mobile, and in no rush to wed." She is looking for strong female role models and is dedicated to achieving her goals and passionate about her independence. She describes herself as a "home-lover, not a clubber" and depends on her peer network for all her life advice. Finally, she finds herself wanting to be carefree and explorative one minute and dependable and responsible the next. It's obvious that this generation of women is ready for anything and believes they can have it all.

Atalanta's role models are not just found in the media's portrayal of single women on such shows as *Sex and the City* and in the movies. The question is, why doesn't the media focus its attention on the positive aspects of Atalantas in its business news? These enthusiastic, energetic women are the future in America. They are role models in their own way as freedom fighters for determining how women will rule the next generation. Women of all ages today are looking to see how other women are doing it and have done it. Whether it's by attending women's conferences to hear the stories of women CEOs or devouring the less-than-frequent business stories found in business magazines and newspapers, or, if they're lucky, looking up the ranks within their workplace, today's career women are seeking inspiration from other women in order to compete and thrive.

The annual lists of top businesswomen, most powerful women, and richest women open up the world of possibilities. For example, this year's "*Fortune* 50 Most Powerful Women" list illustrates the diversity of women and their companies. The first three are the CEOs of PepsiCo, Kraft Foods, and Archer Daniels Midland (ADM). We are immediately made aware that women are being taken seriously at least some of the time. Indra Nooyi, born in India and CEO of PepsiCo since August 2006, brought her custom as a lifelong vegetarian to the healthy nutrition concept the company has adopted. Irene Rosenfeld stood her ground earlier at Kraft when she left the company because she disagreed with top management. The company brought her back as CEO in June 2006, when top management's direction wasn't working. Pat Woertz showed her stuff at Chevron but knew the CEO slot wouldn't open for years, so she took time to research other opportunities. ADM came knocking within months and Woertz became CEO in April 2006.

These women and many more like them cannot be dismissed as rare or eccentric. They are more the norm across America today although our media does little to tell us about their journey. They are women who are serious about their career and work. And they are women who bring the meaning of *vive la différence* to corporate influence.

When asked about what she thinks women bring to the table, Ellyn McColgan, who's president of Fidelity Investments Distribution and Operations and has been on the list of *Fortune* magazine's "50 Most Powerful Women in Business" since 2004, answers, "I'm thinking of a half a dozen of women who work here at Fidelity who are widely recognized as smart and as the people who get a lot done. They work well across divisions because they are so focused and they work so well with other people."

Women are also making their mark out in the marketplace. A 2006 *New York Times* article[4] focuses on the need for American companies to wake up to the consumer power of women. In it, Michael J. Silverstein of the Boston Consulting Group says that women "will earn more money than men if current trends continue by 2008." Women make the majority of buying decisions not only in household goods but also travel, automobiles, education, financial services, and healthcare. Women also make almost half of home improvement and consumer electronics buying decisions. And, by owning almost 50 percent of all small businesses, women are key purchasers of all business products and services.

There is not just diversity in what women versus men want but also in what different women want. When I started my newspaper, I queried advertising agencies about how they targeted businessmen. The answers from agency to agency were similar as they each had a clear profile about what a businessman looked like, what he read, what he watched, and where he traveled. When asked the same question about a businesswoman, no agency had a clear idea of how to reach her. There was no clear profile for a businesswoman. Aha! I knew immediately, I had an opportunity to fill a niche. The point is not to suggest that men are predictable and have no mystery to them, but that women hold the surprises.

This isn't to say that corporate is completely gender blind. One startling "new" idea is that women and men network differently. The passé brainchild of networking your way to new business only on the links or over cognac and a smoke is being replaced, at least at some major companies across the country according to an article in *The Wall Street Journal*.[5]

Profiling women's events at firms such as Ernst & Young, Merrill Lynch, and General Electric, writer Carol Hymowitz reports, "After all, networking over shoe shopping at a Manhattan boutique is no different than playing golf and sharing cigars after a steak dinner is for men." I've attended many women-only networking events myself, including a night at the theatre, an exhibit at the art museum, wine and chocolate tastings, fashion shows, and even a lesson in flower arranging. The point is not that women don't, or can't, enjoy the things men do, but that they enjoy other social gatherings as well, and a smart company will provide alternative occasions to make sure they tap into the passions of all its customers.

So why is most of our country still caught up in a one-size-fits-all mentality? And, why is that one size a white male forty regular? Even he is looking for more choice and opportunity to embrace a *vive la difference* workplace.

CHAPTER 3

A Look Back to Look Ahead

"I think it is time for us Americans to take a good look at ourselves and our shortcomings. We should remember how we achieved the aims of freedom and democracy. We should look back in an effort to gauge how we can best influence the peoples of the world."

—Eleanor Roosevelt

Take a look at this paraphrasing of the National Organization for Women's Bill of Rights, adopted in 1967, and see if you don't end up asking yourself: Is this all there is?

1. That the U.S. Congress would pass the Equal Rights Amendment, which guarantees the equality of rights for all regardless of gender.
2. That women be granted the opportunity for equal employment.
3. That the law protect women's rights to return to their jobs within a manageable time after childbirth without loss of seniority, and that they be paid maternity leave.
4. That there be an immediate revision of tax laws to permit the deduction of home and child care expenses for working parents.
5. That adequate child care facilities be established by law.
6. That women have the right to be educated, at all levels, to their fullest potential and equally with men through the enactment of federal and state legislation, thereby eliminating discrimination and segregation by sex.

7. That women in poverty have the same rights as men in securing job training, housing, and family allowances through revisions in welfare legislation and poverty programs.
8. That women have the right to control their own productive lives by removing language in penal code laws that limit access to contraceptive information and devices, and by repealing abortion penal laws.

What was considered radical in 1967 is today a statement of not only the obvious but also a declaration of what's right. Equality does not mean there are no differences between men and women. It means that we should have the same rights under the law.

History provides perspective for us all. As I researched this book, I realized that what I believed were the radical "bra-burning feminists of the 1960s" were actually an older, more experienced group of women than I, with a greater understanding of the inequities for our gender. I believe the next generation, those up-and-coming women—and men—making their way into the work world have the same disadvantage that my generation and I had in not knowing what had come before us. The lack of knowledge of how women have provided not only comfort but have also worked at every level during wartime in our country's history to then quietly allow themselves to become second-class citizens once the crisis was over must be corrected. This history and its power, or the lack thereof, must be shouted out to every generation. We must not forget the sacrifices of our forbearers—our great-great-grandmothers and the generations of women who have brought us to where we are today: Ready to lead in America.

Every historical advancement of our female ancestors has served as a challenge, not to male authority in self-righteous indignation but to inequality. Each advancement has been a forward step toward equal opportunities for all, the very basis of our Constitution. We are not there yet! It's time for a new women's revolution where women take their collective place equally alongside men and help make this country the best place it can be and continue its path as global leader. For us (America) to take a second place to any country because of its positive position on equality of the sexes versus our seeming inequality is an abomination.

As you'll read later in a discussion on global family leave programs, America ranks almost last out of one hundred and seventy-three countries studied that offer guaranteed leave with income to women in association with childbirth. To be crystal clear, there is no guaranteed paid leave for mothers in the United States in any segment of the workforce. Other countries have learned the importance of a diverse workforce and how to keep talented people on the job. This is a lesson America cannot afford to toss out with yesterday's homework. We must seek out the talent at hand and move in the direction of creating leadership that brings equality across the sexes. We have no time left to continue this lag behind the rest of the world. We must actively seek out the talent at hand and move in the direction of creating leadership that brings equality across the genders. We will all be better for it.

Awareness of the past will get us on the right track. There is a very good reason to study history, whether it's the history of a country, a battle or conflict, or the history of a people. History affords us an opportunity to learn something from the events of the past. Most important, it allows us the opportunity not to make the same mistakes twice. Leaders must build on the knowledge of past events in order to see potential outcomes for the future. It is often said that the definition of insanity is doing the same thing over and over and expecting different results each time. Understanding our history allows us to move ahead rather than 'round and 'round in circles or, worse, backward. Too often we see our leaders fail by dismissing history and assuming that time has changed the circumstances.

Women's history is not spoken or written about enough, in my opinion. Although March is considered Women's History month in the United States, you would be hard-pressed to find much written about the women's movement that began in this country in the early 1830s. I am devoting this chapter to the history of the women's movement and to women's leadership to set the stage for my assertion—that the time is now for women to lead. Men and women must understand the past struggles of their female ancestors to have an appreciation for where we are today and why we are at that moment in time when change must take place. So, don't skip this important look back at women's efforts to participate jointly with men as they stepped foot onto the shores of America.

Since coming ashore first in 1608 at Jamestown, Virginia, and at the subsequent Plymouth, Massachusetts, settlement in 1620, women have contributed at every level of society. (I can't help but note that the first woman to help the earliest Jamestown settlers, all men arriving in 1607, was Native American Pocahontas.) From generation to generation, women have been asked to lead in a variety of capacities at different times in our history. The U.S. census reports that in 1800, 5 percent of women were employed. Married women at this time had a life expectancy of forty and had an average of seven children. By 1900, 21 percent of women were employed, and life expectancy for a married woman was fifty-plus with the likelihood of having four children. By the year 2000, 60 percent of women were employed and comprised 40 percent of all workers. The life expectancy of a married woman in 2000 reached eighty and she produced an average of two children.

The statistics show clearly that as reproductive labor decreased and life expectancy spans increased, women sought more opportunities for work and vice versa. Today, 52 percent of the workforce is female and 54 percent of the ninety-six million singles in the United States are women. Although 90 percent of women statistically will become pregnant, most of them will continue to work, according to the U.S. Department of Labor.

During the Industrial Revolution at the beginning of the 1800s, women's work moved from unpaid housework to low-pay wage work. In the early factories, single women and poor married women played a major role in filling the jobs of making finished goods out of raw materials for low wages. Men secured the higher-paying wages as mechanics and overseers. As the factories grew, there was a demand for clerical work and sales clerks. White literate women took these jobs, which were managed by men. By 1830, department stores were the rage; at first, because women worked for cheap, they were hired for sales positions. But as the role became more professional, women were pushed out into the lower-paying jobs of teachers and librarians that were once held by men. By 1900, women outnumbered men as teachers by two to one.[1]

The 1830s marked the start of the first women's rights movement. As factory workers, their work was critical to the economic growth of the country, yet they had no rights to own property or to control their wages. The first Women's Rights Convention was held in 1848 in Seneca Falls, New York, by Elizabeth Cady Stanton and Lucretia Mott. Three hundred people attended, forty of whom were men. The Declaration of Sentiments, signed by one hundred of the participants, was presented as the convention's grievances and made available to the press. The following were their grievances.

1. Married women were legally dead in the eyes of the law.
2. Women were not allowed to vote.
3. Women had to submit to laws when they had no voice in their formation.
4. Married women had no property rights.
5. Husbands had legal power over and responsibility for their wives to the extent that they could imprison or beat them without impunities.
6. Divorce and child custody laws favored men, giving no rights to women.
7. Women had to pay property taxes although they had no representation in the levying of their taxes.

8. Most occupations were closed to women, and when women did work, they were paid only a fraction of what men earned.
9. Women were not allowed to enter professions such as medicine or law.
10. Women had no means to gain an education since no college or university would accept female students.
11. With only a few exceptions, women were not allowed to participate in the affairs of the church.
12. Women were robbed of their self-confidence and self-respect and were made totally dependent on men.[2]

The media mocked the convention, and when *The New York Herald* printed the Sentiments, the paper's negative intention backfired as the printing gave the opportunity for men and women who had not attended the convention to think about the questions that had been asked.

As we look at the Sentiment's grievances of 1848, it should make us shudder that many of them took generations to be rectified and, in the case of equal pay, we are still on the journey.

By May of 1851, another Women's Rights Convention took place in Akron, Ohio, organized by Frances D. Gage. Both men and women were in attendance. Both men and women were allowed to speak their minds as to how the concerns for equality between the sexes needed to be aired. The only black person attending was Sojourner Truth. Standing nearly six feet tall, she stood out among the crowd and was given the opportunity to be heard. Her words, in a speech known as the "Ain't I a Woman?" speech, spoke of the importance of the women's movement to black women. She rebuked the widely held idea that women were weaker than men.

"That man over there say that woman needs to be helped into carriages, and lifted over ditches, and has to have the best place everywhere. Nobody ever helps me into carriages, or over mud puddles, or gives me any best place... And ain't I a woman? I have plowed and planted and gathered into barns, and no man could head me... I could work as much and eat as much as a man—when I could get it—and bear the lash as well." Sojourner Truth continues today to stand out as a symbol of a strong black woman who worked for equal rights all her life. She understood that her fight was based on her color and her gender, and that equality must be in both areas to be satisfactory.[3]

The Civil War, with women taking up the work of the men out on the battlefield, would set the scene for greater struggle for women's rights and civil rights that often crossed paths. In 1869, the Fifteenth Amendment gave black men the right to vote. Neither the Fourteenth nor Fifteenth Amendments included women. With the passage of the Fifteenth Amendment, many black women felt that black male suffrage was an important first step toward women's rights. Meanwhile, women were left to clean up from the ravage of war, keeping families together, and finding ways to feed them when their men didn't return home. The movement led right up to the women suffragettes' winning the right for women to vote in 1920 with the Nineteenth Amendment—culminating the first wave of a women's movement in America. It would be another forty-plus years before women collectively worked together again to advance their rights and call attention to the need for equality.

World War I once again saw men go to war and women do whatever was needed at home, from working in factories making weapons to populating the battlefield as nurses. The Great Depression of 1929 was a time when one out of every five people was out of work. In some places, it was illegal to hire women, yet many women had no choice—single women, widows, divorced women—they all had to find anything they could to survive. They were allowed only to do what was labeled women's work—laundry, cleaning, cooking, and sewing. Minimal survival was the only right they endured for the ten years leading up to World War II, when women's help became paramount once again.

Then-President Franklin Delano Roosevelt (FDR) campaigned to get all women working, and by 1945 six million women worked in war industries. These women were called Women Ordnance Workers (WOWs). The Rosie Riveter media campaign directed by the government ultimately got nineteen million women working in factories and businesses, on farms, and in the military. Child care centers were set up in factories, or neighbors watched one another's children. It was considered a woman's patriotic duty to work as the men fought the war. In 1942, six months after Pearl Harbor was attacked, FDR signed a bill to create the Women's Army Corps (WAC). The Navy followed with the Women Accepted for Voluntary Emergency Services (WAVES). The Coast Guard and the Marines also allowed women to join their ranks.

When World War II ended, women were asked to go home and leave their jobs for the returning men—even those women who had lost their husbands and now had no support. Polls at the time showed that three-fourths of the WOWs wanted to keep their jobs. Many women found ways to keep working and even learned new skills to change positions. And by 1950, one-third of all women still worked.

Yet the 1950s was a time of prosperity for many. Wartime was over and jobs were plentiful. Although more women than ever worked, the image of a perfect family was an at-home mom with two-plus children and a husband with a good job. Families could live and thrive on one paycheck. It was the *Leave It to Beaver* era that the media likes to perpetuate even today as the perfect role model for happy families, with June Cleaver, the housewife in her shirtwaist dress, waiting by the front door for her children to return from school and for her husband to return from work to the comfort of their immaculate home.

By 1960, however, the need for two paychecks grew as the economy weakened. The women's movement again mobilized in 1961 when then-President John F. Kennedy created a blue-ribbon President's Commission on the Status of Women. The committee was chaired by Eleanor Roosevelt, and it was to focus on the prejudices against women as well as on basic rights. The goal was to give women an opportunity to make a maximum contribution in government and private employment.

Women wanted to work and needed to work. More and more married women took jobs at low wages just to keep the family on par. The 1963 recommendations from the Commission included:

- Making admission requirements at colleges more flexible in order to admit more women,
- To fund child care centers for working mothers privately,
- To provide for paid maternity leave, expand job counseling services for women, and end gender-based hiring and discrimination practices.

Equal pay was also legislated in 1963, when the United States passed the Equal Pay Act, outlawing different pay scales for men and women. Little changed, however, since most men and women didn't work the same types of jobs. What did change was that, up until this point, jobs could be advertised for women or for men and with differing gender-based pay scales. The Equal Pay Act provided women the promise of a fair wage for the first time in history.

The 1963 report was the first time that the status of women in America had been researched. The other most important recommendation of the commission was that each state set up a similar commission. By 1964, thirty-two states had complied and by 1967, all fifty states had set up commissions. The synergy between women's groups helped motivate the passage of the Civil Rights Act of 1964, eliminating discrimination against African-Americans, and Title VII of the Civil Rights Act finally prohibited discrimination by race or gender. Once again, race and gender were combined under an act of discrimination. This act also set up the Equal

Employment Opportunity Committee (EEOC), where complaints could be heard and reviewed. In 1967, the Affirmation Action Executive Order was declared for women and minorities to make sure both had an equal and fair opportunity for employment.

At about the same time, in November, the National Organization of Women (NOW) ratified its Bill of Rights and empowered women across the country to start their own women's groups. It was the second call for the liberation of women. This next wave focused on benefits and workplace discrimination, as well as sexual harassment. In 1971, the National Women's Political Caucus (NWPC) was formed with a mission of inclusivity. Like the suffrage movement, it focused on the women's vote and the opportunity for political power to redirect the nation toward a peaceful goal. At the founding convention in 1973 in Houston, Texas, fifteen hundred came to build a national political movement for women. New York Congresswoman Shirley Chisholm argued that "the NWPC is not to be the cutting edge of the women's liberation movement, but a big umbrella organization which proves the weight and muscle for those issues which the majority of women in this country see as concerns." It was clear: Diversity would be a strong issue that women would and could embrace.

The women's movement of the 1960s and 1970s for the second time in U.S. history had a reason for momentum, and its impact righted the backward progress of previous decades.

By the end of the 1960s, women in America made up:

- 2 percent of the architects,
- 3 percent of the lawyers,
- 7 percent of the physicians,
- 9 percent of the scientists, and
- 22 percent of all teachers.[4]

The 2006 *Databook* on *Women in the Labor Force*[5] reported statistics based on 2005 information that illustrates the dramatic change for women in these arenas as follows:

- 24 percent were architects,
- 30.2 percent were lawyers,
- 32.3 percent were physicians,
- 48.7 percent were biological scientists,

- 45.9 percent were medical scientists,
- 35.3 percent were chemists and materials scientists, with women comprising approximately 10 percent of all engineers,
- 56.8 percent of secondary and postsecondary teachers, and
- 82.2 percent of elementary school teachers.

A lot has changed in forty years, but, as you'll see, a lot has remained the same.

Feminism in America

Feminism in America cannot be pinpointed to a specific date, because as long as there have been women, there has been a feministic point of view. Many times in our history, however, the word has taken on a negative connotation. The movement in the 1960s and 1970s split into several factions, some more radical than others. Issues around the Vietnam War, reproductive rights, civil rights, and sexual orientation burst on the stage through the movement. No history of the women's movement in America would be complete without mention of two women who embodied the spirit of those days.

The first is Betty Friedan, whose book *The Feminine Mystique* in 1963 could be seen as the tipping point for the second wave of the women's movement. For the first time, "the problem with no name" that was afflicting women across America was identified and received maximum attention. Masses of women were seeking assistance from professionals for their unexplained malaise. Friedan acknowledged the problem as frustration and lack of fulfillment by women who could not define themselves as anything other than someone's wife, someone's mother, or, simply, a homemaker. Friedan will be remembered as one of the most influential feminists in the twentieth century as a cofounder of the U.S. National Organization for Women and as a mouthpiece for the emancipation of women.

Gloria Steinem is the second feminist icon who continues to stand for the fight for women's rights through her writings, activism, and magazine, *Ms. Magazine*. As cofounder of the NWPC as well as the Women's Action Alliance, Steinem has walked the talk for women for the past fifty years. She was often designated by the media as the movement's spokeswoman as her moves and voice were sensational and she tolerated the media's mocking. These are just two of the women to whom the media turned its attention in the late 1960s and early 1970s to portray as examples of those who sought to undermine the family. Yet their work spurred women's consciousness-raising groups across the country, where women got together with their friends in small factions to discuss their work in and outside the home. By the early 1970s a sexual revolution had blossomed, and women were demanding their opportunities promised to them by law.

The National Organization of Women (NOW) Convention in 1971 passed the following resolution.

1. Be it resolved that NOW recognizes the double oppression of lesbians.
2. Be it resolved that a woman's right to be her own person include the right to define and express her own sexuality and to choose her own lifestyle.
3. Be it resolved that NOW acknowledges the oppression of lesbians as a legitimate concern of feminism.

Once again, the women's movement and, more specifically NOW, its leader, found itself between causes—the gay liberation movement and the women's movement. The message didn't resonate positively across America, which wasn't ready for the sexual orientation debate. The importance of NOW's history and its impact on the women's movement and women in general explains the ebb and flow of the movement since inception. Its focus on the politics of sexual orientation, and later abortion, disturbed the majority of the country at that time and allowed the media to demonize the organization. These divisions caused an ominous feeling for women who wanted to be considered feminists.

My research of this time brought back to mind Sojourner Truth's dialogue with her "Ain't I a Woman" theme—that of not being a second-class citizen, but a person entitled to all the benefits men enjoy.

By the early 1990s, and specifically 1992, women in many respects had come full circle, or so we are to believe if we accept the media hype of the day. The Year of the Woman, 1992, was the year that more women were elected to the U.S. Senate than ever before. Four women, Dianne Feinstein, California; Barbara Boxer, California; Carol Moseley Braun, Illinois; and Patty Murray, Washington State, were elected to the Senate to join Nancy Kassebaum, Kansas, and Barbara Milkulski, Maryland.

For the first time in American history, six women served in the Senate. In their first year in Congress, these women got thirty pieces of legislation passed. In their second year, another thirty-three legislative actions were approved. The record for any year before this was five. It should be clear from this recounting of history that, with more women serving in Congress, a new perspective and initiative should move forward.

As you'll read in the following chapters, during the next decade and half, women have put their education first, taken advantage of the vote, made their way into the workforce in record numbers, and continued to fight for equality at every level. The organizations that started the rhetoric and got women mobilized are still active and formidable against the opposition. But the struggle continues. Today's young woman sees open doors in her future and opportunities that every woman and man in America is promised. Yet, the reality, as will be mapped out, is not what's promised and, in the end that hurts America just as much as the women it disappoints. The most educated and the most deserving are allowed to see their dreams disappear.

As Speaker of the House, Nancy Pelosi remarked as she took the oath of office on January 4, 2007, "It is a moment for which we have waited over two hundred years. We waited through the many years of struggle to achieve our rights. But women weren't just waiting. Women were working. Never losing faith, we worked to redeem the promise of America, that all men and women are created equal. For our daughters and our granddaughters, today we have broken the marble ceiling."[6]

So, as the debate goes on, women are making history in America every day. Not a week goes by, as a publisher of a newspaper, that I'm not pitched a story of another "first" for women: the first woman chief of police of a major metropolitan city, the first woman head of a major city council, the first woman major university president in the area, the first woman attorney general in the state, and the list goes on. But just because women are making history each day does not mean that each crack in the glass ceiling or the marble ceiling or the concrete ceiling, or whatever the ceiling, is getting that ceiling closer to being shattered. That will only happen when women and men make it their business to bring other women into the pipeline to power. Each "first" must be followed by a "second" and a "third" and a "fourth," and on and on. So, before you become complacent with the history of the women's movement in this country and how each step along the way has benefited you—men and women—read on. We have a lot of work to do before there is equality among the sexes in America.

CHAPTER 4

The Time Is Now

"Women will run the twenty-first century. This is going to be the women's century, and young people are going to be its leaders."

—Bella Abzug

Your first question may be, "Why now? What has changed so dramatically that women are ready to take the lead?" Let me give you some "whys" to consider. When we are in such need of the many attributes women bring to the table—character, determination, compassion, and empathy, to name a few—why aren't more women among our leaders?

When it comes to business, women account for 85 percent of the consumer purchasing power—so why aren't they at the helm of more large enterprises? Women are over half of the U.S. population—so why are they just 16 percent of Congress? More than 65 percent of all graduate degrees are now being earned by women—so where is their path to holding the elite positions at colleges and universities? With females representing more than 50 percent of all law and medical school students—what are the legal and medical professions doing to structure themselves for change? Finally, as the volunteers and, by 2010, as those who control 60 percent of the wealth in America[1]—why aren't women leading the nonprofit and philanthropic worlds? You see, the real question is, "If not now, when will women accept the power that is theirs for the taking?"

Rosabeth Moss Kanter, the Harvard Business School thought leader, says, "Now is the time for women. I think we have a sufficiently large pool of women with experience and credentials to make it extremely plausible. There were many years in which a combination of discrimination and preference and gender segregation of occupations meant that there simply were not many women in position. Now women have earned their way onto the track to top leadership and have proven themselves. We now have more and more work where physical characteristics play absolutely no role in the ability to perform that work. Today, the main skills are mental. Most work is knowledge work."

Let me stop here for a moment and say that women are leading in one area—getting hit harder by inflation than men. According to Merrill Lynch economist David Rosenberg, this is due to consumer prices. The costs for items that women consumers purchase, "including clothes, shoes, cosmetics, jewelry, housekeeping, and appliances, have been rising faster than for typically male products—men's clothing, sporting goods, televisions, and auto parts and repairs," he notes. The result: The "female inflation rate," as Rosenberg calls it, is 3.6 percent year to year, which is eighteen times the 0.02 percent inflation rate for men.[2] As women are encountering greater job growth than men and marrying later than they used to, they are also spending more of their income than single men. The gender-related supply-and-demand inflation rate is clearly a benefit to men but one that should scream to women that once again, at this moment, their achievements still have a negative effect on their future.

Women can't reach parity unless we all, men and women, focus on getting there. We are holding ourselves back every time we don't hire a woman, don't refer a woman, and don't vote for a woman. We can no longer discount half of the talent that is out there ready, willing, and able to lead. Time is no longer on our side. Never before have there been as many women who are as educated, as employed, and as motivated for leadership as there are today. There is power in numbers and women, as 52 percent of the U.S. population, *have* the numbers. The balance of power should be on the brink of equalizing. The workplace should be on the verge of change. Now is the time for women to wield their power and set that change into motion. Let the united force of momentum begin!

For the past thirty years and more, every woman with the desire to lead in corporate America has been described at least once by someone as hitting her head against the proverbial glass ceiling, banging her pretty head against a cement wall, clawing her way to the top, and yes, sleeping her way to the top. Not attractive descriptions for women who have nothing more in mind than to achieve their maximum potential. The women who have made it, however, are scarce in comparison to the number of positions available and to the talent waiting in the wings.

It's time for women to be able to gut it out to stay in corporate America and change the "business as usual" atmosphere that is corrupting the system. It's time for women to show that they're capable of true and equal representation in government at all levels: local, state, and federal. It's time for women to bring the capabilities that make them successful lawyers to the leadership of the firm. It's time for women to go to the head of the class in shaping our future through colleges and universities. It's time women succeed in their chosen medical and science specialties without being held back by stereotyping. It's time for women to take their place with the "other half" and lead in all segments of society, thereby creating even greater strength through more fairly realized unity.

Warren Bennis says, "Letting the self emerge is the essential task for leaders. It is how one takes the step from being to doing in the spirit of expressing, rather than proving."[3] In other words, it is not necessarily the path we choose that determines our ability to lead but how we are able to express ourselves fully. Detoured by the roadblocks on the path to leadership in the corporate culture, women have expressed themselves by starting their own businesses—and their numbers are dramatic. Between 1997 and 2006, woman-owned businesses grew by 42 percent compared to 23 percent growth for all businesses. As Sharon Hadary, executive director of the Center for Women's Business Research, says, "What we heard from a lot of women was that they were leaving their former employer because they felt that they could not make a difference in the organization and that their opinions were not influencing the direction of the organization." Determined to lead, they have found a way to do so—but it is not in corporate America.

I believe that this is the tipping point women have been working toward. As we will discuss later in the book, small business in America is the engine driving our growing economy. Women in 2006 were responsible for 10.4 million privately held businesses—that's two out of every five businesses in the country. In corporate America, women are secure in the ranks of middle management and stand at the precipice of senior management. Women and the women's movement are responsible for the changes that have taken place in corporate America and in their own businesses regarding flextime, family and medical leave programs, onsite day care, and elder care programs. These programs were demanded for by women but benefit all employees. Men are equally the beneficiaries of these programs, as we will discuss later. I have often said that the change in generational attitudes can be described as follows: When I was born, my dad was in the office waiting for the call; when my son was born, my husband was with me in the delivery room; and when my son has his child, he will take time off from work to bond.

It is clear that the days when women were encouraged to give their all and "stand by their man" and hope for the best are over. Smart companies of all sizes depend heavily on women to advance their agendas and contribute to their bottom line. These national as well as global companies have serious programs dedicated to the retention of women. These programs are not in place to placate the demands of women's organizations but because company leaders realize that talented employees are absolutely essential to success. OK, so you ask, why aren't there any men retention programs? Men are certainly essential to corporate America and to the bottom line. Men, however, have what can best be described as the old boys' network at work, where each member of the club automatically welcomes a newcomer.

In their book,[4] *Members of the Club*, Dawn-Marie Driscoll and Carol R. Goldberg describe how comfortable this membership is for men. "It is not an institution that can be found in the telephone book, nor does it have a list of members. No single definition precisely fits The Club, but we know it when we see it." In the early 1990s when the book was written, The Club was "an inner circle of male senior executives and professionals, all of whom know each other, many of whom have shared past experiences in school, the military or their companies." In other words, a place "where everyone knows your name," to borrow a well-known tag line from the familiar television show, *Cheers*. Yet, although more and more women have moved into senior executive and professional positions and are well known to the men at The Club, membership still eludes most.

Of course, there needs to be a safe place to prepare for The Club, and that place is within the old boys' network. It provides an opportunity for men to start their career with a place at the table and the sense that there is a clear career path. The unspoken rule of going along to get along and becoming a member of the team are tactics learned early on, most likely from team sports. As long as companies remain male-dominated, these conditions don't change, not because of bias or discrimination in the workplace per se, but from a lack of diversity. Studies on the effects of having women on corporate boards show that it takes a minimum of three women on a board to change the dynamics of the group. One woman is seen as a token, whether on purpose or by situation. Two women may be able to back each other up enough to be heard but it takes three women to create an impact on the discussion.

The point I am making here has nothing to do with discrimination. Quite naturally, birds of a feather flock together. We unconsciously, and sometimes consciously, feel more comfortable with others who are like us. It is instinctual to believe that those who look more like us think like us and will act like we do. Like it or not, this is human nature. But understanding this is the first step in making sure we do everything we can to value diversity at every level—even though we know we must work hard in achieving what does not come naturally.

When more than 50 percent of the workforce is female, companies must make an extra effort to provide mentorship programs that will meet their needs for advancement and hear their concerns along the way. It is not enough to endorse women's initiatives for senior level and/or mid-level managers. New recruits, both male and female, must feel that there is an equal opportunity for advancement at the firm whether or not there is a current role model of their gender at the "C" level—CEO, CFO, COO, and on. The same must happen in every profession.

In 1988, Bennis wrote in *On Becoming a Leader*, "Where have all the leaders gone? They are, like flowers of the haunting folk song, long time passing."[5] All the leaders we once respected, he says, are dead. He goes on to list many of the greatest leaders in all of history, FDR, Churchill, the Kennedys, and Martin Luther King, just to name a few. No women are on his list. Moreover, today's question is not only "where have all the leaders gone?" but also "why have so many become corrupt?" Why have greed, self-interest, and self-indulgence taken over as the major characteristics of our leaders? And before you accuse me of male-bashing, let's take a look at just a portion of "The Corporate Scandal Sheet"[6] as an example of what can happen in every sector across the country.

- October 2001, Enron: Corporate executives boosted profits and hid debts totaling over $1 billion by improperly using off-the-books partnerships. The company filed for bankruptcy. The employees lost their pensions.

- November 2001, Arthur Andersen: Andersen was convicted of obstruction of justice and ceased auditing public firms by August 31. This case was later reversed but Arthur Andersen went out of business and more than eighty thousand employees lost their jobs.

- April 2002, Adelphia Communications: Three Rigas family members and two other ex-executives were arrested for fraud.

- May 2002, Tyco: Ex-CEO Dennis Kozlowski was indicted for tax evasion and improper use of company funds.

- July 2002, AOL Time Warner: AOL said it might have overstated revenue by $49 million.

I could go on and on with other corporate scandals but you know the stories all too well. You could say I am making the case that these companies, all led by men and controlled by male-dominated, and in almost every case, male-only boards of directors, are corrupt due to their lack of female representation. You would be right. That is exactly what I am saying. I need to take you a step further, however, to make my point. We have created a power structure in corporate America today that has lost its moral compass. By focusing on the assumed desires of corporate shareholders that company profits are more important than anything else, we have created unreasonable pressure on company officials to drive earnings at any and all cost.

Five and more years have passed since the scandals I mention here and yet today we are still immersed in scandals of backdating of options for corporate executives and board of directors and the need for more than half of the *Fortune* 500 companies to restate earnings. So, what about the issue of whether there is a gender difference in ethical decision making? Leslie M. Dawson, professor of marketing at the University of Massachusetts Dartmouth, says, "The more we understand the differences in moral reasoning that characterize the sexes, the better we can appreciate women's impact on ethical decision making in organizations."[7] The research she reported on was based on forty-eight male and forty-two female marketing and sales managers who were given six scenarios involving possible ethical issues and asked to make a decision in each. Four of the six scenarios proved the sexes had statistically significant different viewpoints.

But do these differences automatically mean that the current decline of ethical standards in the business community may be able to be reversed with a continuing influx of women at management levels? Dawson suggests that "what seems more certain is that women's increasing influence in organizations will bring about differences in how ethical problems are perceived and resolved. Women's special traits could readily be seen as improving the ethical climate of a firm in numerous ways: more sensitive and caring treatment of customers, more creative approaches to problem solving, more effective relationship building creating greater trust in interpersonal affairs, more supportive and understanding supervisory styles."

The bottom line is that bringing women's voices to the top where decisions are made can only help ebb the tide of corporate shenanigans. When I'm asked if I believe that women would be less corrupt than men if they held the majority of the power, my answer is that our instinct for being so tough on each other—and holding ourselves to the same standard—might just be the strength that keeps us accountable when we are put in powerful positions. I believe America now depends on it.

How will women change the tone in corporate America? The same way they will change the face of law, politics, healthcare, the sciences, higher education, nonprofit, and philanthropy. With women as the majority in senior level positions in corporations, strong companies will become stronger as people—human capital and not monetary capital—are given the greatest attention. All companies are only as successful as the people who work there. Doing well by doing good will not be a motto on the door but a concept embraced by all management filtered down to every employee. Companies in America cannot afford to dismiss the importance of people—employees, customers, the communities where employees and customers work and live, and even international customers, the people interested in the American way of life and ideals. The governance of these companies, the board of directors and the management team, will benefit by understanding their customer better since their customer is a woman.

The same kind of changes will happen in every avenue for women's leadership. Some of these changes are already happening in medicine, where women's influx into the medical community has helped focus the attention on women's health. Dr. Nancy H. Nielsen, speaker for the American Medical Association's policymaking House of Delegates, says, "Women have energy, passion and a lot of experience at care-giving. Those are great qualities for leaders who can inspire others and demonstrate by their personal behavior what our profession is all about. Throughout the ages, physicians have put the needs of others before themselves. It is truly a profession of service to others."

Of course, women as caregivers is nothing new, but as leaders in medicine and science, the evidence thus far is that they seek only to advance humanity as a whole rather than the spotlight for themselves. Forty years ago, doctors, mostly male, had all the answers and there was little doctor/patient communication. The education of today's patient requires much more communication, and women have been drawn to accomplishing the task. The leadership of both men and women is critical in order to find solutions to the serious healthcare debate going on in America today.

Our nonprofit community has been blessed with some of the most talented women and men for decades, but women are not up to pay parity with their male counterparts. The variety of other career options facing women today puts those low-paying, nonprofit roles in jeopardy. Pay equity across all professions is paramount, and for women at the helm of nonprofits, another day cannot go by without equal pay. We need an army of female nonprofit leaders to work alongside the new majority of wealth holders (women) to guide them with their philanthropic choices.

As America increasingly becomes a place where the rich get richer and the poor get poorer, we need the leadership of women because, as Marian Heard, former president and CEO of the United Way of Massachusetts Bay, says, "While men are sympathetic, I think women have a different level of empathy. Because we have been caregivers and nurturers, we understand the human side of the equation most days. It doesn't get in the way. I think it strengthens, quite frankly, our dealing with people. Women, more so than men, are used to juggling and we can keep different files and different projects and different things going at the same time."

These unique qualities are equally important in the leadership qualities necessary in higher education. Teachers and professors are, in most cases, the second role models, next to parents, that young people have to pattern themselves after. It's time for the tenure process to be transparent. Tenure is one more case where performance matters and the club must be gender-inclusive. Similarly, the legions of women graduating from law school must be able to see a direct path to partner if they join a law firm or the opportunity to rise in the ranks in the judiciary, should that be their aspiration. The enforcement of our laws must have equal gender perspectives in order to be fully just. Our government needs women leaders simply because without equal participation, we do not have equal representation—locally or nationally. Women have as much stake in the future of America as our male counterparts, at home and abroad, and the world is watching us as we work toward inclusion in every area of leadership.

I believe it is in harnessing the talents of the qualified workforce waiting to join the ranks at the top that can bring balance to what currently is an insider club. In Norway, this balance is called the 40-percent rule. Norway's publicly traded firms "have to meet a 40-percent requirement for female board members by 2008 or be shut down."[8] Your first response may be, "Quotas—are you kidding? Women will get there when they deserve to. They will earn their way onto corporate boards by their performance." Really, I say. Do you actually believe that? And, performance, you say? Performance, where? At the Parent Teacher Association (PTA) or on some other volunteer board? Most corporate (paid) directors are found through networking. Do you remember The Club we just talked about? Many directors are CEOs of the largest corporations in America, and we know how many of them are women—eleven when this book was written. Qualified women are easy to find today for these boards through nonprofit organizations like those that compose InterOrganization Network (ION), a group of eight regional organizations from across the country that are advancing businesswomen to positions of power, but that is not happening.

So, back to quotas, because I'm sure you did not let me off the hook that easily, how successfully are quotas working in Norway? According to European Professional Women's Network (PWN) "'BoardWomen Monitor 2006,'" corporate champions are beyond tokenism on their boards. Since the quota system was established, more than 40 percent of female directors are on boards in five industry sectors: "banks, specialty and other finance, telecom services, media and entertainment, oil and gas." Data has also revealed that women on these boards are being selected as employee representatives with a large number of labor union appointees. Most important to the discussion of the success of quotas is the European PWN's biannual monitor that provides both women and companies with "benchmarks of what is being done where and what the results and benefits are." America is ready for a similar system as the needed watchdogs, ION Network and others, are ready, willing, and able to monitor the process.

The country of Norway has also had a gender quota system in place since 1986 for its political parties for government appointments. Norway's Cabinet has been at least 40 percent women, and currently eight out of seventeen Cabinet ministers are women. Women make up 39 percent of Norway's Parliament. But what's good for Norway isn't necessarily good for America. Or is it? Affirmative action programs are not foreign to Americans. The debate goes on daily in every area of business, education, and government. Good, thoughtful people debate the importance of diversity but, at the same time, fairness to all. Perhaps the initiative of Clinton Allen, founder and president of the Corporate Directors Club, an organization with more than five hundred members, of which one hundred are women, will turn the tide in the corporate boardroom.

"I think we haven't gotten there yet in terms of full acceptance of the concept of women on boards," Allen says. "I've gotten to know a ton of women with the Corporate Directors Club very well—top notch, first-rate women—and I would go out of my way to try and get them on boards. I've been on three boards with women, and women tend to do their homework—sometimes more than men. They take their time. I'm not saying men aren't good directors, I'm just saying women seem to dot the 'i's and cross the 't's a little bit more. It's that attention to detail that has always set women apart, and working alongside men is unmistakably the way to get on more boards."

I believe in quotas because I have witnessed the power of affirmative action programs. More than sixteen years ago, I cofounded a regional organization called South Shore Women's Business Network. Its purpose was and is to provide a place for women in business to meet and network with each other and grow their businesses. One of the first things I did as executive director was to reach out to the State Office of Minority and Women's Business Assistance (SOMWBA), for the purpose of finding out what services were available to small women-owned businesses. Massachusetts, just like every other state in the union, has a program that allows women and minorities and disadvantaged businesses to become certified as such in order to have the opportunity to compete with much larger, well-funded businesses. The prime contractors with state contracts must hire a percentage of these Women Business Enterprises (WBEs), Minority Business Enterprises (MBEs), and Disadvantaged Business Enterprises (DBEs).

I personally know of dozens of women-owned firms with small operating funds who were able to navigate their way through the bureaucratic maze in order to present themselves equally to prime contractors. The Big Dig, regardless of its later problems, was an opportunity for small firms of all types to offer up their services for a project of incomparable potential. A contract with the Big Dig guaranteed a payday and perhaps a pay decade, depending upon your work.

Two stories related to the Big Dig come to mind. First is a woman-owned sand and gravel company with an earth removal permit that was SOMWBA certified. Trucking was a big part of the Big Dig since what was unearthed to prepare for the tunnel in turn was used to build a sewerage treatment plant, a golf course, and more. O'Donnell Sand and Gravel took its business to a new level due to the opportunity provided by affirmative action. "We built twenty-plus-year relationships with the primes," says Mary O'Donnell, who started the company. "They needed the minority set aside, and sand and gravel wasn't something they did in-house. It was a piece of work that they could give away, and the fact they could give it to a woman's enterprise was a bonus."[9]

In the construction arena, the primes, all male-owned firms, had the big projects wrapped up. So how did a woman compete with this group? O'Donnell competed by having the chance to show she had the right stuff to get the job done on time and under budget. A $7 million contract to supply all the rock over and under the Third Harbor Tunnel put O'Donnell Sand and Gravel on the map, so to speak, and proved that the company could deliver.

Affirmative action programs provided that opportunity as well for Judith Nitsch Engineering, now Nitsch Engineering, founded in 1989. Starting her firm during the real estate crash, Nitsch attributes her success to taking advantage of public-sector/private-sector market swings, putting network-ing to work, seeking outside input, and ensuring a marketing culture in the firm. The civil engineering firm had the people and the talent to do the job for the state in the Big Dig project. But as a small company, it would need to act as a subcontractor.

The Big Dig, billed as the "largest, most complex and technologi-cally challenging highway project ever attempted in America's history," had a federal 11-percent DBE hiring mandate that included women and minority-owned businesses. The project allowed Nitsch Engineering to quadruple in sales in 1993, and the experience increased the in-house ca-pabilities as well. In 1996, Nitsch achieved prime contractor status. "We grew from one person to a company with a COO, a CFO, a marketing director, an HR manager and department managers," Nitsch says. "To grow the business, we've always taken advantage of the opportunities out there."[10]

Today, Nitsch Engineering is the largest WBE civil engineering firm in Massachusetts and provides public and private development in twelve states and four countries. Nitsch Engineering serves as a prime contractor on many jobs, and this is all due to the opportunities afforded to them once upon a time—because of affirmative action. It is clear that these programs give small companies a chance to do the job and to be seen as competent partners to the largest firms. It didn't take long for Nitsch Engineering to be seen in this way.

When women have the chance to prove they can get the job done just as well as their male counterparts, they are more likely asked to be part of the team the next time around. This is exactly why we need to do whatever we can to infuse corporate America with more talented women in senior executive ranks and at the board level—to give the boys a chance to see us in action. Here is where quotas come in. It is time to stop the "opting-out" talent drain in our major companies. I believe that with role models and proven leaders of both genders at the top, change will trickle down and the leaders of tomorrow will work together more inclusively to meet the demands of a changing workplace.

The Women's Business Enterprise National Council (WBENC) was founded in 1997 and is the nation's leading advocate of women-owned businesses as suppliers to America's corporations. It is also the largest third-party certifier of women-owned businesses in the United States. More than one thousand U.S. companies and government agencies rely on the WBENC certification for their voluntary supplier diversity programs. Its president, Linda Denny, notes, "Women-owned companies have participated in supplier diversity programs in growing numbers over the last ten years and have become a powerful voice in the supplier diversity community. That community also includes minorities, disabled veterans, and various other kinds of groups."

Yes, I can read your skeptic's mind at work. Affirmative action programs cause controversy in every industry. Whether it is women or minorities, there is a supposition that any assistance causes unfairness for someone else. The truth, in my opinion, is that in order to ensure equality in the workplace, we must introduce new faces and ideas every chance we get to make certain that all groups have a turn at bat. Here's the problem. The leadership path for men is clear and visible. All we have to do is look at the example of the platform that has been created for Barack Obama, a very talented and articulate man that the Democratic Party and the media embraced in 2006. What did we see? Am I saying that the respect and attention for Barack Obama was without merit? Not at all. What I am saying is that talent can be seen from far off and must be embraced as early as possible to realize its contribution in the future. Where are the young women leaders of tomorrow? Why does the media constantly reinforce only negative stereotypes of young women—the young celebrity types with money and no responsibility? Yes, the media provides us with negative male role models as well, but the differences are clear. The women chosen are shown as stupid, irresponsible, anorexic, selfish, and self-involved. The young men have their faults yet also seem to have greater purpose and potential for turning themselves around.

Young women, in reality, excel in sports, in the arts, in school, and in the community. As a former president of the sixth largest council of the Girl Scouts of the USA, I can state with complete confidence the extraordinary leadership abilities of those thousands of young women every year who attain the Gold Award, an honor similar to the Boy Scout's Eagle Scout Award. But what awaits these young women as they enter the workforce and even make it to the middle ranks of whatever they choose, be it an attorney, a politician, a businesswoman, a hospital administrator, a scientific researcher, or a college professor? Nothing more. That's it. At least that is how it is now for the majority of women, and their inertia is not due to lack of trying.

The time for women must be now. It is time that we get involved and make things happen. Again, there's no sitting back and assuming that women's swelling numbers in just about every sector will change the leadership ratio. Take the Equal Pay Act, for example. Passed in 1963, there's still a wage gap almost forty-five years later. This gap begins just one year out of college, when women working full-time already earn

80 percent of what their male counterparts earn, according to the April 2007 "Behind the Pay Gap" report released by the American Association of University Women Educational Foundation. Ten years after graduation, the gap widens to women's 69 percent of what men earn—even though women outperform men in school. If women don't take this personally, and if we all don't take this seriously, who will?

Evelyn Murphy says, "The EEOC (Equal Employment Opportunity Commission) has always been underfunded, and it continues to have layer upon layer of responsibilities such as pregnancy issues, disability issues, and more put upon it. There will never be enough funds to enforce the law."[11] So it is up to us to initiate change. The future of America is in embracing women's talents, championing fairness across the board, and making America the greatest country on earth for future generations. Before you say America is already the greatest country on the earth, I want to remind you that we can't rely on the reputation from previous generations forever.

The lesson of the previous chapter illustrates clearly that we must learn from history so as not to repeat the same mistakes over and over again until the pain of doing so finally moves us to change. We must pay attention to the competition we see around the globe as education has become critical and accepted as the way to compete, particularly in many parts of Asia and India. Today, 65 percent of all graduate degrees are earned by women. As a nation we must utilize the talents of the best and the brightest and not allow stereotypical ideas of the past get in the way of progress.

And then, to assure that the time is now for women's leadership, work/life balance must be seen for what it can be. Family is important to both men and women. To assume that the birth of a child affects women more than men in the same occupation sets up a bias that is unfair to both genders. Family, and more important, a healthy family, is essential to our country's future. Business, government, law, higher education, medicine and the sciences, and the nonprofit arena must support families in every way possible—not because it is in the best interest of women (and men) but because it is in the best interest of America. Without procreation there are no future leaders and no need for goods and services, fair and just laws, improvements in healthcare, or applicable educational advances. It is that simple. Therefore, it's up to us to put families first, and that means more flextime, more day care, and more attention to the details that allow us all to move forward. These are all practices that benefit both men and women.

It's time for America to reconnect with all its people and address the problems currently stalling progress in business, politics, healthcare, education, and philanthropy. It's time for women to join men in leading in America. Your first response to this claim may be, "How can putting many more women in charge solve the nation's problems?" Or, if you are like me, you may ask, "Why has it taken so long to embrace the obvious and utilize the talents of 52 percent of the population?" When it comes to women in national government, the United States—with sixteen out of one hundred senators and seventy-one out of four hundred and thirty-five in the House of Representatives—ranks sixty-sixth among one hundred and eighty-nine countries, and behind countries such as Mozambique, Uzbekistan, and Pakistan.[12] Unfortunately, the story at the state level is even less encouraging, with just 23.5 percent of female lawmakers in state government. Perhaps, the 2007 record results of fifty-eight women being elected to their state senates, houses, and assemblies is a sign of hope for the future.

Swanee Hunt, president of Hunt Alternatives and director of the Women and Public Policy Program at Harvard's Kennedy School of Government as well as former ambassador to Austria, says women tend to bring greater senses of integrity and honesty to the political process. "Most women perceive politics as a dirty game. They are right. Two-thirds of one hundred and fifty-nine countries surveyed by the World Bank in 2005 had serious corruption. Increasing the number of women in politics may be an effective measure against corruption. A growing body of evidence suggests that female government leaders tend to be more transparent and honest than men. Research sponsored by the World Bank found that the greater the representation of women in government, the lower the level of corruption."[13] What more information do we need to vote for a woman every chance we get?

When we asked how he envisioned the country with more women leaders, management guru Tom Peters said, "Women are more focused on relationships, women are more thoughtful, all of those things are astonishing strengths and it sure as hell would make a difference if women were running the United States of America, etc. I really do think we would have a more peaceful planet. But, on the other hand, guys get away with their thoughtlessness, just because they are the ones that step forward and it's tough, it's called Life 101. Every strength contains within it a weakness, whether you are male or female. If you're a relationship person, you do things more slowly. Relationships are a more thoughtful affair. I happen to think that works in the long haul. I happen to think that works in the short haul. If you believe *The Female Brain*, seven weeks after conception, you and I are the same and then the great divide begins at literally the speed of light. I get whacked by this incredible wave of testosterone in the eighth week and I lose my relationship ability and begin to develop my competitiveness skills ability. That's the hard science of 2006."

The hard reality today is that America is in need of relationship building, of thoughtful action, of women at the helm. Whatever your response, the rest of this book will tell you why the time is now and why you—woman or man—have an obligation to participate in the change.

CHAPTER 5

"Business as Usual?" ... Try "Business as Exceptional"

"An empowered organization is one in which individuals have the knowledge, skill, desire, and opportunity to personally succeed in a way that leads to collective organizational success."

—Stephen R. Covey

There is no "business as usual" anymore. Corporate types are looking over their shoulders in the aftermath of Enron and other such scandals. Sarbanes-Oxley has put public companies under the gun to ensure that their leadership understands their fiduciary responsibility to shareholders and the general public. Women are often profiled as the whistleblowers in corporate scandals, which has us wondering: Would we see better character and values reflected in business if women had an equal role at the table?

My answer, as I'm sure you know by now, is a resounding "Yes!" Women bring compassion to leadership and greater collaboration to business. I'm not the only one to think so. During the ten years I have been profiling women in business, women consistently walk the talk as they define power differently than men. Women see power as something that should be shared. They have worked hard to get to the top and, once there, they reach out, not always to other women unfortunately, but to others to be more inclusive and to create a flatter organization.

As you'll read ahead, CEO women time after time choose to work with others to lead rather than dictate the direction. Character and values are clearly important ingredients for the company's success—and very likely for bigger profit margins. The 2004 Catalyst Study, "The Bottom Line: Connecting Corporate Performance and Gender Diversity," indicates that companies with the highest representation of women on their top management teams had better financial performance than the companies with fewer women in these positions. The study was careful to point out that it could not unequivocally say that gender diversity causes increased financial performance, but only that the data certainly can support a clear case for it.

Sharon Allen, who was recently elected to her second four-year term as chairman of public accounting firm Deloitte & Touche USA, does say unequivocally that having more women at the top—and more women in general—improves the bottom line. Deloitte's Women's Initiative (WIN), undertaken fourteen years ago when the company realized that its women were not reaching the partner level as expected, has worked successfully at retaining and advancing women ever since. In 2006, according to Public Accounting Report's survey of women in public accounting,[1] Deloitte & Touche USA topped the country's Big Four accounting firms in the percentage of women partners, principals, and directors. *Fortune* in 2007 named Deloitte to its "100 Best Companies to Work for" list for the eighth time.

Since the U.S. Labor Department statistics show that by 2008 women will make up nearly half of the labor pool and will earn 57 percent of all accounting degrees, retention is increasingly becoming a top priority in the profession. Replacing high-performing professionals can, and does, cost more than twice that individual's salary, so focusing on retention of women and men is not just practical but a tremendous boost to the bottom line as well. "We're not doing this just because this is the right thing to do," Allen says. "Without question, it has converted to improved financial success. Retention rates have improved significantly and it has positively impacted recruiting costs, which are very significant to us. As women move up into the ranks of our organization, the retention of the really good and strong leaders improves our operating results. We're convinced, absolutely convinced, that we are a larger organization and a more profitable organization as a result of our initiatives."

So, why aren't more businesses catching on? Certainly, some women are making strides into senior management and into the corner office. But once they get there, do or can they bring change that can be quantified and be held up as a reason for more companies to look to the promotion of women as the path to increasing profits and growing shareholder value? Catalyst's "The 2005 Catalyst Census of Women Corporate Officers and Top Earners of the *Fortune* 500—Ten Years Later: Limited Progress,

Challenges Persist," says it all in its title. The findings were disappointing, to say the least. But that was before the 2006 Census,[2] which found women holding 15.6 percent of *Fortune* 500 executive positions, down from 16.4 percent in 2005, with the number of companies with three or more women in the C-suite also decreasing. Because women's numbers went backwards, the forty years to parity predicted in 2005 among *Fortune* 500 corporate officers has become forty-seven years. Worse yet is the seventy-three years—seventy-three years!—it will take to get women in equal numbers on *Fortune* 500 boards. Even though little changed in the numbers of women overall year to year—14.6 percent in 2006 compared to 14.7 in 2005—that tenth of a percent translates into a decrease in the number of companies with one or two women directors as well as an increase in companies with no women directors at all. And the differential resulted in an additional three years to parity. That's right. Women are *actually* moving backward, not forward, in their quest to find equality in corporate America.

Other discouraging findings in both the Catalyst 2005 and 2006 updates: Women are still more than twice as likely to hold staff positions, almost guaranteeing their likelihood of missing out of advancement opportunities to C-level positions. Men, on the other hand, are equally represented in both staff and line positions. It's the line positions that affect the bottom line and are therefore the positions from which corporate America promotes. There was a glimmer of good news: Women in top-paying positions rose to 6.7 percent in 2006 from 6.4 percent in 2005, and women directors' participation on compensation and nominating/governance committees increased from 9 percent and 14.2 percent respectively in 2005 to 10 percent and 14.7 percent respectively in 2006. I did say, "glimmer."

What will get more women to the top in greater advancements than tenths of a percentage point? A reality check, for one thing. Since 1970, according to *The Economist*, two out of every three jobs globally have gone to women.[3] Combine that staggering statistic with the fact that women will soon be the majority of wealth holders in this country and, as Tom Peters says, "There is a demographic tsunami that is going to make this stuff happen whether guys want it or not. It's going to happen. Whether or not women are populating the C-suite, they are more than 50 percent of managers, well more than 50 percent of human resources and 50 percent of admin officers, so while the big company executive suites are still short on women, the infrastructure below is on the border of becoming women-dominated."

Here's Peters' take on the evolution of leadership over the next two decades: "The statistical reality is that, if boomers hold all the top jobs today and 80 percent of boomers in the top jobs are men, 80 percent of the boomer top job men jobholders will retire in the next twenty years and, at the next level down, most of the people who will be in line for the promotion statistically will be women, period. And women are going to be ten times harder to ignore in the course of the next twenty years than is even the case today, let alone years ago. It's stunning. That's why I'm presenting it like, what the hell choice do you have?"

Before we all sit back and say time will simply take care of any women's leadership issues, however, let's focus on what will still be in the way of women's leadership progress no matter how many women populate the payroll. "It will never work if companies work on this as if 'it's the correct thing to do,'" says Myra Hart, Harvard Business School professor, corporate board director, and one of Staples' four founders. "They have to address it as an economic imperative, and then things will happen."

Women's Retention/Pipeline

In our chapter, "The Time Is Now," we looked at just some of the reasons women are ready to take the lead. For the past thirty years, women have taken on every challenge offered in corporate America, and they are on pace to be equal with men in MBA programs by the time this book is released. Women have the ambition and the drive necessary to get to the top but continue to get sidetracked by corporate structures that haven't kept pace with their European and Canadian counterparts in accommodating their needs—and in reality, most everyone's needs. Companies in certain parts of the world have developed the support systems people require to juggle 24/7 work and family responsibilities, but this is not the case in the United States, where change has already been a long, slow process.

It was 1986 when then-Colorado Congresswoman Patricia Schroeder introduced the Family and Medical Leave Act (FMLA). It was purposely drafted to include both mothers and fathers. Finally passed in 1993, the act allowed three months unpaid leave within two years after the birth or adoption of a child for either men or women. Although the leave was unpaid, the job and its accompanying health benefits were guaranteed during and on return. The final act included only companies with fifty or more employees. Both men and women in the United States have taken advantage of the law, but the majority has been women. If, after the leave, the woman or, although this is not likely, the man, does not return to work, there is no further commitment by the employer for future employment or benefits.

The Project on Global Working Families report[4] concluded in 2007 that the United States lags far behind in family policies—not only all other wealthy countries but also most low-income countries. One hundred and seventy-seven countries were researched and their public policies for families were measured. When it comes to childbearing, one hundred and sixty-eight countries (out of one hundred and seventy-three) offer guaranteed leave with income, and ninety-eight of these countries offer fourteen or more weeks paid leave. Let me again be crystal clear. There are no guarantees of paid leave for mothers in the United States. Men's paternity leave is also considered a positive advancement in many countries. Sixty-six countries either pay paternity leave or offer the right of paternity leave to fathers, and thirty-one of these countries offer fourteen or more weeks of paid leave. Fathers have no guaranteed paid paternity leave or paid parental leave in the United States (see Figures 5.1 and 5.2).

Other areas studied and measured by the study were time allowed for breastfeeding, work hours, and leave for illness and family care. In each area, the United States rated close to the bottom in providing families the time they need to care for each other.

Figure 5.1

Maximum Paid Leave (Maternity and Paternal) Available to Mothers in Countries Providing Paid Leave.

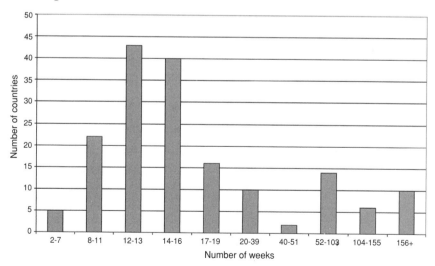

Source: Jody Heymann and The Institute for Health and Social Policy at McGill University, "The Work, Family, and Equity Index," the Project on Global Working Families (January 2007) (used with permission).

Figure 5.2

Maximum Paid Leave (Paternity and Parental) Available to Fathers in Countries Providing Paid Leave.

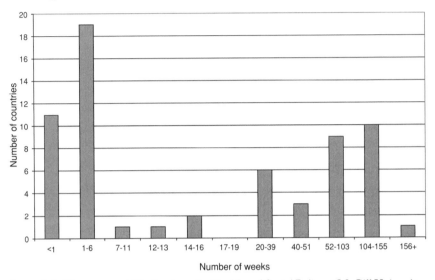

Source: Jody Heymann and The Institute for Health and Social Policy at McGill University, "The Work, Family, and Equity Index," the Project on Global Working Families (January 2007) (used with permission).

It is important to say that some U.S. companies are moving in the right direction in this area, however. As already noted, companies understand the need to retain talent because they know that training can cost in the tens of thousands of dollars and the loss of an exceptional employee, male or female, can cost upwards of one hundred thousand dollars or more. And they know that the women they lose are among the best and the brightest. That's why they hired them in the first place. In researching their tentatively titled, yet-to-be-published book, *Assuming Control*, Harvard Business School's Myra Hart and coauthors Candida Brush and Patricia Greene have found a significant number of MBA women stepping out of full-time, fast-paced careers. "So the question is, 'Do you have to slow down or leave?' That has a lot to do with how work is structured. If you choose to exit, how do you reenter when you're ready? That's a huge challenge, and it's not yet resolved," Hart says.

Deloitte happens to be answering the "slow down or leave" question, but then the company has long been ahead of the curve. Deloitte began on its retention-advancement course correction by studying why women were not being promoted to partner at the expected rate as well as what accounted for such high turnover throughout the organization. A need for flexibility for work/life balance, the natural assumption, turned up on the what's-wrong list—but so did: (1) not giving women the best assignments out of fear that they would depart and leave clients hanging and (2) a dearth of mentoring opportunities. Addressing all three as a starting point—work/life balance, better assignments, and mentoring—Deloitte took one more initial step, Sharon Allen says: "Specific action. You can't just assume that when you create these opportunities that women will always step up automatically and take them. You have to take special action and special initiatives to allow for the training." And very possibly most important, the company had the necessary at-the-top buy-in to make the changes. Tom Peters says, "They put real muscle behind this thing. They put it at the CEO level and at the advisory board level and in an annual report on progress with the women's initiative."

These days, Deloitte is going a step further. Its latest initiative is career customization, which allows men and women the opportunity to accelerate and decelerate their careers in keeping with their personal needs. "Our hope and our expectation is that this is going to allow us again to retain a much higher percentage of talented women who will not only find the right balance of their work and their life at any point in time but will stay with us for a longer period of time and excel and become the next role model," Allen says.

The smart company will address ASAP the pernicious cycle of losing its investment and its talent, and here's more reason to do so: The Graduate Management Admission Council projects that business schools' outreach targeting women will only increase their numbers in MBA programs—to 64 percent full-time, 47 percent part-time, and 50 percent in executive programs. But is the next generation willing to step up to the plate without this "whole life balance" thing changing? What's so inviting, after all, about the work world when you hear Hart describe what she sees as needing to change to get more women to stay. "I believe we have to rethink the structure of work. As a society, we have accepted the assumption that high quality work can only be done on this rapid-fire, 80-hour workweek schedule. It's what we hold up as the model. Whether on Wall Street or in the media, it seems that the people we define as truly successful are always available, have their Blackberries in hand around the clock and never say no. Frankly, that may win you the prize, but it's no way to live."

So, if you build it right, will they come? Yes, and in droves. The Simmons School of Management survey, "Optioning In versus 'Opting Out': Women Using Flexible Work Arrangements for Career Success," released in 2007, finds that 88 percent of the four hundred women respondents are using flexible work options—telecommuting, flexible hours, and the like—to stay in the workplace while managing their complex lives. What's more, these women say they did not sacrifice financial success when carving out their options. The ultimate result? A new model in which women are acting as "career self-agents" in negotiating their own terms for employment and, rather than opting out, are opting in.

This points to the fact that, once the right retention initiatives are in place, then, of course, it's up to the individual to take the bull by the horns and wrestle his or her way up to the top. Joseph Fanning, a senior manager at Ernst & Young in Boston, confirms that the system can allow for a quick rise for talented men and women if the right steps are taken.

"Accounting firms are looking for an army of talent in the first few years out of school, recruiting a diverse group of ethnicities and genders," he says. "During the first three to five years, a new recruit will work hard and study to fulfill the requirements for the CPA exam. It is a rigorous but clear path and it is a testament to how one will further his or her career with the firm. It shows respect for the job. The 'army' little by little is whittled down by the workload, the required skill sets, the responsibility, and the exam itself. Once you have reached the manager ranks, the path to partner starts to become more apparent. Aggressively seeking challenging assignments and high-profile roles, along with having a mentor to help navigate your career, can assist in accelerating the process. The average age to make partner is anywhere from thirty-four to thirty-eight years old, depending on the practice."

Flextime and the possibility of working from home for all employees are actually helping the women who take advantage of the offerings to attain partner as people can find fulfillment personally and professionally. "Public accounting firms want a diverse partner group, including women, and if the desire is there, women can and will make it," Fanning says. Interestingly, he notes that few men, that he knows of, take full advantage of his company's work/life balance programs, although he says everyone in his practice, male or female, takes advantage of some portion of the flexible work environment that his firm offers.

The New York office of Ernst & Young tackled the perceived shame in taking time off for family by displaying a nine-foot poster, visible from Times Square, which featured the promotion of Rob McLeod after he took paternity leave. The same poster also hung in every Ernst & Young office throughout the United States for the greatest impact inside the organization. The company's approach in focusing on men with this work/life program is aimed at retaining and promoting women, and it is in addition to the mentoring and concierge services that are offered.[5] The truth of the matter is, once men and women are comfortable in their skins and once they're sure that corporate is supporting them in—and not punishing them for—their individual needs, the move to leadership parity can begin.

So, why are there so few women rising to the top even when they're in a supportive environment? Fanning suggests, "There are the traditional reasons, including the desire to stay home and raise a family, and, that aside, other major drivers that would include not asking for or receiving the proper assignments, not communicating their worth and not having the right mentors. My superiors have mostly been women coming up through the firm and I have had great relationships with all of them, including from a mentor perspective. I believe one of the most significant contributing factors to my success in the firm thus far has been the counsel and guidance of my mentors. Male or female, to get ahead it really helps to have the guidance of someone who is where you want to go."

So there it is. Women need the confidence to promote themselves, the smarts to find and follow through with a mentor, and the willingness to take advantage of the programs available to them that will help them achieve their goals. Certainly, more women at the top serving as role models and willing mentors will make a huge difference for younger women beginning their climb—if they actually begin the ascent.

The Media

Even today, the media continues its mantra of a glass ceiling to get across the point—that ambition isn't a feminine quality—and, when that image doesn't discourage women, the new drum beat becomes "women opting out." It is important to understand that when corporate America reports losing women in large numbers, it is not that they are going home to nest. The truth is that after a long battle to advance, many women realize they have a better chance of succeeding by developing their own business model. Learning once again that we have a choice today in how we work and with whom we work, women take the risk for doing it on their own. And the corporate woman CEO is still depicted as the person who has sacrificed it all to get to the top. This myth must be rebuked. Doing so is the main reason I started a business newspaper profiling women senior executives and women business owners.

Four years into publishing the paper, I attended a luncheon at which the keynote speaker was Ellyn Spragins, talking about the misfortune of successful women. Her point: They either had no husband in their life or he was a househusband and not an equal intellectual partner. Looking around the room and seeing many successful women that I knew well and knowing the successful, talented men they were married to for thirty or more years, I spoke up and immediately took our speaker to task.

"As publisher of a newspaper profiling women in business, my experience is just the opposite," I said. "My experience is that successful people are determined people and that determined people put great effort into everything they do. That includes work, marriage, and family. The successful women I know, and several of them are in this room, are married for many, many years and have children and grandchildren who are strong, successful individuals."

With this, the speaker asked me about my own family and, particularly, my husband. "I am married thirty years (it is now thirty-five years), my husband is a financial advisor and I have a son twenty-five-years old (now thirty years old) who is in technology sales. My husband is my financial advisor and my biggest fan, and I am his. We have a successful marriage and family because we work hard at everything we do."

Out of this conversation, Spragins interviewed me for a piece she was writing in the *New York Sunday Times*.[6] I panicked for several weeks before it came out. I knew that she had an agenda and I feared my husband's reputation as a financial expert would be jeopardized. Fortunately, the article made a short reference to him and concentrated more on how I choose my own portfolio of investments. I have been investing in stocks since I was ten years old. I wasn't married then. What the article did not say, and what of course one could only partially read between the lines, was that as a smart businesswoman I may choose what stocks I'm interested in but I'm not foolish enough not to take the advice of the person who cares most, besides me, about my financial stability. My point is, the media has an angle and an agenda with much of what it writes about women in business, and both men and women must be aware that it just isn't that simple. Reader beware!

In the same vein, later that same year, I got a call from a major network's local affiliate. The producer of the nightly television show *Chronicle* was interested in doing a show on successful businesswomen and their trophy husbands. That's right, I was asked to identify the region's women with the greatest achievement and their househusbands who made it all work. Now, you might say, doesn't that prove the point that women have made it if television wants to tell their story? I'm afraid not. And, you should know better than that. Creating the picture that successful women must find men who are ready, willing, and able to fulfill the household chores and give up on their own dreams is the media's way of telling young women that they might just have to pay too high a price for success. Viewer beware!

This is a perfect time to let you know that I am a true believer that women who stay at home and raise families, help their husbands achieve success, and/or provide hours and hours of community service work all deserve and have my absolute respect. And I just as strongly support the men who take on that same role. People, male and female, have the right to choose their dreams and pursue what fulfills them. But it is reprehensible for the media to control the image and enforce a preconceived picture that continually downgrades women's leadership capabilities and, at the same time, the person who might be supporting them in ways other than financially.

I could spend an entire chapter, no, an entire book, on how the media distorts the power and influence of women in everything we do in America. It is never enough that a woman CEO leads a multimillion dollar company, employs hundreds of happy workers, and provides the best in medical, dental, and retirement benefits. She must also be struggling with a debilitating disease or have a handicapped child, or, like my friend Shirley Singleton, CEO of Edgewater Technology, experience a massacre of seven employees by one disgruntled software engineer. Is this the way to have to get media attention if you are a woman leading a $10 to $100 million company? Of course not.

Singleton cofounded Edgewater Technology in 1992. I met her in 1997 when the company was still small but starting to tick in the technology boom. In 1999, Edgewater was acquired by StaffMark, a publicly traded billion-dollar staffing organization. Singleton remained as president and continued to grow the company. Until the tragic event of December 26, 2000, she had very little media coverage. None of us can imagine the thoughts that must swirl through a leader's mind at such a time of crisis, but Singleton proved herself to be the finest leader any company could ask for by keeping the company on track through not only the heart-wrenching episode but also the ensuing technology bust. Over the past seven years, Singleton has received a lot of attention for a variety of reasons, mostly for the tremendous motivation she gave to her employees to stick together and make it through. But I also know she often feels too much attention is paid to her. My advice to her and other women is that we need them to keep the spotlight on themselves for whatever reason so that the achievements of all women will have the limelight. I admire Singleton and other women like her for not allowing the media to paint them with a broad brush and to stand up and give voice to all the women leaders. We cannot allow the media to define women only as victims or as those who succeed only against immeasurable odds. Sometimes women are successful just because they work hard and know what they are doing. What a concept!

Just take a look at how Carly Fiorina, former HP CEO, was and is handled by the media. In a 2006 *Financial Times* interview,[7] Fiorina admits to feeling like she was "operating in a fishbowl of media and public scrutiny" all the time she led HP. "People have their point of view based on their stereotypes. You have to cut through that. In many ways I was a caricature. Gee, she has laid off people, therefore she is heartless. She wears nice clothes, she must be superficial." Her autobiography, *Tough Choices: A Memoir*, was written not just to tell her side of the story but also to tell how business really works. "It occurred to me that people didn't really understand how business operates. People don't understand that you set goals, you rally people around a common goal that is worth achieving. People think business is mechanistic. It is a very human activity. To change, to get results, it is about changing people." For the five-and-half years she ran HP, Fiorina was held up as a role model for women—with or without her or other women's permission. She declares in her book that she did everything she could to reject questions about her gender but nothing she did allowed her to escape them. Since Fiorina was the most powerful woman in business in the United States, the media was not about to focus on the business issues facing the company only.

By the time of her announcement of Compaq's acquisition, Fiorina thought the media's attention would finally focus on the plan itself but there was never a letup on her gender and how that played with the public and company directors in such a crucial decision for the then-struggling company. In the same 2006 *Financial Times* interview, she says, "I don't believe that I lost or that I failed. I think I was fired. I don't feel like a victim in this. I took a set of decisions that I am accountable for. I feel that I made the right choices for the business. I think the results [since then] have demonstrated that."

I remember Fiorina's firing well. I was inundated by calls from both newspapers and television that day to comment on her fall. "Was she fired because she was a woman?" "Was it a sign for businesswomen that there was no chance to succeed at the top?" "Did women not have what it takes to succeed?" No, no, and no. CEOs in public companies are hired and fired every day across America. They serve at the favor of the board of directors. If and when the board feels the CEO is moving in the wrong direction, the decision is made to find someone new.

So did Carly Fiorina's five-and-half years at HP help or hurt women? Unfortunately, not a month goes by that some man, business or otherwise, doesn't say to me, "What a shame for women that Carly Fiorina got

fired from HP. It shows women don't have what it takes to be CEO."
Really. Isn't it interesting that we don't blame all men for the behavior and
decisions of Tyko's Dennis Kozlowski, Enron's Kenneth Lay and Jeffrey
Skillings, Adelphia's John Rigas and his sons, Timothy and Michael, and
the list can go on and on. No one would begin to suggest that their
behavior indicates that all men are selfish and regularly put their own
self-interest above those of the company and of the shareholders. What
we need are lots of women at the top. It's then that we won't have the
opportunity to shake our heads and cluck our tongues over the dismissal of
one rare woman CEO. (And, if the media will revisit Fiorina's insistence
on merging Compaq with HP, it could very well be that she did "good" for
the company and that the board of directors did the disservice.) But how
to get more women to the top is the pressing question.

For decades, we have heard that getting women into CEO positions
was all about filling the pipeline. A December 2006 *New York Times*
article[8] follows the story of Carol Bartz, the former CEO of Autodesk
who worked her way through the male-dominated technology industry in
Silicon Valley in the 1980s. Throughout her climb, she often found herself
skipped over or dismissed by other men in the room who assumed "she was
an office assistant." Things aren't all that different today. "There have been
women in the pipeline for twenty to twenty-five years. Progress has been
slower than anybody thought it ever would be," says Julie H. Daum, North
American board practice leader for executive search firm Stuart Spencer,
in the same article.

In 2006, more women had reached chief executive in the *Fortune* 500
than in any other year with the addition of Irene B. Rosenfeld, CEO
of Kraft Foods; Patricia A. Woertz, CEO of Archer Daniels Midland
(ADM); and Indra Nooyi, PepsiCo chair and CEO. But the overall feeling by these women and others is that they want to be seen for their
"accomplishments rather than for being women."[9] Perhaps, and in my
opinion it is very unfortunate, they learned from watching Carly Fiorina
struggle to get her message out while doing her best to sift through the
questions directed at her only because she was a woman. The media's preconceived view of a woman CEO, then and now, prevents these leading
women from publicly speaking their minds on an array of issues. Other
potential female and male leaders are the losers when the media puts its
own spin on women at the top.

Clearly, the working woman's mantra is: We must see it to believe
it. We must believe it to achieve it. It may be tough running a *Fortune*
500 company whether you are male or female, but the responsibility of
shouldering all the attention as *the* woman in this position is more than any

one, two, three, and perhaps all eleven women can bear. Scrutiny, however, hasn't stopped the women who are at the top, nor has it prevented women like Sherron Watkins, a vice president at Enron, from blowing the whistle on corporate wrongdoing. Watkins was the first to e-mail Kenneth Lay about the problems she knew about firsthand, pointing out misstatements in the financial reports in the company. She exemplifies everything the media wants in a hero or a shero and everything most companies stay clear of.

As was mentioned in an earlier chapter, the corporate scandals and particularly the year 2004 will go down in history as the most corrupt year in corporate dealings. Or will it? The fact that more than six hundred public companies overstated their earnings and had to request time to restate their earnings in 2006 puts a new microscope on what's happening in corporate America. Backdating of options will be the scandal that will keep the focus on what and why corporate America—men's corporate America—can't keep its house in order. Am I suggesting that with a balance of women in senior-level positions there would be a difference in character and values? Yes, again, I am willing to take a stand and tell you that it is a matter of checks and balances. More women in top leadership positions will change this. If *Fortune* 500 and *Fortune* 1000 companies had 50-percent female leadership, you would see a very different dynamic.

Women on Corporate Boards

Sarbanes-Oxley and its strict compliance measures may be responsible for a slight blip in women's representation on corporate boards that some say they are now seeing. "Board membership has become so professional these days. It's no longer the kind of bring-your-friends-aboard-and-play-golf thing that it was twenty or thirty years ago," says The Corporate Directors Club's Clinton Allen, who has served on public boards since 1976. "It's very important that directors understand what their responsibilities are and what their responsibilities to the shareholders are. When you are in an environment like that, to me, it doesn't matter if you are a man or a woman."

Still, the corporate board is another numbers game. If CEOs are the mainstay of board membership, and women aren't getting to CEO, then guess where else they aren't getting. Ditto for any other C-level position. "So what?" you might ask. "Why do we need more women in the board-room?" Corporate America is not just about jobs, it is also about your investment in America. The value of your investment portfolio—mutual funds, 401(k)s, IRAs, pension funds, and, yes, even social security—is based on the success and/or failure of public companies. So we are all very much affected by the inner workings of these organizations. What's more, these are the companies that are most visible and transparent in terms of operation. For those on the outside, diversity of thought translates into credibility and reliability by shareholders and consumers alike. On the inside, diversity at the top gives credence to the opportunities for anyone with the ability to rise to the top. And we need women in the boardroom, and the executive office, and everywhere else throughout the organization, for their understanding of half of the country's population or, put more simply, for better profits.

Let's look at the facts. Women are the major consumers in America, not only of consumer goods but also of all business goods and services, totaling $44.5 billion.[10] It is clearly in the best interest of corporate America to have its major consumer perspective reflected at the board level. The 2004 Catalyst study mentioned at the very beginning of this chapter isn't the only study to make the link between women's participation and bottom line performance. Toni Wolfman, in her 2007 *New England Journal of Public Policy* article, notes six other studies from 1998 to 2005 that, as she says, "demonstrate a correlation between the presence of women in positions of corporate leadership—on boards of directors or in senior executive positions, or both—and superior financial performance."[11]

The most recent study that Wolfman, president of InterOrganization Network (ION) and Executive in Residence of the Women's Leadership Institute at Bentley College, notes is the 2005 study by Citizens Advisers that analyzed the two hundred and ninety-eight companies in the Citizens Index. Each of those companies had at least one woman or minority on its board of directors or in the upper two levels of its management. Citizens Advisers "found that the total and average annual return on the stock of those companies with the highest gender diversity was several percentage points higher than that of the companies with the lowest gender diversity and also had less volatility or risk than those companies with fewer women," she writes. "While these studies do not purport to demonstrate a causal relationship between the presence of women in positions of corporate leadership and stronger financial performance, at the very least they show that the two go hand in hand. As such, they reinforce the conclusions of those who advance the case for diversity as a common sense response to the increased economic clout of women and their growing importance as corporate stakeholders of every kind."

Anecdotal evidence—conversing with other people—points to more women on boards outside the *Fortune* 500 in the last three to four years, but we're still talking about a mere 14.6 percent of the directors sitting around the *Fortune* 500 table in 2006. Clinton Allen notes seeing an increase of women on boards over three decades, but even he says, "I don't think there's full acceptance of the concept of women on boards. There are an awful lot of boards that are just men, and diversity issues don't come up all that much, to be perfectly honest. It still is a bit of an old boys' club. It hasn't flipped yet."

That isn't to say that Allen and others like him aren't trying to get more women on boards. He has nominated women for membership on the boards on which he serves—not because they're women but because of the skills they bring to the table. But somehow, some way, these women had to get to one board table in the first place.

Gail Deegan, who is a director on the boards of both EMC Corporation and The TJX Companies, is a perfect example of once you're in, one board leads to another. Before beginning her CFO trek to multiple companies and back when she was treasurer at Eastern Gas, Deegan would make presentations to her company's board. She got to know one of the members, the CEO of Houghton Mifflin, who asked her to join the Houghton Mifflin board in 1989 to add needed financial expertise. A year later, she was asked to join the board of what is now PerkinElmer through similar circumstances—the then-chair of the company was also on the Eastern Gas board.

"In both cases, the senior people saw me in action," Deegan says. "There was a comfort level and they felt comfortable recommending me. Whether they're sponsoring you for a promotion or a board, it's a little more risky for them because they're saying, 'Here's a woman' and the response is, 'We've never had a woman on the board. How do we know she can do this?' and they respond, 'I know because of such and such.'"

Altogether, Deegan has been involved in five corporate boards over the past twenty-five years. Sometimes she has been the only woman. Other times, she has had company. One of the boards brought in another woman at the same time as Deegan to make their entry more comfortable as two. Today, Deegan is the only woman out of eleven on the EMC board, but is one of four women out of ten directors on the TJX board. She doesn't see a different dynamic board to board, no matter how many women comprise its membership. "Once you get past the initial gender 'there's a difference,' it becomes a much greater sense of what are the experiences and the expertise that you bring to the board and how does the board function as a board," she says.

Myra Hart sits on the public company boards of Ahold, Office Depot, and Summer Infant as well as several private boards. She's among four female directors on a supervisory board of seven members at Ahold, whose stock is traded on the New York Stock Exchange (NYSE) and the Amsterdam Stock Exchange, and is one of the four women out of twelve directors at Office Depot. "I don't have first-hand experience with being the first woman on a board," she says. "I have never found it difficult to get attention or be heard if I have something to say. There is no sense that women are anything but first-string members of the team."

A study out of the Wellesley Centers for Women,[12] however, found that a critical mass of three or more women could cause a fundamental change in the boardroom and improve corporate governance when interviewing fifty women directors, twelve CEOs, and seven corporate secretaries from *Fortune* 1000 companies. "While a lone woman can and often does make substantial contributions, and two women are generally more powerful than one, increasing the number of women to three or more enhances the likelihood that women's voices and ideas are heard and that boardroom dynamics change substantially."

The study's report also heard from interviewees that women were more likely than men to ask the tough questions. Salespeople can confirm this since women are known to ask the detailed questions around wanting to understand every aspect of a particular problem or fact. Men are less likely to question another man on the facts. The results of the Wellesley Centers study imply that even one woman serving on a board makes a constructive contribution. Even when seen as a token in the room, one woman can bring a new perspective. Two women on a board have the opportunity to back each other up, creating a larger impact on the board. Just because two women serve on a board, however, doesn't mean they will agree. Three or more women on a board change the dynamic of the meeting and the women tend to blend in and be seen as people rather than for their gender.

The study report found that three or more women on a board allowed women to speak and contribute more freely, and men were able to listen with more open minds. "As one woman director interviewed summarized it, 'One woman is the invisibility phase; two women is the conspiracy phase; three women is mainstream.'"

I have always said that we women are our own worst enemies because we don't give an inch without questioning each other. If only men had this talent. In the case of board leadership, this talent of questioning everything has merit. My own personal experience goes like this. While sitting on a regional board, I attended quarterly meetings. At each board meeting, I brought up the subject of not getting board materials, and particularly financials, in advance of the meetings. Each time, I was given an excuse for why the financial statements were not available earlier. It is important that board members have time to review the lengthy statements and compare any inconsistencies that might crop up from quarter to quarter. A director cannot sufficiently do this during the meeting itself. The board chair, a man, seemed more angered at my question than at the CFO, who was clearly negligent. Finally, I got other board members who understood that it was their fiduciary responsibility to understand the financials and to approve them as written, and to question the chairman as well. One week before the next board meeting, all board materials, including financial statements, were mailed to directors. It may have started with one voice but it took many to insist that a change be made.

There are many stories of women who have joined corporate boards and asked questions for the first time only to find out that they were questions that had never been asked before and that none of the current board knew the answers. Asking questions is something women do. It does not show ignorance but curiosity. We need more curiosity on public company boards, and yet women's place at the table is diminishing. Similar to Catalyst's 2006 findings, ION reported in February 2007 that corporate boardrooms had ignored the requests from advocates for sound governance and others for greater diversity in their boardrooms. The report, "Women on Boards: Missed Opportunities," showed that women held just 10 percent of the board seats of the one thousand, one hundred and twenty-six public companies studied and that 38 percent (four hundred and twenty-seven) had no women on their boards at all. Most shocking, these numbers changed negatively for women from the year before.

Wolfman, ION's president, told us, "What in the world are all these nominating committees doing? Too many appear to be doing the same old, same old. Maybe they are now using search firms. But how are they using search firms? How many of them are feeding names to search firms and ignoring the other candidates the search firms suggest, while publicly citing the recruiters as the source of their nominees? And how many search firms continue to promote the same candidates over and over without taking the time to expand their pools of potential directors? I don't know the answers to these questions, but it certainly appears that the traditional old boys' network still plays a very important role in the nomination process."

When asked why it is so difficult for women to get onto public company boards, Wolfman, as an extreme example, recounted a recent conversation she had with the male chair of the nominating committee for a large Massachusetts publicly traded company. "When I told him that I had learned that his board was looking for a director with a specific set of skills and experience, and that I knew a woman who met all of the criteria, he flat out told me that he wasn't interested in hearing anything more from me. He went on to tell me that the only way that a candidate would be considered for nomination would be if a current director made a recommendation based on a personal relationship. And I said, 'Even though I could introduce you to several women who have all of those characteristics you're looking for, you would not accept their resumes and you wouldn't be interested in meeting any of them?' and he basically told me, 'That's the case.'"

So, I guess we can't call it discrimination since the company in question has one woman on its board. And we can't say there aren't any qualified women for the position or that the chair of the nominating committee can't find them because ION has done its homework on finding qualified women for corporate board membership and is ready with the list. The truth is, the majority of these public company boards are happy just the way things are. Some are willing to open the door a crack and allow a woman in but not to the point of changing the good old boy appeal of the group. So, again I say, here's what needs to change in corporate America. And how is change to come about? Read on.

Follow the Money

Best Buy is getting "in touch with its feminine side."[13] With women consumers influencing 90 percent of consumer electronic purchases in an $80 billion market, Best Buy was in danger of losing a good part of its customer base. Women were complaining that they weren't getting the help they needed and they didn't feel as though they were being treated with respect. The company first responded by offering more personalized service and then redesigned the store. Now Best Buy is focused on changing its workforce. Anna Gallina, general manager at a North Palm Beach, Florida, store, is quoted as saying, "Women consumers are seeing a lot more women in our stores and that makes it less frightening and less intimidating."

At this writing, 40 percent of Best Buy's employees were women. "We are working with the Girl Scouts, with private female colleges, and with others to recruit amazing women so we can delight our women customers," says Best Buy VP Julie Gilbert. What a refreshing concept—corporate realizing the benefits of having women feel acknowledged once they've shown them they understand them. This information is important for men and women as the bottom line affects us all. We all need to put our money into mutual funds and reliable investments of worthy companies for our future. We are in need of more diversity on our corporate boards for the greater perspective—the 360-degree perspective that men and women bring to very dialogue. When women are no longer considered outsiders, they can have greater influence on a board. Today's corporate boards will benefit from new points of view and tough questioning. Shareholders, investors, and our entire economy are ready for change in the boardroom. So how do we get there? Are we in need of quotas?

This was the topic of the Women's Forum's Conference in October 2006. The chief executive officer of Nestle, Peter Brabeck, spoke about how women, "with their different attitudes and intelligence, are significantly contributing to creating a new corporate mindset in the twenty-first century." When asked how many women sit on Nestle's board and on its executive committee, however, Brabeck's answer of two on the board and none on the executive committee was met with heckles. The question of quotas quickly became the debate. Many companies talk about diversity but have not truly addressed it specifically with a plan. The question of quotas, nonetheless, receives a negative response from both male and female CEOs. "I don't think you'd like to be here as part of a quota, but because you are professionals," Brabeck said, and he explained, "I think it [quotas] humiliating." It was clear during the three-day conference, however, that without some type of aggressive action, women would have decades to wait for parity.

The debate for quotas around the world has strengthened since Norway initiated a requirement that women comprise 40 percent of the boards of listed companies by 2008. Whenever I mention quotas to women in business, they immediately shun the idea and respond: "We must get there on merit alone," "Quotas give the impression that the position is not earned," and "Quotas bring us all back in time to when women couldn't measure up." When asked, Tom Peters noted that affirmative action for civil rights was "absolutely necessary, absolutely reasonable—and the time has past. I certainly think there should be goals that I set as the human resources officer male or female, but federally mandated numbers I think are a bad mistake in 2007."

Still, I'm not backing down from my stance on quotas. The quota system in Norway and Scandinavia shows that a quota system does work. By looking outside the typical recruitment arenas, corporations there have found qualified women to fill the positions needed to fill the quotas, and the result has been progress for businesswomen in this region of the world.

To be sure, hiring targets are working—in the U.S. companies that choose to institute them and then follow through with measurement and analysis for any potential course correction. Deloitte & Touche USA works as an example here. Sharon Allen notes, "Sometimes, if there's an option between two equally talented candidates, you choose to put a woman in a position in order to create the role models and leadership opportunities necessary to change an environment that otherwise may have inhibited women's progress. We did that. We were careful not to create quotas or situations where women got the position only because they were a woman. In my view, that works against you. But we did assure that women were given opportunities that created the change which moved them up into the leadership ranks."

Ilene Lang, Catalyst's president, notes the positive changes at the companies that have seen the light. "All of the programs that we have worked with, that we know about, that have won a Catalyst award are companies trying to become more diverse and more inclusive, particularly in their leadership. They do have targets. They do have goals. They typically look at representation and they say, representation and meritocracy go hand and hand, and that means that if the top of your company doesn't look like the middle or the bottom, then there's something wrong because we know that talent doesn't discriminate. We know the kind of talent that comes into the workplace out of colleges and graduate schools today, so if the cream that rises to the top doesn't look like the feeder pool, then there's a problem. So, these companies set those targets. Those are not quotas and the difference is that quotas motivate a kind of behavior that is just about the numbers and what we see is targets."

We certainly applaud the companies that do recognize the value of their women employees right up into the executive offices, and we are grateful for the exposure that Catalyst lends to the right kinds of efforts that will strike down the current forty-seven year and seventy-three year predictions for parity. This year, 2007, Catalyst recognized three corporations for doing things right for their women consumers, customers/clients, and employees: PepsiCo, PricewaterhouseCoopers, and Scotiabank.

Here is my problem. I don't see five hundred out of the *Fortune* 500 on the awards list. And I'm not picking on Catalyst. Look at any list—Best Places to Work, Best Companies for Women of Color, Working Mother Best Companies, and the like—you won't see every single company's name on the list that should be on that list. When organizations celebrate the companies that are doing well by women, we all applaud. But what about the majority of companies that aren't getting it? Are we waiting for the media to go after them and expose their bias and their discriminating practices? At newsrooms across the country, particularly at newspapers where the investigative reporting is best known, the skeleton crew left after cutback after cutback barely has the time to uncover the daily national and local news. To assume that the media, or a watchdog group, will rise up and insist that the *Fortune* 100, the *Fortune* 500, and the *Fortune* 1000 reward employee performance with the opportunity of advancement regardless of gender is, in my mind, naïve.

Until all one thousand of the *Fortune* 1000 companies can be celebrated, the time for quotas is now. Nothing less will accelerate women's participation in senior management and on corporate boards the way a mandate will, especially because there are plenty of women who are so close to making the leap to the very top level.

In this decade, women will become the majority of middle managers, the majority of entry-level workers, and the majority of older workers. Therefore, certainly, Lang is correct when she says, "By 2014, 60 percent of the entrants to the workforce will be women and people of color. That means that by 2050, the majority in the U.S. workforce will be women and people of color, not white males. This is why this leadership question is so pertinent and why the companies that tap into the leadership now are assuring the sustainability of their companies in the future."

The pipeline is filling and it *must* lead directly to the top positions. With all this talent and energy, companies must take advantage of the best and the brightest, men and women, and make sure they are equally represented at the top in C-level positions and corporate boards. When the consumer can see herself reflected at all levels of business, she will know her business is respected and she is respected. America's economy depends on the retention of women, women's purchasing power, and women's ability to build business, lead business, and be role models for future generations. But, I say, the time for all this to take place is now—not in 2014, or 2048, or 2082. *Now*.

Just Imagine

Half of those leading in corporate America, filling corner offices and C-level positions, are women. They make sure that shareholders can be proud of the company they support and of the policies they provide to the people who labor across all lines of the business. These women ask questions in boardrooms and make sure guidelines are followed carefully. As corporate board officers, they work to build the company by reflecting the needs of the company's prime consumer—other women—and understanding her concerns. America gains economic strength in the face of global competition with women leading Big Business.

CHAPTER 6

Women Entrepreneurs:
The BIG Engine That Could
and Does

"Aerodynamically, the bumblebee shouldn't be able to fly, but the bumblebee
doesn't know that so it goes on flying anyway."
—Mary Kay Ash, Mary Kay Cosmetics

Small business is what is driving our American economy, and women are
driving the bus when it comes to starting small businesses. Little attention,
however, is given to those choosing to take the risk in establishing their own
businesses and providing opportunities for employees, vendors, and more.
Before continuing on, let me point out the common misconception—
perhaps, when I say "small business," you immediately visualize a hair
salon, a retail store, an interior design studio, all great businesses, to be sure.
But the areas of major growth for women's businesses today are actually
in construction, manufacturing, technology, and healthcare. These are
businesses that have scaleable models, and they are businesses that require
leadership qualities in order to grow. It is estimated that by the year 2008,
more than 50 percent of all American businesses will be woman-owned.
They many not be *Fortune* 500 companies (at the moment!) but these
companies will continue to employ more than twice what the *Fortune*
500 employ and therefore will be the teachers for the next generation of
business leaders.

Nearly half of all small businesses in America—businesses up to $100
million—are majority women-owned. That's 10.4 million companies versus men's 11.7 million.[1] Women-owned firms are growing at two times

the rate of all firms—that's 42 percent versus 23 percent. And out of all women-owned businesses, companies grossing over $1 million are the fastest growing sector. Women have turned to entrepreneurship as a way to fulfill their idea of success and at the same time to provide the ability to design their work environment. The women whom the media portrays as "opting out" of corporate typically turn up a month or two later "opting in" with their own businesses. So don't listen when you hear the media talk about women and their choice to leave corporate careers. And what about the number of working one-parent families? There are no white knights rescuing them. They, like the rest of their cohort, have the education and the determination to thrive in business and, if choosing to opt out/opt in, they succeed by doing it their way. And for those who have never opted in—they simply have "entrepreneur" encoded into their DNA.

All of these women, no matter what their path to entrepreneurship, are doing it incredibly well. Women Presidents' Organization (WPO) members, for example, in a survey done in September 2006, had owned or managed their businesses for one to thirty-four years, averaging in at 12.8 years. The majority of the respondents had annual revenues of $1 to $5 million; 16 percent, between $6 and $10 million; 10 percent, between $11 and $20 million; 9 percent, between $21 and $50 million; and 3 percent owned or managed companies over $50 million. "I believe that entrepreneurship is the great equalizer for women, that the story is not the story in corporate America but in small business America, that women can shatter the glass ceiling in small business ownership," says Marsha Firestone, founder and president of the WPO. "The average age of our members is forty-nine, so they tend to start their businesses a little later— after they get some experience and they learn from that experience that there is a place that they can do better."

Women are starting their businesses first and foremost out of an entrepreneurial idea, or as Sharon Hadary, executive director of the Center for Women's Business Research, says, "They see something that they're looking for, a product or service, that nobody is providing and it's a unique opportunity to provide that product or service. Or they see a product or service being provided by others, including their employer, that they think they can do better on their own."

A perfect example of such a company is SmartPak, a $35 million company initially providing packaged daily allotments of supplements for horses in 2000, which now offers an array of products for all kinds of equine and canine needs. The company was born out of frustration by Becky Minard. Unable to have the barn where she boarded her horse give the animal its proper dosages of vitamins and supplements, Minard turned her questions of "How can this be so hard?" and "Why can't we just put it into little packs and send somebody a month's supply and send it every month?" into a business that has a potential market of $500 million. The idea was so popular with horse owners that they were soon ordering smaller amounts of supplements for their dogs, and so began SmartPak's entry into the canine business. Through catalogue, Web, and bricks-and-mortar stores with online ordering kiosks inside, the company sells barn supplies and tack for horses; toys, food, and gear for dogs; pharmaceuticals and supplements for both; and apparel for people. With a background in life sciences, consulting and operations, as well as a Harvard MBA, Minard is building the SmartPak brand and reach as chief marketer to her husband's role as CEO.[2]

Lois Silverman turned improving on a service into a public company. The founder and former CEO of Comprehensive Rehabilitation Associates (now Concentra Managed Care), she started her company in 1978 out of seeing something that she could do better. While working in the 1970s for a large insurance company providing medical management services for injured workers, Silverman saw an opportunity for going a step further in managing workman's comp care. The new business would provide medical, vocational, return-to-work, and cost-containment services and thereby mitigate losses on the part of carriers and employers. Seventeen years later, she led the IPO. "We had had rapid growth, new services and solid gains in the market. We were the industry leaders in terms of a privately held company and it just felt like it was the right time," Silverman says.

To build liquidity for the final boost in positioning, Silverman and her business partner had brought in investors but they retained 51-percent control of the company in order to remain at the helm. In 1995, Silverman was the first woman to take a company public in Massachusetts. She built a $100 million company with two thousand employees. Silverman learned from experience the isolation women particularly feel being wrapped up in growing their businesses out in the corporate world and so, today, she ensures peer support systems for women through the nonprofit she founded, The Commonwealth Institute.[3]

Some women entrepreneurs are not interested in employing people. They choose instead to be sole proprietors and understand the need to juggle the "doing the business" with the "marketing and selling to customers" part of the business. Seventy-five percent of all firms and 81 percent of women-owned firms have no employees. Sole proprietors can grow their businesses using outside contractors. As of 2004, women-owned firms without employees generated $167 billion in annual sales, according to the

Center for Women's Business Research. I know dozens of women who started their consulting businesses by leaving the company they worked for and offering to consult on a project basis, which gave them the opportunity of starting their businesses with one very impressive client.

Women can also start their own businesses out of frustration in the workplace, where they aren't influencing the direction of the organization as they'd like on a strategic level. And there's the flexibility mantra and being in control over their time. Annette O'Connor started her company, Clearhead Consulting, after eighteen years of working in major corporations in human resources and in strategic consulting positions. She describes the culture promulgated at the time this way: "There was a lack of willingness to speak the truth about the impact day-to-day business decisions had on the average employee. The last competitive advantage is people, and if you (the company) don't understand this, you are foolish."

O'Connor recognized that she had the resources necessary to design her own model of a company that would allow her to work on her own and out of her home—two goals that were paramount to her. It was clear that midsize companies, twenty to seventy-five employees, needed to outsource their HR work and that she was at the right time, right place with her niche business. It was 1996, there was a technology boom and companies were growing fast. O'Connor had been in positions all her career life where no female peers existed. A business of her own would also allow her to expand her networks and seek out women in business as associates and colleagues.

"I figured that a worst-case scenario would be that I would do contract recruiting for $50 per hour. But, once I put the word out, getting business was never a problem. Companies were desperate for building infrastructure for growth and designing employee policies and benefits that could grow with the organization. I was valued as a resource to CEOs and COOs and I leveraged that ability to bring in other strategic professionals, such as those in compensation. I tripled my corporate salary in my first year of business."

Of course, owning your own small business has challenges. The Number One challenge for any businessowner is isolation. "Finding confidential people to share feelings with and learning to forge relationships with other women was also a struggle," O'Connor concurs. "But I learned to be a team player and put my years of knowledge into simple solutions and practical approaches." Ten years later, her business has new challenges. "The world is changing rapidly, and retention is a huge issue for all companies. Generational issues are the major topic of HR discussions. I have to constantly test my model."

Other women, who are intent on building not only a company that employs people but one that also impacts the lives in its environs, build a company that can support its employees and the community at large. A woman who has taken this very different direction in her business is Trish Karter, president and CEO of Dancing Deer Baking Company. From investor to temporary participant to fully involved partner to majority owner, she has risen to the challenges thrown her way.

In what began in April 1994 as an all-natural wholesale bakery, Dancing Deer has built a national reputation and brand with its direct-to-consumer Web business, wholesale distribution business, and corporate delivery channels. In addition to the usual profit motive, Karter has what she calls "environmental objectives" and she also incorporates employee ownership into her business plan. "I don't want to just push cookies out the door," she told *Fortune Small Business* when she was a 2005 Winning Workplaces Best Boss. "We have to have a greater impact on the community."[4]

In 2002, Dancing Deer introduced the Sweet Home product line to put 35 percent of the retail price of each order toward helping homeless families find jobs and move into their own homes. The program came from a partnership with the nonprofit, One Family. In 2005 alone, Dancing Deer donated $30,000 to the homelessness eradication effort. "I thought One Family's mission to end homelessness was compatible with our mission to do good in the world," Karter says. "That ties in with our employee base at our location in a low-income area. My concept was to focus our philanthropy efforts to be more meaningful, to save ourselves some time and to design something to enhance our marketing strategy. The Sweet Home line made an impact on our branding, but I didn't expect it to have such a strong visceral impact on people. If other companies did what we do on a similar percentage basis, the world would be turned upside down!"

Taking an unusual tack, Janet Kraus and Kathy Sherbrooke started their company on a business principle and then searched for the right service to flesh out their philosophy. They met at Stanford's Graduate School of Business and found instant synergy. "We took a 360-degree view of business, which is all about the different impacts that you have in the market on customers, on employees, on business partners," says Sherbrooke.[5] After graduation, they set off in different directions but planned to team up in the future to build their company. In 1997, they did just that by starting Circles out of Kraus' extra bedroom. Understanding the time-starved professional, they began the trial-and-error process of trailblazing a new, untried, but immediately welcomed concept in lifestyle support at the *Fortune* 500 level.

Raising money and getting to profitability was difficult during their first four years. But by Q4 in 2001, after landing $26 million in four capital rounds—friends and family, angels, and two institutional rounds—they hit profitability. Circles, now with six hundred employees, $45 million in revenue, and offices in Boston and Canada, is a concierge company that offers sevices to large corporations as a benefit to increase employee loyalty as well as provides a program for customer loyalty that adds a benefit/enhancement to the high-valued customers of credit card companies and private wealth management firms.

Ever evolving, these days Circles is broadening its reach with a new high-end, direct-to-consumer service. Kraus and Sherbrooke took a friendship, an interest in working together, and a business principle versus a predefined product or service to creating their dream company. Their revenue model is endless, as individuals and companies will never run out of the need for convenience in getting services done efficiently for themselves and their customers. The point here is, as Kraus says, "Every woman entrepreneur should think that the world is small instead of thinking that it is so big."

But deciding to build a company early on, as Kraus and Sherbrooke did in graduate school, is different than realizing later in your career that perhaps your job, as you have always known it, is coming to an end. That realization and the ensuing entrepreneurial bug struck Suzanne Bates in 2000. An award-winning television news anchor and reporter in several markets across the United States for twenty years, Bates was longing to start her own business. "I noticed that many of the people I admired were getting paid for what they know. I wanted to transfer my skills and teach what I know," she says. So she launched Bates Communications, a strategic consulting firm specializing in executive and professional development in communication skills.

Since its founding in 2000, the company has established a national reputation for its outstanding executive coaching program as well as innovative workshops, training, and development. Bates has also verbalized her special expertise in her book, *Speak Like A CEO*. "I made a transition out of choice," she says. "Even if it is not your choice to start your own firm, you can embrace it with gusto. The positive attitude that you bring to your business is key to your success. My advice is to commit yourself to it and jump in with both feet."[6]

So we have examples of women starting businesses because they opt out of corporate America and feel they can do it better. Then there are others who feel that not only can they do it better, they can do it by building a company that gives back to the community that supports them. We see other women who meet early on in their careers and know instinctively that their synergy can create a company to be reckoned with and yet others who have spent years developing their craft and know that entrepreneurship is the way to take it to the next level. These are just a few stories that show the great diversity in what women want to achieve when they start out on their own. All of these women are role models to many for many reasons, but mostly they are examples of women who have started a business out of the determination to be exactly who they are and have that reflected in their businesses. Each is also a role model for others when it comes to providing the best workplace for employees. Small or large, these woman-owned firms understand the need for flexibility for their employees, as they too must have work/life balance to perform at their best. And they're cognizant of the importance of benefits. The Center for Women's Business Research, in its Top Facts listing on its Web site (http://www.cfwbr.org/facts/index.php), notes that women-owned businesses spend an estimated $546 billion annually on salaries and benefits.

The newest category to this list of entrepreneurial whys and wherefores is the corporate woman who leaves corporate America in order to help other corporate women in more than just one company. Having worked in benefits and sales at Johnson & Johnson and then going back into human resources at State Street Bank & Trust Company, Mary Gegler has spent her career working at and learning from corporate America. She started MBG Associates Leadership Consultants to help those still traversing the corporate mentality. She understands the corporate dynamics and is able to assist other women in making their mark on the organization.

"I learned to be good at identifying the next generations of leaders. Leaders are not born but need to be trained and developed," she says. "I saw a lot of talented people with horrible managers, particularly women who wanted to advance in the company but too often weren't given the opportunity to do so. They left and advanced elsewhere."

Gegler, like many executive coaches, doesn't need to market herself. Her clients come from personal relationships and referrals from those who have worked with her. "They know I understand the corporate environment, from both the sales and HR arenas and particularly my expertise on compensation issues. I tell my women clients they must fight back—negotiate their compensation. Men aren't shy. They negotiate." Understanding how the system works is Gegler's value. Understanding how women can get ahead is her greatest asset.

Finally, there is the serial entrepreneur who's unable to sit still as she constantly has ideas of companies that must be built. Sue Welch has created three companies so far, each one more complex than the last. Today, as founder, chair, and CEO of TradeStone Software, she's tackling global sourcing's most complicated problem to date by unifying domestic and international buying in one view, no training needed to tap into the system. She first saw a dire need in global sourcing when she was working in imports at Zayer Corporation in the 1980s and has been on sourcing's cutting edge ever since. IMC Systems Group, founded in 1984, was a pioneer in international supply chain business applications for PCs. RockPort Trade Systems, started in 1992, introduced Windows to international buying. Today, TradeStone brings the Internet to the supply chain in a first-time anywhere-to-anywhere solution.

IMC was ahead of its time, and when the venture partners got impatient for their return on investment (ROI), they replaced Welch. Undaunted, she opened RockPort's doors the next day, served out her noncompete time by consulting, and mulled ideas for a new tack for sourcing. The technology she came up with was so innovative that QRS bought RockPort for $100 million. A year later, Welch intended to retire but instead spent the first of this two-year noncompete traveling to understand the Third World supplier's import/export perspective. The conundrum of separate systems for domestic and international buying as well as the small supplier's inability to tie into the buying engine led to conceptualizing TradeStone. "Quite frankly, I didn't think I'd come back to this," she says. "I thought, how could I redo it again and do it so it's fresh and exciting and different? When you start getting ideas again, you say, 'Let me just go back and look at it one more time.'"[7]

Peg Feodoroff's story is a twist on the serial entrepreneur—one of a woman whose business is cooking along when she realizes she has a greater mission in life. A successful commercial interior designer for twenty-five years, Feodoroff's company, Inspired Interiors, worked with the best companies in Massachusetts on their office environments, not to mention, very often, the CEO's home. The idea for her second company arrived just after she was diagnosed with malignant melanoma and during treatment. The value of her idea was confirmed by her sister, who had been diagnosed with colon cancer six months earlier. Feodoroff was appalled at the hospital gown offered her during treatment. Out in the waiting room, only the patients were labeled what she calls "defective" by the johnny versus others' street clothes. Offering real clothing with hidden openings for treatment would take away the stigma and the humiliation, she believed. As Feodoroff says, "Anything that the johnny was, we went against." The company, Spirited Sisters, with its patient clothing line, Healing Threads, gives back dignity to those who need it most. "We're doing this for a reason," Feodoroff says.[8] At this writing, the fledgling company is hitting its stride. There is a need, there is a will, and there is a way. Feodoroff is a survivor, in business and in cancer, not a quitter. Entrepreneurship is what gets more than twenty-two million Americans out of bed in the morning and will continue to be the driving force in our economy.

The Workplace Revolution

Women today are meeting their needs to work successfully by creating their own work environment—and, in the process, they're revolutionizing the workplace with the very practices that corporate is slow to adopt. The 2005 "National Study of Employers" by Families and Work Institute found that small businesses (those with fifty to ninety-nine employees) compared to large companies (those with a thousand or more employees) "are significantly more likely to offer flexibility to all or most employees than employers of other sizes." The survey was conducted across a broad spectrum of one thousand and ninety-two for-profit and nonprofit companies, with 73 percent of the sample being defined as having women in the "C" level positions. The report revealed that the small company employer understands from experience the need for "work to work" for both employee and the company.

Putting the employee in control of his/her starting/quitting time, paid/unpaid overtime hours, full- or part-time hours, working onsite or off-site, and job sharing are choices the small business employer and, therefore the women business employer, provides. Although she isn't able to provide as an extensive a benefit package as the larger companies, today's small business employer offers her employees a work/life balance as best she can—and often better than the corporate workplace she might have left. A Women Presidents' Organization survey revealed that 57 percent of its members regularly "investigate and adjust salaries to ensure pay equity for positions of equal qualification and responsibility," confirming that women business owners understand the need to stay on top of the wage gap.

Women tend to create the kind of workplace that is the opposite of the corporate culture they fled or that reflects their vision of what a workplace should and can be. At the beginning of her eighteen years with the Center for Women's Business Research, Sharon Hadary still remembers one particular conference panelist whose comments back then were a harbinger of what has become an emerging company practice. Hadary recalls, "She said, 'You know, most people in business equate quality with the number of hours worked. We equate quality with quality.' And then she went on to say that, instead of losing an employee who wanted to stay home with her new baby, her company gave the employee a computer so she could work at home. Not only were these women saying they wanted the flexibility for themselves, they were now creating cultures that encouraged that flexibility for their employees."

Hadary adds, "Our research indicates that women-owned businesses are more likely than men-owned businesses to have a gender-balanced management team and workforce, and that, as men-owned businesses grow, the workforce becomes much more heavily weighted with men, whereas women tend to keep that balance even as the company grows."

As we've noted before, women are not opting out of corporate and staying home as the media would like us to think. In fact, corporate's loss is entrepreneurship's gain. "Corporations are losing the best and the brightest, and that is too bad. We need women's leadership in the corporate world," Hadary says. "I'm glad, however, that entrepreneurship is here as an opportunity for women who, for whatever reason, feel that the corporate environment is not appropriate, whether it's lack of flexibility, or lack of ability to move up to the most senior levels, or just the culture of the company itself."

The female entrepreneur is in control of her work environment and her time. She doesn't work less but on her own terms and she delegates her responsibilities in a new way. Woman-owned businesses are generating nearly $2 trillion in revenues and 12.8 million jobs—"that's 12.8 million people putting food on the table, paying a mortgage, or sending a child to college because of a business owned by a woman," Hadary notes. "Women are creating business leadership by creating jobs, and even the ones who don't have employees frequently are creating opportunities for others to gain economic independence by using contractors."

Even so, every small business must compete with the mammoth corporation. Male or female, that competition isn't easy, but successfully competing is all about connections. Women typically, as we note throughout this book, have not had the connections or the networks that men have had for generations. Over the last thirty or so years, supplier diversity programs, which grew out of the civil rights movement, have offered women and minorities the opportunity to compete on a so-called level playing field with their larger competitors. Certifying women-owned companies for these programs are national organizations such as the Women's Business Enterprise National Council (WBENC). Its certification guarantees that the company in question is a woman-owned, operated, and controlled company—a women's business enterprise.

Today's voluntary and mandated diversity supplier programs grew out of the federal government's concern that it was not doing business with disadvantaged companies. Federal contracts began to require the large prime contractors to subcontract a percentage of their subcontracts to the smaller diverse supplier. The goal was to make sure that small companies were given the opportunity to perform and to be ranked by performance rather than by size or connection. Soon the larger companies realized the value of their diversity suppliers and began voluntary in-house diversity supplier programs for all of their contracts. "They were finding good suppliers offering good products, good services, with on-time delivery at very competitive price. These smaller companies could also be more responsive to changes if they were needed," says Linda Denny, WBENC's president.

For the past ten years, WBENC has provided access to markets for women-owned companies as its certification is the most commonly accepted and valued by America's corporations. In turn, Denny believes that "corporations have learned that women can bring a different perspective to a product or a service. Women have a different point of view when it comes to how they make buying decisions, how they build relationships, especially if it is a consumer or a business-to-consumer company." Denny says there's phenomenal room for growth in supplier diversity programs these days outside of the United States. "We're going to work with our women's business enterprises to help them understand how they can benefit in the global marketplace. Many of our certified businesses operate internationally because the corporations they are serving want them to go with them to India, China, or someplace else."

Some would call these supplier diversity programs a quasi-quota system, meaning they provide special opportunities for those that participate. On closer inspection, however, you'll see every certification program of this type is more appropriately seen as a seal of approval for the firms that perform the due diligence in getting the certification. It is not as simple a process as you might think. Every part of the business is scrutinized, from ownership, to employees, to vendors, to customers. Women Business Enterprises (WBEs), Minority Business Enterprises (MBEs), and Disadvantaged Business Enterprises (DBEs) must solidly verify themselves and their firms to become certified. Perhaps if this much scrutiny were performed on all companies, we would have less fraud. But the important point is that it takes a lot of work and a reliable company to gain certification. The certified companies then can offer their services to large corporations with this seal of approval and have the opportunity to get the experience and the income needed for growth. In many ways, supplier diversity programs can be looked upon as mentorship programs offered to the smaller company from the bigger corporation. It is that experience of working together that can catapult the growth of the WBE.

All this said, there's tremendous room for improvement. Sixty percent of *Fortune* 1000 corporations spend more than $1 billion with outside suppliers each year, but only 4 percent of that goes to the WBE. Yet, those WBEs with $1 million or more in revenue, in comparison with their smaller counterparts, are more likely to have corporate (34% vs. 12%) and government (31% vs. 8%) contracts.[9]

Of course, not all women-owned companies choose or need to become certified. Many entrepreneurial women see their reflection in other entrepreneurial women and believe that by utilizing their services they further the cause for women's success. They typically seek out other women-owned businesses as subcontractors and are much more likely to employ women, thereby reaching out and pulling up to continue the growth of the sisterhood. Yes, sometimes women can see the expertise and value of other women, and support women's small enterprises.

If we look back about eighteen years, before the beginning of the surge of woman-owned businesses, we see that the United States was just beginning a recession. The Dow Jones dropped more than 25 percent on October 19, 1987. Black Monday is the name given to this day as similar enormous drops occurred around the world. By the end of October, stock markets in Hong Kong had fallen 45.8 percent; Australia, 41.8 percent; the United Kingdom, 26.4 percent; the United States 22.68 percent; and Canada, 22.5 percent. It was during this time that the savings and loans began to collapse and unemployment hovered at 7 percent. A large percentage of white-collar jobs were lost in the 1980s and early 1990s, and men, many of whom had never been unemployed, found themselves unemployable. As unemployment insurance ran out, many chose to label themselves as consultants out of necessity. Home-based businesses took on a new meaning. Once thought of as only an alternative for women looking for a hobby, home-based businesses grew rapidly. According to national research firm IDC, there are between 34.3 and 36.6 million home-based businesses in the United States, estimated as generating $427 billion each year.

These facts are important as it took the men who established home-based businesses to provide the credibility for women who had made them their bread and butter for years. Today, home-based businesses are almost as likely to be run by women as men. This phenomenon reminds us that it is not just women in business who are isolated. In 1991, when I cofounded a regional women's organization, the South Shore Women's Business Network, for the purpose of providing a place for women to come and share ideas, learn from each other, and work together to become successful, 12 percent of our membership was men. Today, the organization still exists and thrives, not only because it works to help women achieve their dreams but also because it is open to all those who want to work together to succeed. My point is that so much focus is given to the large companies in America—the *Fortune* 100, the *Fortune* 500, and the *Fortune* 1000—that we forget that the true engine driving the economy in our country is small business.

What's more important is the fact that women are now the ones driving the model for entrepreneurship. They're the role models for the next generation—our sons and daughters—and for other business leaders, particularly the men who need prodding in accepting gender equality. To get to that kind of comfort level, Hadary notes, "These business leaders have to look around and say, 'You know what, I see this woman or that woman in this kind of leadership position, so it's OK if I want to bring someone into my senior advisory group who looks like that woman instead of someone who looks like me.'"

I started my newspaper, *Women's Business*, for this very reason. Having been brought up in the newspaper business with my brother who started the *New England Real Estate Journal* in 1963, I was always disheartened by the lack of women who wanted to be quoted in the commercial real estate world. My experience in the early 1970s and then later in the early 1990s proved that women were part of the equation but uninterested in getting the press. I would go to industry meetings and very often be the only woman in the room. But I knew that other women were very much a part of this industry and would eventually be the leaders because of their innate talents in the business. Having been in real estate myself, I knew women genuinely wanted to fit the client with his or her needs. Residential or commerical, women are an asset in the real estate business. But knowing and doing are only part of the equation. Without visibility, even the most successful businessperson cannot rise to the top. I learned from my brother that visibility is everything in business—the real estate business and every business. He encouraged me to set out and start my newspaper to profile women in business and to change the way women in business were perceived in the region, Massachusetts, New Hampshire, and Rhode Island, and, eventually, New York, New Jersey, and Connecticut, and, through a sister publication, in Ohio, Kentucky, and Indiana. The stories of women's success are endless and they provide the reader with the role models for the present and the future.

Role Models

The motivation of our next generation of women business leaders is critical to our economic growth. The study "Teen Girls on Business: Are

They Being Empowered?"[10] investigated the perceptions of teen girls toward business and career. Again, the pipeline must be filled by women as well as men since they continue to seek education in the largest numbers. The girls' negative opinion of business as a career, however, was a stunning outcome of the study. It was found that although boys and girls share the same basic ambitions toward work/life balance, only 9 percent of girls listed business as a first-choice career compared to 15 percent of boys—a 40 percent difference. Girls, 75 percent to boys' 55 percent, suggested that "helping others" was a key ingredient in what they wanted to do for the future.

The study of more than four thousand teens found that girls were much more likely to choose a career in law or medicine than business. Entrepreneurship was considered by girls as the most desirable business option because they perceived it as providing more flexibility and control. The scandals in the news at the time were clearly a reason that both boys and girls had a negative image of business. When asked to describe business, the teens used words such as "finance," "accounting," and "making money." Girls felt their strongest skill was listening whereas boys chose decision making. The end result of the study was that there are few female role models for girls to copy.

The media plays a large part in teens' perception of the world and the media must begin to reflect what real women in the business world are achieving. The problem that Candida Brush, Paul T. Babson Professor of Entrepreneurship at Babson College and quite likely the first person to do an academic study of women entrepreneurs in the United States, has with the media is what she calls "hero worship," and, although it affects all ages, she speaks specifically to the lack of role models for the female entrepreneur. Bill Gates, she points out, is constantly portrayed as if he built Microsoft all by himself—forget the team, the collaboration, and all the other factors along with taking a risk that go into starting and building a company.

"The whole worship thing is so pervasive, and what that does, when you start to think about it, is set role models for women entrepreneurs, women who don't necessarily fit the psychological trait envelope that is portrayed as the key to success, so they have no role models," Brush says. "My criticism is that the general media often gets hung up on things that are really detrimental to anybody other than the person the story is about because it doesn't portray an accurate picture of what that person did to succeed."

It's fortunate that organizations such as the Girl Scouts realize the value that women role models can provide with face-to-face meetings in programs such as CEO Camps. Organized in the summer as part of the Girl Scout experience, these camps invite female CEOs to share in a variety of workshops focused on giving girls insight into what the life of a woman leader is like. This is just one of the many programs across the country helping to build girls' enthusiasm for business. Today's girls are tomorrow's women leaders and women business owners.

And adult business women need role models, too. Networking organizations like the Women Presidents' Organization provide a venue for role modeling both from the standpoint of learning from those who have made it and from those who are going through similar circumstances. Second stage entrepreneurs, according to research done by the Edward Lowe Foundation, learn best from one another. Notes WPO's president, Marsha Firestone, "A peer advisory group allows the entrepreneur to grow some of her best ideas from her peers and brings the genius out of the group—to accelerate growth of the company and enhance competitiveness."

VCs, Angels, and Others

Access to capital is still an issue for company growth and particularly for women-owned enterprises. Venture capital, angel investing, friends and family, and bank loans are all important to getting a business up and running. In the venture capital world, it's rare for women to find the pot of gold at the end of the fundraising trail. In fact, women entrepreneurs are seeing a steady dwindling in their one-time barely increasing success in raising venture dollars. According to 2007-updated calculations by Dow Jones VentureOne, companies with women founders raised:

- 6.7 percent of the $26.7 billion invested in 2006,
- 7.37 percent of $24 billion in 2005,
- 7.73 percent of $22.5 billion in 2004,
- 7.99 percent of $19.7 billion in 2003,
- 8.05 percent of $22 billion in 2002, and
- 9.4 percent of the $36 billion invested in 2001.[11]

Candida Brush spent eight years working on the Diana Project along with her colleagues, Nancy Carter, Elizabeth Gatewood, Patricia Greene, and Myra Hart, looking at the venture capital (VC) industry itself to understand why women are getting such a tiny amount of money. Part of the attracting-VC-dollars problem for women entrepreneurs, the Diana Project researchers discovered, is how few of their gender are in the venture capital industry itself: less than 9 percent in 2000, with 64 percent leaving the industry from 1995 to 2000. For a platform that requires contacts and referrals if a business proposal is going to make it over the transom, "women entrepreneurs have less chance of getting to the negotiating table," the project's executive summary says.

Springboard Enterprises was founded to coach and connect women seeking venture capital, yet only one hundred out of two to three thousand applicants a year received funding, Brush notes. The glass-half-full news is: "Springboard, however, has proved that there is a large enough pool of women who are qualified, who have the right experience, who have a business that has protectable IP, that is scalable, and is a good possibility for equity funding of some kind," Brush says.

The Diana Project also pointed to the types of companies VCs will fund: "In today's market [2000], the most attractive venture capital candidates are those who have expertise in fields that traditionally have been dominated by males, such as engineering, biotechnology and physics." The same holds true today. Myra Hart says, "Because the vast majority of companies that are venture funded have a technology component to them, women are at a significant disadvantage. The problem begins at the undergraduate level, where women represent less than 20 percent of the engineering and hard physical science majors. There are relatively few women who have the technical training to lead a large, scalable enterprise that is technology-driven."

These women do exist, even if they're far and few between. Christina Lampe-Onnerud is exactly the type of founder and CEO that Hart is talking about. She thought big—the multibillion-dollar portable power sourcing market, that is, the battery market. She had the technology credentials—a leading innovator in battery design, she holds fifteen patents with six pending at the time of this writing and, prior to starting Boston-Power, worked on polymer batteries at Bell Communications Research and then set up and ran Arthur D. Little's world-renown battery lab. The Sonata next-generation lithium-ion battery that hit the market in HP laptops in summer 2007 advances portability with previously unheard of recharge time, lifetime, safety, and environmentally friendly features. Even when those in battery design didn't see Lampe-Onnerud's plan for the new version as one that would succeed, venture capital took to the concept immediately. From her initial idea-dabbling start in 2004, Lampe-Onnerud had raised $23.6 million by early 2007.[12]

Still, for most women, hitting the venture capital trail is so daunting that there's quite possibly truth in the rumblings that there aren't all that many women VC-seeking candidates in the first place. "So it's the choice thing," Brush says. "A lot of people argue that women don't want it, and there is some evidence to support that."

Angel investors are another alternative for the emerging entrepreneur but, once again, it is all about connections. The good news is, while there are few women venture capitalists, more and more retired senior executive women are turning to angel investing not only to seek a healthy ROI but also to lend their expertise through hands-on participation in the scaling of the business. There are plenty of angel-investing networks that are both male and female, but only a few female-only groups, like Golden Seeds, are focusing their attention solely on woman-owned firms by using their business skills and their money to fuel small business growth.

Artemis Woman LLC is one such recipient of angel attention. Founded by Ann Buivid and Lisa Kable, Artemis is dedicated to creating home spa and beauty products for women. These two founders brought more than thirty-five years of combined experience in *Fortune* 200 companies, including General Foods, Black & Decker, and Remington Products, to planning the high-growth enterprise, which in turn helped attract the angels to their door in 2003. They did try the venture capital route first. "We had to beg people for money," Buivid says.[13] One venture capitalist, she relates, asked her, "I have no idea what this microdermabrasion product does, but can I use it to polish the tires on my car?"

Where the VC community saw no hope, angel investors like Stephanie Hanbury-Brown, Golden Seeds' founder, saw opportunity. "It was one of the first companies we invested in," she says. "We liked the company immediately and knew that the founders knew the consumer goods, retail and manufacturing business well." Artemis Woman achieved profitability in its third year of operations with nearly $4 million in revenue. What female angel investors saw in the consumer products concept and the management team eluded the traditional male investors who were more typically interested in technology opportunities.

Educating more women around participation in high-stakes investing is another way more women-owned companies will reap the rewards of investor infusion, Brush says. She believes the link that "is missing is not just more women. It is women needing to learn more about financial options, so if we can get women where they're least populated—venture capital, angel investing, and hedge—then women can participate more fully in wealth creation. Women entrepreneurs need access to all the resource providers and one way to do that is to make sure that the composition of the resource providers is not a homogeneous group." At the time of her interview, Brush was in the midst of planning a Power Investing Roundtable to raise the bar in women's management of their personal investment portfolios and, at the same time, diversify the funding resource pool.

Hanbury-Brown is actively supporting women-owned business with the angel group that she founded. After twenty years in financial services in Sydney, London, and New York, mostly with JP Morgan, she founded Golden Seeds purposely to support women's ventures and provide them strategic business advice as well as access to capital. "By identifying women-led ventures with potential to grow into multimillion-dollar businesses, we can provide early stage funding and enable accredited investors to invest with us," she says. "We support women to utilize both their intrinsic and financial capital to its full potential."

For women entrepreneurs requiring more modest funding, the good news is that the banking relationship for women-owned businesses has improved dramatically since 1992.[14] In 2006, 57 percent of all women business owners reported having a line of credit for their businesses and 41 percent said they had a commercial bank loan, whereas in 1992, only 35 percent were satisfied with their banking relationship. Women business owners have built relationships with bankers and other financial experts, and these relationships are paramount in assisting them with growth. Yes, women could say, "We've come a long way, baby, in getting banks to pay attention, but we've got a long way to go to impress the VC community." Regardless, with or without venture capital, women will continue to put one foot in front of the other and build their dream business and lifestyle to accommodate their needs. Small business in America today is more and more woman-owned and represents the future for our economy. It is in our economy's best interest when all the resources at hand are put in place to encourage the growth of small business. The benefits for small business employees in America are already happening as women increasingly become entrepreneurs and assert their conscience in the understanding that their employees are people who want to succeed both for the company and their respective families.

Just Imagine

Women own the majority of businesses in America. There is a true understanding of what families need in regard to child care and elder care needs. Men and women are comfortable with telling the truth when it comes to taking time out from work to attend their children's events or their elder's healthcare appointments. Flexible work arrangements are the norm. The wage gap disappears—at least in small business—as wages are based on performance and not gender, and particularly not face time. The differentiation of the CEO's salary to that of the entry level employee is by a matter of a few zeros rather than multiplied two hundred and forty times, which is the 2005 difference. Productivity and loyalty are appreciated and compensated. Human capital is the priority and retention is the most important focus for human resources.

CHAPTER 7

Legally Blonde—and Black, Brown, Red, and Gray

"Society as a whole benefits immeasurably from a climate in which all persons, regardless of race or gender, may have the opportunity to earn respect, responsibility, advancement, and remuneration based on ability."
—Sandra Day O'Connor

You might first ask, why a separate chapter on the legal profession? Law is a part of the business sector, you can argue, and can be covered in the chapter on business. Perhaps, but the large law firm works in a very different manner than most business enterprises. First, compensation is based on billable hours. The only other profession that operates in this way is the accounting profession, and we have discussed their issues and how the focus on women's retention has dramatically changed in just the past few years. This hasn't happened for women lawyers. The legal profession also has a system of management that is very different from other businesses. Law firms are managed generally by committees of partners. How one attains partnership, again, is one of the vivid issues that women need addressed if they are to be well represented, either as clients or as professionals participating in the practice of law.

"You need diverse people giving advice if you want to make sure you're getting the most balanced, comprehensive advice possible," says Lauren Stiller Rikleen, a senior partner at law firm Bowditch & Dewey who, after authoring *Ending the Gauntlet: Removing the Barriers to Women's Success in the Law,* became president of the resulting follow-on Women's Institute at her firm. "People with diverse backgrounds bring different perspectives, and that's healthy."

What's more, in the argument for a separate chapter on law is the diversity of career paths for someone with a law degree: corporate law, private practice, in-house counsel, academia, and public service. In fact, twenty-four of our forty-three presidents were lawyers before taking up residence in the White House. Women are 30.2 percent of the legal profession and comprise nearly half of all law school classes today.[1] Out of the nationwide class of 2004, according to the National Association of Law Placement, 56 percent of women chose private practice, 10 percent went into business, 11.9 percent sought out government, 12.8 percent became judicial clerks, 6.1 percent joined the public interest ranks, and 1.7 percent became academics.

But what opportunities await them within their new career paths? For an advanced degree that draws such large numbers of women, the juris doctor in many cases still leads to a profession in which women struggle to attain leadership positions. In the corporate law firm, women are 44.1 percent of the associates and only 17.3 percent of partners.[2] At the *Fortune* 500 and *Fortune* 1000 respectively, just over 16 percent and 15 percent of in-house general counsels in 2006 were women. Across the country, women comprise 23.3 percent of district court judges and 23.6 percent of circuit court judges, according to the ABA Commission on Women in the Profession's "A Current Glance" compilation. Out of fifty-three chief justices, seventeen or 32.1 percent are women.[3] Only one woman today serves on the nine-member U.S. Supreme Court. And, just as visibly, there has never been a woman president.

This isn't to say that the legal profession hasn't undergone dramatic changes for women in the past thirty or so years after more than a century of snail's progress. Women entering the field today have aspirations beyond anything most women of my generation could even imagine. Growing up in the 1950s, I never heard my parents, or anyone else's parents, suggest that their little girl would one day be a lawyer. It was not that we weren't encouraged to get a higher education and potentially advanced degrees. The legal profession, back then, was seen as stuffy and male and very few women need apply—an environment that permeated law until only recently.

Back in the 1860s, women began to fight for a career in law through lawsuits and changes in the law. Apprenticeship at the time was the path to a law career, and gender discrimination was "deeply rooted in the legal system."[4] Law schools emerged in the 1870s but it wasn't until 1920 that they first opened their doors to women. The last law school to admit women, Harvard Law School, did so in 1950. Still, career options for women were limited. Sandra Day O'Connor, the country's first female U.S. Supreme Court justice, serving from 1981 to 2006, graduated from Stanford Law in 1952 among the top of her class. Unable to find a law firm in California that would hire her as a lawyer—one firm did offer her a position as a legal secretary—she turned to public service.

Ruth Bader Ginsburg is the second woman and only other woman to serve on the U.S. Supreme Court, appointed in 1993 and remaining on the bench today. The only way she was able to get a clerkship with a district court judge upon graduation from Columbia Law School in 1959 was through heavy lobbying by a professor. As the story was told at the Symposium Celebration of the Tenth Anniversary of Justice Ruth Bader Ginsburg's Appointment to the Supreme Court of the United States, the professor broke down "the judge's reluctance to hire a woman clerk, particularly one with a young child, by guaranteeing him a male backup as a replacement should he be unable to work with her, and threatening to cut off the judge's future supply of Columbia clerks should he be unwise enough to refuse to give her a trial run."[5]

Women's numbers in law school began to grow significantly in the 1970s, and by 1985, more than 40 percent of law students were women. Numbers, however, haven't improved parity in salary if looking at women's versus men's weekly pay, according to Bureau of Labor Statistics calculations.

- In 2002, the mean weekly paycheck for men lawyers was $1,547 compared to women lawyers' $1,073, a weekly difference of $474.
- In 2003, men earned $1,610 compared to women's $1,237, or a $373 disparity.
- In 2004, the difference paycheck to paycheck was $455 a week, with men earning $1,710 versus women's $1,255.
- In 2005, it was men's $1,748 versus women's $1,354. That's a near $20,500 annual difference in 2005 alone.

Making partner doesn't improve pay for women, either. According to the 2006 "National Survey on Retention and Promotion of Women in Law Firms"[6] by the National Association of Women Lawyers (NAWL), there's an $80,000 annual pay disparity between male equity partners and female equity partners. "I tell people all the time, it's not as though anyone is going to cry that women equity partners make $429,000 and men make $510,000," says Cathy Fleming, a partner at Nixon Peabody in New York

City and president of NAWL. "The truth is, regardless of the amounts involved, there should be equal pay for equal work at all levels. And with the profession becoming increasingly female, I joke—although it is only half a joke—that when it becomes much more of a women's profession, being a lawyer will become less prestigious and will pay less."

In a roundabout way, law firms' move into advertising—something that was once considered too flamboyant or perhaps crass for such a distinguished profession—may help women's salaries improve, thanks to newer transparency. Today, most law firms know only too well the importance of advertising. In order to distinguish themselves from the hundreds of thousands of firms, they must make every effort to brand themselves effectively to counter competition. Lawyers are required to bring in business in order to cover their pay. Rainmaking, or developing business, is the key to making it to partner. Therefore, compensation for new recruits at law firms has also become competitive. I remember in early 2000, when the cover of *The Boston Globe* business page reported that former Boston law firm Testa Hurwitz & Thibeault had declared that it would raise the starting salary of all new recruits to $155,000. The decision was in reaction to the increased competition from high tech firms in the region that were offering colossal salaries and often signing bonuses as well as stock options to those graduating from law school. The result of Testa's news immediately caused other law firms of similar size to do the same. The visibility of wages at law firms for new recruits, I believe, makes for transparency in the hiring process and helps attract more diversity.

Another major problem for women in the law profession, particularly in corporate law, is fitting a life into a career coupled with the firm's perception as to how a woman can fit her career into her life. Billable hours—the hours an attorney charges a client—have increased from seventeen hundred hours annually in the 1970s to today's twenty-three hundred hours or more, making for seventy- to eighty-hour workweeks.[7]

Catalyst's 2001 "Women in Law: Making the Case" explores why legal employers are not retaining women in equal numbers to men. The ultimate conclusion: Employers who provide women with mentors, control over their work, and development and advancement opportunities have a better chance of retaining women. "These women are saying they want high-profile assignments, advancement opportunities, and flexibility to get the job done on their own terms," noted then-Catalyst president Sheila Wellington. The study found that more than two-thirds of women and nearly half of men agreed that family responsibilities represented the most significant barrier to women's advancement. Both men (66 percent) and women (68 percent) found it difficult to balance the demands of work and personal life. Interestingly, men are beginning to make the same career choices as women, according to the study. Although 34 percent of women said they had worked part-time compared to 9 percent of men, 45 percent of women and 34 percent of men selected their current firm to accommodate work/life balance.

Let's look at an example in which the names have been changed to protect the individuals and the firm that hired them. Bob and Sue are recruited from the same law school for ABC LLP. Both begin at an entry-level position at the firm and at the same salary. During the next three to five years, both do whatever it takes to be seen as potential leaders in the firm. Both are mentored by others and are put on the fast track for advancement. During this period, both marry and start families. Both welcome into their respective families what could be the next future president of the United States. Bob takes just two weeks of paternity leave to help with the birth of his first child and is promoted as he is seen as a mature member of the firm. Sue takes the twelve weeks she is allowed for maternity leave and the management team doubts her return.

Now, before you leap to conclusions as to my point here, let me just say that both Bob and Sue are respected by the company and that no bias has ever been shown one way or the other. But Bob's mere two weeks of paternity leave presented a major hardship on his family, as his wife is CEO of her own company and cannot possibly stay out of work for more than two weeks. Bob could have asked for more time but realized that two weeks was the perception for time off for men with a new child. He returned to work knowing full well that it would be a major hardship to his family, who must now depend on outside child care. Oh, and Sue? She returned to work twelve weeks later with child care in place and ready to catch up to where she left off, only to find that her path to partnership was no longer as clear. Her direct reports were happy to have her back, but her superiors gave her less important client work to help her handle what they perceived as her lack of sleep and need for flexibility. None of this was discussed with Sue. It was all just assumed that it was in her best interest.

My point is that it isn't Bob's behavior or Sue's behavior that has to change. It is the behavior of the firm that needs an overhaul. We cannot presume to know how our employees will be motivated to perform. We can only give them the tools to do the best job possible. Family is important to men and women and must be important to the law firms that employ them. As Rikleen points out in her book, women have a higher than average attrition rate at law firms and "their continued departures are ignored at the profession's peril."[8]

So what can and has to change for women to see opportunity in corporate law firms? First, attitudes toward part-time work. The Association for Legal Career Professionals (NALP) reports that 14 percent of professionals in engineering, medicine, and architecture work part-time while only 5 percent of attorneys do. Law firms have a structure that has been around for two hundred years and, in that time, our society has changed dramatically. Both men and women have needs for part-time work. Issues such as child care, elder care, health concerns, and one-parent families affect men and women. The legal profession must work to create a work environment and structure that works for today's attorneys. As technology has created a 24/7 world of work, face time should not continue to take precedence over quality work time. As a service business, the legal profession is dependent on the needs of the customer—the client. Work done at home doesn't negatively affect the client and should not impact an attorney's place of importance to the firm. Yet, law firms continue to struggle with the notion that those at their desks the longest are the most deserving.

And then there is the pervasive perception that women can't take on the stretch assignments because of their family demands, so the firm never approaches them in the first place—not unlike the bugaboo Deloitte discovered in its own women's retention difficulties noted in our chapter on business. NAWL's Fleming, who has worked at several law firms, relates this story from a previous workplace: "I've heard male partners say, 'Well, I have to ask Joe because Maryann has a one-year-old at home and she can't do it,' and I'll always say, 'That's her choice. Offer her the opportunity. Don't make the decision for her. Do you want that to happen to you: 'Gee, he's too old to go do this?' What woman ever unilaterally redirected work because 'he's a father and he needs to get home?'"

Says Rikleen in a telephone interview, "It's not a very smart business model to be graduating large numbers of women who get out into the workplace and then don't feel there are opportunities to succeed. The notion of one spouse in the workplace and one staying home is fading very quickly so you then have to think, as a society, we want to raise healthy children, we want to be good at what we do in our jobs, we are going to have to have a workplace that recognizes that there is fluidity that is required. The legal profession, of all places, ought to be doing that because in a service business, you generally can do much of the work at different times of the day. I call it family and flexibility, the importance of the 'F' words. It really is about the workplace flexibility that's needed to address the very changing world that we live in.

"To me, it all comes down to flexibility," Rikleen emphasizes. "What kind of workforce do you want to try to create to make sure that those who work there are as productive as they can be and how can the workplace take some of that stress out of people's lives? So much can be managed if companies would be more willing to be flexible around how people manage their lives. I do think that having a balanced-hours policy that makes it clear that people can succeed and be promoted while working reduced hours is critical. I think that so many women leave what they're doing because they're working on a reduced-hours schedule that is either ineffectively implemented or seen as doing somebody a favor. It should be because the workplace feels it is a smart thing to do."

It is true that law firms have made some adjustments to the increasing numbers of women associates, who are quicker than men to raise concerns about balancing work and family, partners at several firms say. For example, when Judith Thoyer in 1974 became the first woman partner at Paul, Weiss, Rifkind, Wharton & Garrison, the large New York firm had no flextime or part-time schedules. Now, she says, it has adopted both.[9] A Lawyers in Transition task force is a newer trend that helps either gender return from work after parental leave, care for an elderly or ill family member, or a retirement that turned out to be temporary, say Valerie Yarashus, a partner of Sugarman and Sugarman in Boston, and Denise Squillante, a solo practitioner in Massachusetts. They find that the numbers of attorneys who must make a transition back into work full-time from being out of the office altogether is likely higher than those who keep at it part-time. "Over and over again, lawyers in these situations stress the need for support and services, including ongoing career services and mentoring," they say.[10] The fact of the matter is, the large law firm will suffer unless it accommodates today's growing demands for tolerable work/life balance. Notes Rosalind Chait Barnett, senior scientist at the Women's Studies Research Center at Brandeis University, "People are leaving law firms, and the numbers are astonishing. They're not going home to bake cookies. They're going to be in-house counsels or they're going to small firms where they have more control over their hours."[11]

The current state of women's retention and their path to partner also stymies their rise to managing partner, the equivalent of corporate's CEO. In the previously mentioned 2006 NAWL study, out of law graduates in 1996, when women were 44 percent of law students, only 24 percent have become equity partners at the firms surveyed by the association. It should come as no surprise, then, that female managing partners only make up 5 percent of top law firm leadership across the country. The problem for women begins at the beginning, says Meredith Moore, director of the Office for Diversity at the New York City Bar Association.[12] Junior attorneys, particularly women, "slip through the cracks very easily in their early years at law firms. Firms need to groom talent from a very early point." And then, Moore adds, mentoring is just as important once women become a partner.

Regina Pisa, the youngest law partner, never mind the first woman, to be named a managing partner and chair of a major law firm, was mentored for leadership by Goodwin Procter at a time when the elder statesman (emphasis on "man") was the one elected to lead the firm. Pisa, truthfully, was surprised that her gender versus her age caught the public's attention as the "first" to celebrate. "Actually, I thought that being as young as I was, forty-two, was more exceptional than being a woman," she says.[13] It wasn't until Pisa was deluged with letters and e-mails from both girls and women telling her what a role model she was that she thought of her new position in terms of a milestone for other women.

The newest spin on improving diversity's lot is the client mandate for a diversified team handling its account. A recent move by Wal-Mart is just one more reason today's leading law firms will need to pay closer attention to those they charge with handling client relationships. The national big box retailer announced in July 2005 at an Atlanta conference on legal diversity that it would limit its legal business to law firms that had "at least one person of color and one woman among the top five relationship attorneys that handled its business."[14] Wal-Mart's general counsel, Thomas Mars, recognized that he had to act when he found that eighty-two of the top one hundred relationship law partners handling the retailer's business were white men. With legal spending of more than $200 million, the company's move to diversify its legal partners sent a loud message to the law firms it did business with—diversity matters. Wal-Mart isn't the only company determined to pressure their outside counsels to diversify their relationship team. At the same conference, the general counsels of Visa, Del Monte, and Pitney Bowes, to name a few, agreed that it is not just about making sure minorities and women are employed at the legal firms they do business with—they must also be part of the client relationship management team.

Team player, then, becomes the first step in answering the diversity problem in the law firm but it doesn't address the wage gap. As Fleming notes and ballyhoos during her one-year NAWL term, the compensation structure within the firm must also change for women's equality to become a reality because, in fact, team player is not part of the salary deal. "Origination," that is, who brought the client to the firm in the first place, is generally the most important factor in almost all law firm compensation systems, she says, so even if a client is now demanding diversity on the team, that woman is not going to get the paycheck credit for building the relationship and retaining the client.

"Where clients now demand diversity to keep using a firm, the compensation structure should reflect the diverse attorneys' contribution," Fleming says. "Simultaneously, compensation systems do not reward for team sharing and introducing those coming up in the ranks to the client—in other words, rewarding those attorneys who make the client an institutional client. Finally, firms should encourage diversity in the ranks of governance in the firms. Women need to be on the key committees such as the compensation and executive committees. While women appear to be making great strides, there still has to be some sort of adjustment or plan to get where women are leaders in their firms with influence in their firms as opposed to appearing to be leaders but lacking in real clout."

And not every major corporation in America has recognized the lack of diversity as a problem. James A. Hatcher, senior vice president for legal and regulatory affairs at Cox Communications, says, "I try to include the white male in this—white males fear diversity efforts."[15] To this I would respond with the famous words of former President Franklin Delano Roosevelt, "The only thing we have to fear is fear itself." White males are not in jeopardy of losing their position in the legal profession to minorities or women in this century or ever. Let's be practical and understand the importance of having legal recommendations rendered by those who reflect the attitudes and needs of the customer. The changing demographic in America requires a change in the make-up of our legal team.

In-House Counsel

The law firm workplace may be driving women out and into alternative practice, but even the role of in-house general counsel is no panacea in terms of balance. The 2001 Catalyst "Making the Case" study notes that of the 57 percent of women trading the law firm for an in-house counsel position in the hope of better work/life balance, 66 percent did not find it. Judging from Sharyn L. Roach's report, "Men and Women Lawyers in In-House Legal Departments: Recruitment and Career Patterns," a study of workplace differences for men and women lawyers working in variously sized in-house counsel departments in the Northeast, women pretty much found the same old circumstances.

Roach notes in her summary: "The findings suggest that women in-house counsel do not enter the same type of practice or organizations, obtain the same positions or earn the same salaries as men." The differences in practice areas, she concludes, are due in large part to the rewards and training offered as well as to the recruitment strategies. It's the firm that dictates men's and women's place at hiring and during subsequent work-allocation decisions. Those decisions provide the different experiences and expertise that then "constrain future employment options."

With regard to the type of company women lawyers shooting for in-house counsel should join, Sue Reisinger writes that "financial services firms offer women the best shot at heading a large in-house legal department, according to *Corporate Counsel*'s 2005 survey of *Fortune* 500 companies. Of the top twenty-five female general counsels in the survey, ranked by the size of their legal departments, twelve are at financial firms or at insurance companies offering such services. Information technology and healthcare were tied for a distant second, with two women in GC (general counsel) positions in each field."[16]

Katherine O'Hara is general counsel at $1.5 billion publicly traded PerkinElmer, a technology innovator in health sciences and photonics, where she has found, not less work certainly, but a more predictable schedule. Switching from high finance to law early in her career, O'Hara was soon switching out of corporate law for the in-house legal department. "I thrived on the tremendous responsibility the firm was willing to give me quite early in my career but eventually I became frustrated with the lack of control over my life because of the unpredictable demands of practice with a private law firm," she says. Working in-house seemed like the right lifestyle move, so O'Hara in 1994 looked for a role in a consumer products company, a challenge in Manhattan. But she did land a job at Avon Products as a regulatory lawyer responsible for compliance with the rules enforced by the Food and Drug Administration (FDA), the Consumer Products Safety Commission, the U.S. Environmental Protection Agency (EPA), and other regulatory agencies.

In 2005, O'Hara learned about the general counsel opportunity at PerkinElmer. Her title at Avon at that point was vice president and associate general counsel. Since the general counsel at Avon was fairly young, she knew she would need to move on if she wanted to be a GC anytime soon. "And to be the general counsel of a public company such as PerkinElmer—it's a fabulous opportunity," O'Hara says. "It's every in-house lawyer's dream to be in this position where you have responsibility for everything: all aspects of the work, both the substantive areas whether intellectual property or commercial contracts or employment, litigation, or M&A, plus the managerial responsibility and the fun of working with a terrific team." Going forward, O'Hara sees herself at PerkinElmer for quite a while. "It's the in-house lawyers who get to translate the legal answer into something that works from a practical business standpoint," she says. "It's that junction between the legal answer and the business reality that I find challenging and enjoyable."[17]

O'Hara's career path exemplifies what the search firm representatives who present at NAWL's General Counsel Institute tell the senior women who aspire to the GC office. Cathy Fleming has been in on the planning of the Institute and has sat in on the presentations. The most important pieces of information she hears out of the search firm reps are: "'Make sure every one of your moves makes sense in terms of increasing your responsibility and your potential to have the top job.' And then, 'When the company tells you that you have to relocate for three years, you've got to go.'"

What Fleming hears from the women in in-house departments is that today's general counsel faces pressures and stressors that aren't that much different than the private practice lawyer's. "This isn't your mother's corporation anymore," she says. "In-house counsels work just as hard, they work the same hours and there's the same level of expectation in producing, although they're producing results and cost-savings while the private lawyer is producing numbers and dollars."

Fleming adds that there is less opportunity for upward movement within the company. "In theory, a law firm would be ecstatic if they had fifty partners who had $10 million books of business. That's not true in a corporation," she says. "There are limited numbers of managerial positions and only one top managerial position."

Here Come the Judge

Gender diversity on the bench is critical to the majority's civil rights—remember women's 52-percent population figure. Having women in the court system equal to their numbers ensures the very core of our democracy. Women here are faring better than their other legal profession counterparts, but there's still a way to go in terms of equal representation. Even the media's choice for judges on television has been about four to three men versus women, with Judge Judy perhaps the most well known. In real life, as noted earlier in this chapter, women do not yet represent a quarter of district court or circuit court judges. At the chief justice level, however, at 32 percent, women are edging toward the 50-percent mark. And once a second woman has, according to a state's constitution, either been appointed or elected to a supreme court, women's numbers steadily increased.

A native of South Africa, Massachusetts Chief Justice Margaret H. Marshall tells us, "My becoming a judge, and particularly becoming chief justice, is a great tribute to this amazing democracy that we call the United States of America. In this country, if one comes as an immigrant with no ties or connection, it really is possible to succeed at the highest level." Marshall was appointed chief justice by the governor in 1999 and, according to the state's constitution, will serve until she turns seventy. She was appointed a justice in 1996, when she was vice president and general counsel of Harvard University. Previously, she was a partner at law firm Csaplar & Bok and then Choate, Hall, & Stewart.

"I should be frank and say that I did not have in mind that I would ever become a judge," Marshall says. "In fact, if you had asked me, I would have been quite startled at the idea." The second woman to be appointed to the Massachusetts supreme judicial court (in 1978, Ruth Abrams was the first woman in the state to be appointed a justice in three hundred and four years), Marshall ticks off the leadership roles women currently hold in the Massachusetts court system: chief justice of the superior court, chief justice of the district court, chief justice of the land court, and chief justice of the juvenile court. At one point during her tenure on the supreme judicial court, four of the seven members were women. To Marshall, the value of women in court leadership is in the judiciary's reflection of its citizens. "It's not that women judges or African-American judges or Chinese judges will interpret the law differently, but that all public institutions should be institutions in which everyone can and does participate."

Marshall's own value as a woman in a very visible role comes through in this anecdote.[18] "Every morning in hundreds of courthouses in my state, jurors are shown a video that explains the process. At the beginning of the video, there is a welcome by the chief justice. Soon after I was confirmed, our jury commission started receiving many telephone calls from jurors who said, 'We served on jury duty and we were welcomed this morning by a male chief justice. We know we have a female chief justice.' The video was not of my predecessor or of his predecessor, but of a chief justice who served decades back. No one had ever noticed it before. . . That's what it's like to be the first woman."

Wisconsin Supreme Court Chief Justice Shirley Abrahamson describes what it felt like to be the only woman for so many years. Appointed a justice in 1976 to fill out a vacancy, she was elected to a ten-year term in 1979 and reelected to two subsequent ten-year terms in 1989 and 1999. She became chief justice in 1996 because of her seniority in accordance with her state's constitution. ". . . [It] wasn't until the '90s that a second woman joined me on the bench. We met at our first dinner party for the new court. When she got up to go to the ladies' room, I quickly followed her, checked all the stalls and said, 'I've been waiting for you for seventeen years.'"[19]

At the other end of the spectrum, Mary Ann G. McMorrow, who in 2005 finished a three-year term as chief justice on the Illinois Supreme Court, has this interesting twist on gender envy: "In Illinois, approximately 35 percent of our judges are women. Men are so fearful of running against a woman that two or three men I know have changed their names to very feminine names. Now, that's a complete reversal from prior years, so I'm not complaining... [b]ut I really look forward to the time when no one will notice if there's a man or a woman sitting on the bench."[20]

Aren't we all! Or at least we should be. So what will get more women on the bench? There is no particular path to judge or chief justice, Marshall tells us. "Somebody once said, 'Becoming a judge is like being struck by lightning but it's helpful if you are standing out in the middle of a field.'" She recommends hard work, excelling at what you do, involvement in the bar and other associations that in turn provides visibility and valuable networks, and experience in the particular court where you hope to serve. And, of course, putting your name in the ring, whether that's for election or for appointment. When Marshall served on her state's judicial nominating council, she would rectify the lack of women on the list by asking judges for the names of the highly competent women appearing before them and then telephoning these women attorneys to recommend strongly that they ("must") file an application. She was, in fact, following the example of Justice Ruth Abrams, who had telephoned her when ambivalent about submitting her name.

"Today, I think there's an assumption that women will rise to the top automatically. But while the numbers are better, we have to keep making sure that women are being encouraged to apply as judges," Marshall said in a *Perspectives Magazine* panel discussion. "One can't assume a bench reflecting the full diversity of the population will just happen automatically."

A Proactive Restructuring

The new surge of women lawyers should put women in line to be the shared keepers of the networks and information that other women will need to succeed. Of course, that is if they are given the opportunity to thrive in the first place. The current structure of American law firms leaves little room for women to prosper once brought on board. Too often once hired, women are put into straitjackets and held back from performing at their highest levels. Although law is a lucrative profession, women are being left off the gravy train. But because the opportunities that lawyers provide for business people can be so extraordinary and the nature of the work they are privy to can be so influential, women must fight to remain in the know.

My point is that lawyers have a great deal of power. There is power in information. As a businessperson and business owner, I know that it is not just legal advice I seek from my lawyer but access to the networks she or he can deliver. In my experience, lawyers are the most well-networked individuals in business, particularly those working in any area of business law. Remember that those high hourly fees you pay—and for a business lawyer today the range can be anywhere from $250 to $650 and maybe more per hour—include access to all the knowledge your lawyer possesses. Success in business is all about knowing where to turn and when. Please understand, I am not in any way suggesting that confidentiality isn't paramount in the legal profession. My experience is that nothing is more important in the legal profession than the confidentiality of a client's information. I am telling you, however, that knowledge is power and we all present advice on the information that we have. Lawyers are the most knowledgeable of any professional when it comes to knowing what is happening in your business world.

Things have to change, therefore, if we are to keep these knowledge-keepers in the firm. Today's graduates expect to have a life outside of a career. Men and women coming out of law schools plan on making partner but have no plan of giving it all to the company. Too often, a talented lawyer, within a few years of making partner, leaves the firm that has invested hundreds of thousands of dollars in him or her in order to go to a position as in-house counsel for a client. The lawyer may or may not find a work/life balance worth attaining, but the firm is left with a very large hole not easily filled.

Really, the structure of the legal profession as a whole must change. Let's not forget those lawyers who choose other areas of practice besides business. Since most everything we know is based on laws, you can't get married (prenuptial), divorced (court), sick (health proxy), retire (trust), or die (estate) without a lawyer. And, of course, our courts, from district to federal to supreme, have lawyers prosecuting, defending, judging, and sentencing. Again—lawyers are powerful people. Women must have every opportunity to succeed in this profession.

In turn, the legal profession needs the perspective that women bring to the law. Women and men need a profession that is proactive in restructuring itself to fit a new world and a new way of doing business. Today's technology-induced 24/7 work world should benefit the legal profession rather than cripple it. More and more documentation of the turnover and poor retention of both men and women should only prod the legal profession to change. That change will not be for women but because of them.

Just Imagine

Women leave law school with all the opportunities afforded to their male counterparts. With encouragement to go into politics, private practice, in-house counsel, and public service, women thrive in the legal profession in numbers equal to their representation.

CHAPTER 8

Women in Healthcare and the Sciences: Prescription for Change

"Never doubt that a small group of thoughtful, committed citizens can change the world; indeed, it's the only thing that ever had."

—Margaret Mead

Although the integration of women into the medical profession began in the 1960s, it is only recently that women are a percentage point shy of comprising 50 percent of all U.S. medical school graduates. The history of the earliest settlers in the 1600s was the last time women dominated this field. Until the 1700s, women cared for the sick with plant remedies and folk medicine. Then medicine became more of a profession and men took over. Eventually, medical schools and state licensing regulations were imposed, and the profession became only for men.[1]

The first licensed female physician, Dr. Elizabeth Blackwell, graduated first in her class in 1849, yet she was refused an association with any hospital. Eventually, Blackwell began her own practice at home to treat women and children. Later, she opened the New York Infirmary for Women and Children and was the first woman to operate a hospital. Blackwell is known as the pioneer blazing the trail for the women who followed. Women remained a minority in medicine throughout the 1900s, however, making up 4 percent of medical school graduates in 1905, comprising 12 percent in 1949 and then plummeting to 7 percent in 1965. Women's numbers tripled between 1970 and 1980, and by 2002–2003, 49.2 percent of medical school applicants were women.

The Association of American Medical Colleges provided a snapshot of how women were represented in medical academia in 2005–2006, which is as follows:

- 50 percent applicants to medical school,
- 48 percent of first-year students,
- 49 percent of medical students,
- 49 percent of graduating medical students,
- 42 percent of residents and fellows,
- 32 percent of medical faculty members,
- 38 percent of assistant professors,
- 28 percent of associate professors,
- 16 percent of full professors,
- 19 percent of division/section chiefs,
- 10 percent of department chairs,
- 43 percent of assistant deans,
- 31 percent of associate and senior associate/vice deans, and
- 11 percent of medical school deans.

It's clear that the percentage of women choosing the medical field and administration leadership in medical schools continues to increase. And career options for anyone with a medical degree are numerous. "The good thing about medicine is there are many, many more choices to make now that there used to be," says Corinne Broderick, executive vice president of the Massachusetts Medical Society. "You see people going into life science research areas, academics, a balance of administration and clinical research, medical publishing, technology—there are so many other things to choose from. I think the choices and the breadth of what's available in medicine can give people more opportunity to have a variety of what they can do than the traditional path of what we used to see of working your way up through the system to become chief of whatever."

Yet with all this progress, women are nonetheless underrepresented in senior leadership positions. In 2006, fourteen women headed one hundred twenty-five medical schools across the country. None of the nineteen pharmaceutical companies in the *Fortune* 500 are run by women. Nationally, women comprise about one-fifth, or 21.4 percent, of hospital presidents.[2] Only 3 percent of those awarded the Nobel Prize in Science have been women. So, what's to blame? Is it a matter of wait and time will tell a different story? Not likely. Like many other sectors, healthcare and the sciences are rife with the same barriers and biases that hold women back.

Ellen Zane, president and CEO of Tufts-New England Medical Center in Boston, laments that, given "the workforce is 85 percent female in healthcare, at least at hospitals, you would think there would be more women in leadership, but there aren't. It's kind of lonely. There are lots and lots of meetings where I sit in a room with twenty people and I'm the only woman in the room." Tufts-NEMC is the second hospital where Zane has led a dramatic turnaround. Her path to the presidency was atypical for an academic medical center—usually the top spot is reserved for a doctor—but Zane says women in positions like hers and of her generation typically get to the top through unusual circumstances. For Zane, it was a community hospital CEO's recognition of her managerial talents that catapulted her up the ladder from her start as a speech therapist until she was proving herself at the helm of hospital turnarounds with a stint in managed care leadership in between. Critical mass, Zane believes, is changing women's path to the top. "Today, as women think about it and say they want to get into leadership, it's often female physicians who like the administrative side as well," Zane says. "I think over time you will see more women aspire to these jobs and get them."

But will they? According to England's Royal College of Physicians' 2004 "Women in Medicine Key Issues" statement, women are not well represented in the upper echelons of the profession, or in all areas of the profession, for that matter, because they choose medical specialties with more predictable work schedules or that allow for part-time hours or job sharing. "Despite more women now coming into medicine, the statistics show that for whatever reason, they are not moving into the whole range of medical specialties," the statement notes.

The question may be: Is the structure of the medical profession, like that in the legal profession, in need of a revamp to keep up with the ever-changing needs of the professionals it attracts as well as the changing world in which we live in? In order to get more women to participate at the top levels of the healthcare system, where time requirements bump into family commitments, the need for a structure change is apparent. The Royal College's key issues statement calls for a different career pattern in response to the numbers of women entering the profession as well as new pathways to move women into leadership positions. The situation in the United States is no different. The question is: Now that women are here and are ready to lead the way, how will the profession and the healthcare system change?

Lifestyle has become a determining factor for both men and women in choosing their career paths in medicine. Broderick says, "I think it is a shared value. Part of the acceptance of it [lifestyle] probably has been driven by the situations facing women trying to balance childrearing and dealing with medical debt. I think it is more accepted for men and women coming into medicine to look at the overall approach that is going to best fit both their lifestyle, their values, and their needs."

Dr. Rhonda Rockett, a family practitioner working three days a week in a Massachusetts group of three doctors, says she chose her specialty with family balance in mind. The two other doctors in her group are men; one works four days a week and the other, five days a week. Although she once worried that patients wouldn't select her as their primary care physician if they knew of her limited schedule, Rockett has recently closed her practice because she had too many patients. Her colleagues, she says, are just as family oriented as she is. When it comes to vacation time, they take turns taking the time off because they're dealing with the same school vacation weeks.

So, while there is opportunity for flexibility in primary care and even in psychiatry, the other specialties present a different story. According to the Women Physicians Congress of the American Medical Association, twenty-four specialties in 2004 had more than one thousand women compared to only seven specialties in 1970. In 1970, there were 25,201 women physicians; in 2004, 235,627 doctors were women. The Top Ten specialty choices for women in 2004 (see Table 8.1), in order of popularity, were internal medicine, pediatrics, general practice/family practice, psychiatry, obstetrics/gynecology, anesthesiology, pathology, emergency, diagnostic radiology, and general surgery.

Specialties like orthopedics, neurosurgery, and urology see few women. Discrimination, or at the very least incredibly discouraging remarks, are part of the reason for women's limited numbers in these fields. In recounting an American Medical Women's Association member's experience, Dr. Susan Ivey, president of the organization, says the female neurosurgical resident dropped out because the atmosphere was so toxic. "It's sad to me to hear that there's still that kind of internal tension and discrimination that keeps women who are clearly capable of successfully making it into surgery from doing so," Ivey says. "Another young woman who's a colorectal fellow—which means she's made it through her five years of surgery, was chief resident, and made it into this fellowship—is now facing this same sense of discrimination in that they don't want her when she finishes. So even though she made it to the top of the heap, there's this environment where she's not one of the boys and doesn't belong there long-term. It's a

Table 8.1

Percentage Distribution of Female Physicians and Specialty—2004

Specialty	Total Women	Under Age 35	Age 35–44	Age 45–54	Age 55–64	Age 65-Plus
Internal Medicine	46,245	31%	33%	25%	8.2%	2.1%
Pediatrics	36,636	30%	32%	24%	11%	3.5%
Family Practice	26,305	29%	36%	26%	6.8%	1.8%
Ob-GYN	17,258	29%	34%	25%	8.5%	2.7%
Psychiatry	13,079	17%	24%	35%	21%	9.6%
Anesthesiology	8,370	16%	32%	31%	15%	5.9%
Pathology	6,037	16%	27%	32%	17%	8.0%
Emergency	5,987	34%	32%	24%	7.9%	1.6%
Radiology/Diagnostic	5,126	23%	34%	30%	10%	1.6%
General Surgery	5,173	43%	31%	20%	5.3%	1.4%

Source: Physician Characteristics and Distribution in the United States, 2006 edition. (c) 2006, American Medical Association, (used with permission).

'we'll just train you but we don't want you as faculty' type of thing. There are still a lot of stories like these that are playing out and may keep other women from choosing a specialty because they perceive it as being very difficult to be successful there."

Dr. Barbara Rockett, Rhonda Rockett's mother-in-law, has defied the usual throughout her career, so it can be done—and it could be accomplished even in 1958, when she was the first woman surgical intern at Boston City Hospital at a time when few women went into surgery at all. Pregnant during her residency, she was only asked once in an interview during her career what she'd do if she became pregnant. "I had one child by then and so I said, 'I'd be pregnant.' I still got the job." In 1985, Rockett became the first woman president of the Massachusetts Medical Society and then, in 1986, the first physician and woman elected to a second, consecutive term. "I guess I have a tendency to say what I think. I never tried to fashion what I said to win votes," she says.

Trained in general surgery, Rockett now assists her neurosurgeon husband and so, these days, she can somewhat control her schedule. Finding child care for her five children was her greatest challenge when they were young, she says, and then, when they were older, she did things like serve as the team physician to attend their games. Rockett also took to leadership in organized medicine: along with deep involvement in the Massachusetts Medical Society, she also participates on the national level as a director of the American Medical Association Foundation and the chair of the Massachusetts delegation to the American Medical Association, and was a former nine-year member of the AMA's Council on Legislation.

Dr. Nancy H. Nielsen is in her second elected three-year term as speaker of the AMA's principal policymaking body, the House of Delegates, and is the first woman elected to the post. An internist, she is a clinical professor of medicine and senior associate dean for medical education at SUNY's Buffalo School of Medicine and Biomedical Sciences. To her, organized medicine is a means to improving the quality of healthcare in this country. "It is my personal crusade to seek health coverage for all Americans," Nielsen says. "I have personal, painful experiences with being uninsured or underinsured. In graduate school, I had two babies through public health clinics since my health insurance plan excluded pregnancy benefits. One of my daughters was very ill, and there was no family coverage. I will never forget what that was like. It is to our shame that we allow this to continue, and that the number of the uninsured grows yearly."

Her own opportunities for leadership in medical organizations—"and there have been many of them"—Nielsen says, have been the result of having a passion for something, volunteering on committees and task forces, and being in the right place at the right time. "So when it comes time for the leadership roles, one is already known as someone who is hardworking, trustworthy, and fair. The ability to work collaboratively is a plus," she says. So is having a sense of humor about navigating a male-dominated organization. "One piece of advice was given to me by a terrific woman physician: She said that if I wanted to understand an organization, I should make it my job to learn about the finances. I am not normally drawn to financial issues, but her advice was very sound. If you understand the finances, you are treated with more respect in groups. But don't negate pure luck. It also helps if you like and understand sports—no joke!"

Mentors and opportunities will get more women to the top in organized medicine, Nielsen says. "Once the glass ceiling is shattered in an organization, it is easier for other women to follow. That is a pivotal event in an organization and is really much more important than just a personal achievement of the first female to be in a highly visible leadership role."

To sum up, while the numbers of women pursuing medical degrees and the fact that men for the most part appear just as interested as women in flexibility bode well for a profession with the capability of across-the-board work/life balance, there should be no complacency about pushing the envelope on a livable workplace. Sure, time might finish up the job in areas where work still needs to be done, but women only hit the 50-percent mark of medical school applicants in the 2005–2006 school year. Compare that to women comprising just slightly more than one quarter of all doctors in 2004. If we simply wait for women to hit the physician's 50 percent—the argument for "change will happen, just hang in there"—then we're in for a long wait.

The Sciences

The number of women in the sciences is another area of concern since far more men than women go on to get master's degrees and PhDs, with women only more recently coming into the attainment of advanced degrees.

- In 2004, women in all science and engineering (S&E) fields earned 50.4 percent of bachelor's degrees, 43.6 percent of master's degrees, and 37.4 percent of PhDs, according to tabulations by the National Science Foundation (NSF).

- Women broke the 40-percent mark in S&E bachelor's degrees in 1988. Nine years later, in 1997, women were 40 percent of those earning both master's and PhD degrees for the first time.

- Women were best represented in biology/agricultural sciences, psychology, and the social sciences and were particularly underrepresented in mathematics/computer sciences and engineering.

- In 2004, women earned 42.1 percent of physical sciences bachelor's degrees, so perhaps their numbers will boost their attainment of master's (35.5% in 2004) and PhD (25.9%) degrees.

- Here's an interesting twist—out of all the sciences individually tabulated, only math/computer science is seeing a decrease in women's numbers and yet there's sustained interest here at the master's level. Women earning math/computer science bachelor's degrees peaked in 1985 at 39.5 percent and have steadily decreased year over year to 29.1 percent of bachelor's degrees earned in 2004. The good news is, women are sticking with the field or perhaps switching into it at the master's level, where their representation in math/computer science master's degrees has hovered in the 30- to 35-percent range since 1983. The downside: Women's numbers at the PhD level have fluctuated in the 20- to 25-percent range since 1997.

What does this mean for the workforce? According to NSF, in the year 2000, the science and engineering industry employed nine hundred, ninety-four thousand, and four hundred women compared to just over three million men. Experts agree that it goes back to the classroom where boys continue to be encouraged in the sciences more than girls. Shirley Ann Jackson, president of Rensselaer Polytechnic Institute and the 2007 recipient of the National Science Board's Vannevar Bush Award, says youngsters "need the involvement of their teachers, their peer groups, of people who can serve as role models."[3] But, if role models are required, we need more women to go into the field to provide the mentoring and the role modeling necessary to encourage girls to pursue the field. And then the question becomes, once women get there, can they be sure that they will be treated fairly?

In 1994, Dr. Nancy Hopkins, a research scientist at MIT, brought what was probably the first public attention to how her gender was holding her back. She joined the MIT faculty in 1973 after receiving her graduate degree and postdoctoral fellow at Harvard. She had moved through the ranks at MIT alongside her male peers not particularly aware of any gender bias. After all, "science is about truths," she has said, and therefore how could gender discrimination take place? Deciding to change her research from viruses to the development of zebra fish, she requested an additional two hundred square feet of lab space. When her small request was denied, she decided to take a look at how much space her fellow scientists, both male and female, were using. Her findings spawned a revelation that now has made history. Hopkins, a full professor with tenure, had fifteen hundred square feet of research space while her male counterparts averaged three thousand to six thousand square feet. Even male assistant and associate professors had an average of two thousand square feet.

After ten months, when she was unable to make any headway with her request, she realized it was time to get the support of other female faculty members. Having never thought about the number of women faculty up to this point, she again was surprised to find only fifteen tenured women compared to one hundred and ninety-four men. She collected her data and put it into a letter to the then-president of MIT, Charles Vest, and asked all of the other women to sign it. All but one did. Vest immediately began an investigation into any and all potential areas of gender discrimination at the school. When the report was ready to be released, Vest insisted on complete transparency so that other colleges and universities could begin to take the subject seriously, and so MIT could begin to tackle the problem. One could say that, when it comes to the debate about equality for women faculty in science and engineering, Hopkins was responsible for the shot heard 'round, not the world, but every college and university in America. Since then, MIT and at least eight other universities have agreed to meet regularly to review salaries and the proportion of other university resources provided to women faculty. The Ford Foundation funded MIT's Gender Equity Project in recognition of the university's public acknowledgement of gender bias.[4]

This story points out how easily gender discrimination can go unnoticed and how detrimental it can be not only to the women involved but also to society, which depends on the opportunities researchers have to do the work. The positive piece is the call-to-action reaction, but can we assume that discrimination for women scientists has now disappeared? Unfortunately not, since women still lag far behind men in patents, according to a study published by the journal, *Science*. Out of four thousand, two hundred and twenty-seven biological scientists working at U.S. universities between 1967 and 1995, women were about 40 percent as likely as their male peers to apply for patents. In 2004, U.S. universities reported nearly $1.4 billion in patent licensing income and royalties on product sales of $1.1 billion, so the importance of being listed on a patent is important for both recognition and advancement in the institution. The study concluded that it was a lack of connections that was holding women back from the patenting process and that awareness of the problem was the first step to removing the obstacle.[5]

Susan Ivey, the American Medical Women's Association (AMWA) president who's an associate professor adjunct and director of research at Health Research for Action at the University of California, Berkeley, had to fight for the right to put her name on her own research. When the Massachusetts General Hospital online newsletter asks in a July 2006 article[6] why women remain underrepresented among medical science investigators, the answer can quite likely be found in women's stories that parallel Ivey's—except that the others might not have bucked the system, or worked the system the way Ivey did. Principal investigator status at most academic medical institutions is extended to the tenure track only, a track that is populated with few women. So if you are writing a grant and publishing research but are not on the tenure track (remember the earlier-noted Association of American Medical Colleges' 16 percent of women full professors), it won't be under your name, but under the PI who can "sponsor" your work. The "Percentage of Women" article notes the dearth of women "lead authors" but doesn't see the problem as endemic to academia's structural hierarchy and women's place in it.

Ivey chalks up her personal activism to closing in on forty when she was faced with chasing after PI sponsorships. A family practitioner for thirteen years before earning the degrees necessary to teach and research health policy at University of California, Berkeley, she says, "I didn't have the time to cotton to somebody to let their career shine while I was trying to build mine, so it really was an urgency that I felt that maybe a younger researcher wouldn't have felt." By reading through job descriptions, Ivey found a position where she could be a principal investigator on an approved project-by-project basis. Once she attained that status "with a lot of fighting and bureaucracy," she "went back to the drawing board to pass the sniff test" to be the PI on all of her projects. "It's a funny system where there aren't a lot of people who are thinking about pushing women ahead, and so if you're not advocating for yourself and pushing yourself, no one else is necessarily thinking about doing it for you," Ivey says. Here again, the system needs changing if women are to be rewarded and recognized for the work *that they are actually doing* but that remains hidden in an antiquated scheme for professional status that, basically, retains the gender status quo.

The Business of Science

Advocating for yourself is also part of the mantra for women aiming for leadership in the pharmaceutical industry. "Female employees must realize that to reach the upper echelons, they must take an active role in their own advancement. Those who sit back and wait for corporate structures to guide them or who lack a clear focus of what they want to achieve, what skills they need and how they intend to reach their goals will likely find themselves disappointed," notes the Healthcare Businesswomen's Association in its "Power" study.[7] At the brink of the new millennium, fewer than 10 percent of senior managers in some forty pharmaceuticals were women, and fifteen of those companies had no women at all in their top positions. Things can't be much better today. The release of the "HBA E.D.G.E. (Empowerment, Diversity, Growth, & Excellence) in Leadership Study" was anticipated sometime after the writing of this book. Its purpose is "to identify for the first time key insights and benchmarks that will allow companies to accelerate the progress of women into the most senior position in the pharmaceutical and biotechnology industries." The expectation is to update findings hereafter every few years and to evolve into an industrywide investigation of all of the life sciences.

In the 1999 study's survey, 77 percent of women felt they had yet to achieve equality with the men at their companies while just over half of the men felt women had achieved equality. General consensus among respondents was that women maintained the minority status at the top because of a lack of training and opportunity to gain line management experience. The outlook of many women was bleak: Thirty-four percent of women in upper management and 43 percent of women in middle management thought there was more opportunity for rising to the top at pharmaceutical companies other than their own and even greater opportunity for advancement outside of pharma altogether. Seventy-eight percent of the women surveyed believed pharma undervalued women—and half of the men agreed. To advance, the survey study notes, "Many women still believe that to be promoted to senior management, they need to be more successful, skilled, educated, and hard working than men. In doing so, they feel they must be aggressive without appearing 'pushy.' Men do not see themselves under this self-restriction."

Interestingly, men and women agreed on the need for better work/life balance in the face of sixty to eighty hours a week on the road—mostly for their personal welfare but also for their family lives. There wasn't much hope held out for change. According to the report, "One respondent noted: 'Until more senior managers lead more balanced lives, they will not see the value of it in others' lives throughout the company.'" In fact, and here's a huge problem for the future leadership of the country's pharmaceuticals, only 5 percent of those who said they aspired to top leadership were willing to sacrifice their personal lives to get and stay there. Four out of ten would be willing to make some sacrifice, and one in four would not make any further sacrifices to get to the top. The report notes, "An upper management woman responded: 'Until two years ago, I would have answered that I was more ambitious and would willingly sacrifice more of my personal life than I would currently be willing to do. Having hit the glass ceiling, I'm no longer willing to sacrifice for this company.'"

There was also unity of the sexes in recommendations for making work/life more bearable. "Interviewees also call on senior management to provide less lip service and more action, and to lead by making decisions that offer all employees day care, senior care assistance, European-style vacations, and other mechanisms that can help restore a better balance between office and home life. When companies implement such actions, respondents claim, everyone benefits: women and men, young and old."

Self-advocacy, however, doesn't play much for the male managers in chemical companies when it comes to advancing their women reports, according to the NSF's "It's Elemental: Enhancing Career Success for Women in the Chemical Industry," out in March 2007. The study is the first to look at what advances and what holds back women in science, technology, engineering, and mathematics (STEM) industrial settings, which represent the largest employer of STEM graduates. While managers, and particularly male managers, rated the ability to relocate higher than women did as a factor for career success, women noted "blowing your own horn" and "to be on highly visible projects" as the keys to promotion. Women also noted sexist discrimination, although those who felt positively about their workplace reported lower levels of discrimination. "While women are taking on leadership roles in STEM industries, the number of women in those roles and the rate at which it is happening is disappointingly slow," concludes Judith Giordan, a program director for NSF's Integrative Graduate Education and Research Traineeship Program.

In the NSF survey, both men and women called mentoring hugely important. Deborah Dunsire's story is a case in point. With a mentor who complemented her own drive, she rose through the ranks of global drug development with such aplomb that in 2005 publicly traded Millennium Pharmaceuticals recruited her to become its president and CEO. Charged with leading the transformation from research to manufacture/distribution, she's continuing to find her own power in, as she says, "moving the boundary forward." Dunsire began her career as a general practitioner in South Africa and fell into drug development by happenstance. Planning to switch to ophthalmology, she filled in time between selling her practice and starting the residency by answering an ad for a clinical research position. Although the transition was difficult at first, once she was exposed to the global scope of drug development, Dunsire was hooked. Her boss/mentor gave her opportunity after opportunity to push herself out of her comfort zone as well as suggested that she get international experience.

From a line position at then-Sandoz Pharmaceuticals in South Africa, Dunsire moved to headquarters in Switzerland for a product rollout and then returned to a line role, this time in the United States. After Novartis acquired Sandoz, she led the U.S. oncology business and then the North American division. Millennium recruited her and since then has brought its first oncology drug to market. So there is potential for women in top leadership in the sciences—as well as great reward. A passion for the better good is what keeps Dunsire motivated. "Over time," she says, "I'd like people to say that Millennium is an innovative company that creates great medicines and thrives in the economic environment of the United States."[8]

As a newer industry, is biotech more accommodating to women than the big pharmas? Perhaps. Mara Aspinall, president of Genzyme Genetics in Massachusetts, believes that there's less history to get in the way in a relatively new industry like biotech. "It's not about everyone who's known each other for thirty years and their father's father who has been in the industry," she says. "Most biotechs are relatively small companies, with twenty or fewer employees. Smaller, younger companies don't have the inbred politics and processes that may discourage women in senior management." Aspinall came to Genzyme with business development and consulting experience backed by an MBA. She joined Genzyme in 1997 as vice president of corporate development and was president of Genzyme Pharmaceuticals for four years before heading the Genetics business in 2001. Genzyme Genetics has more than tripled in size since Aspinall's start and is one of the country's largest diagnostic testing companies. Hard work, a great team, and a culture of meritocracy are the foundation of her leadership success, Aspinall says.

While Genzyme has promoted numerous women into leadership roles, elsewhere in the industry there is still a lack of women in leadership. "Biotech, as a new industry, has been more open to women but, as yet, there are few women CEOs," Aspinall points out. "Women are entering the sciences and junior management ranks in greater and greater numbers. Biotech, however, is not as successful as it should be at retaining talented women over the long haul in senior positions."

Aspinall also notes that there aren't enough women founding biotechs. Part of the problem can be in landing the funding, asserts Springboard president Amy Millman: "While women in biotech have zero difficulty defending their product or technology to their peers, they have a hard time selling their capabilities, their expertise and their ability to execute to anyone outside their comfort zone."[9]

Nonetheless, women are finding ways to start their own businesses without outside capital, just as they did in the early days of women's business entrepreneurship when banks, never mind the venture capitalists, wouldn't fork over a loan. Bootstrapping her company, Jean Qiu chose biomedical research in late 2002 precisely because of its emerging status and self-funding potential. Today she's founder, president, and CEO of Nexcelom Bioscience, a Massachusetts company revolutionizing the lab with the first disposable vs. glass slide and subsequent follow-on innovations.

In anticipation of running her own business, Qiu, an electrical engineer, honed her skills at 3M in Minnesota. First she helped develop the first blue-green semiconductor laser for reading CDs (marking the beginning of the dozen patents that bear her name) and then went on to second and third careers within 3M, developing advanced plastics into new product concepts and commercializing the Healthcare Group, her purposely chosen entry into the healthcare field. All the while, Qiu was absorbing the 3M way of "make a little, sell a little" for her own purposes. By 2001, she was ready for her entrepreneurial leap. She chose biomedical research—"if you want to do a start-up, you have to work in a field that doesn't have a lot of barriers for small players"—and moved to Massachusetts for its biotech strength. The slide she developed is actually quite high tech. "We're doing nanomanufacturing, creating a very microscopic nanoscale feature on the plastic," she says.[10] By 2006, Qiu had introduced a benchtop automated reader that replaced "eyeballing" an estimate or using a huge, lab-shared machine, and was breaking the million-dollar revenue mark.

Again, as we saw in our business chapters, women in science and engineering are making their way in fields still dominated by men. The same holds true for women in medicine. And again, we can't rely on the theory that women's increasing numbers will fix any inequities over time. Time's ticking away. Scientific advancements aren't going to slow down until more women can bring their talents to the bench. Drug development isn't going to wait until more women are at the top of businesses that turn advancements into tangible, available, lifesaving, and health healing products. Patients aren't going to hold off on making appointments until they have more women physicians to select as their practitioners and specialists. We need change now.

Women's Health

Women's impact on the sciences is most dramatic in the area—the new area—of women's health. The increasing female participation as physicians in medicine has caused a sea change in the care for women. This evolution has sparked a dramatic overhaul as to how women's health is viewed by the profession. In 1991, then-President George H. W. Bush appointed Dr. Bernadine Healy director of the National Institutes of Health. As the first woman appointed to the position, she launched a $625 million Women's Health Initiative involving one hundred and fifty thousand women in a fifteen-year study on preventing heart disease, breast and colorectal cancer, and osteoporosis in postmenopausal women. Up to this point, very little research had been done on women's health. In 1993, a law was passed requiring no bias in medical research. Since then, there has been a dramatic push for educating women about their health and the health of their families. The 2005 "Women and Diversity WOW! Facts" reports that women are the decision makers for 67 percent of healthcare spending and 92 percent of long-term care insurance decisions in the country. So whether it's her health or his health, women are the driving force.

This new focus on women's health spurred an industry of women's health centers across the country. Many centers decided to care for women with women physicians only. More and more women demanded to be cared for by women, feeling that their health issues would be given greater understanding. I was fortunate to work with a pioneer in the establishment of women's health centers, Rina Spence. In 1995, Spence opened the first Spence Center for Women's Health in Cambridge, Massachusetts, followed by two more in that state and one in Washington, DC. The plan was to roll out forty more centers across the country. As the coordinator for business development, I saw incredible demand from the beginning. Women who had not been to see a doctor since giving birth came to the Spence Center to be seen and heard by a female physician. The ability to have in one place all of their care—gynecology, mammography, bone density, X-ray, cardiology, gastroenterology, dermatology, as well as what was considered at that time as nontraditional care: chiropractic, acupuncture, and massage therapy—was appreciated by women.

It was the beginning for women in recognizing how they should be treated by the healthcare system. Unfortunately, Spence Centers didn't have the opportunity to expand around the country due to the disparity between the reimbursement for care by the insurance companies and the cost of that care. The fee-for-service part of the business couldn't make up for the lack of reimbursement for traditional medical services. But the concept was a model for others in the healthcare world to build on. Today's push and success of concierge medicine is a direct result from the type of care Spence Centers and others, Canyon Ranch for example, provide. The build-it-and-they-will-come motto was proven, yet the cost coverage for adequate healthcare remains a national problem.

Women's health is now a specialty and has inspired greater attention by the biotech and pharmaceutical communities as well. Just look at the shelves in grocery stores and drug stores—you can't miss women's cereals and women's vitamins, the very basics of health maintenance. And the advancements for women's health have been huge. Heart health is perhaps the best example. Today it's commonly recognized that men's and women's heart attack symptoms are different. Newer is the discovery of the different roles plaque plays in causing heart failure in men versus women. All of this is because of women initiating the focus on women in clinical testing and health advancements versus the old school men-only models. Still, our healthcare system continues to be a national problem in need of an overhaul, and it is clear that as patients, physicians, scientists, and policy leaders, women could very well be the major drivers in the solutions for its future in America, if only given the chance.

Women's Progress

If we look closely at the top where scientific achievement is measured, the Nobel Prize in Science, we learn that just 3 percent of those receiving this prestigious honor have been women. If somehow after reading this far in this book, you can still consider the supposed innate abilities of female versus male, remember that it was not until after the 1920s that women were even allowed to pursue higher education in mathematics and science. That is your great-grandmother's, grandmother's, or your mother's generation, depending on how old you are. Then it is important to note that up until 1970, women interested in working in research in universities did so as volunteers without pay. Yes, Marie Curie, probably the best known, if not the only known female winner of a Nobel Prize for Science, worked for years without any compensation or position. The Federal Equal Opportunity Act passed in 1972 reversed state laws and university rules that previously had banned the hiring of wives of university professors, even though most of the research teams at the time were made up of husbands and wives. According to the book, *Nobel Prize Women in Science*, in 1998, 70 percent of American women physicists were married to scientists. Only the men in these research teams received the pay, the position, and the accolades as the wife was assumed to be an assistant on the project. But the wives' passion for the research kept them engaged and, just as with Nancy

Hopkins' story, these women believed their work would speak for them and their performance.

Likewise, academia's tenure track in the sciences poses much the same quandary for women as you'll see in higher education in general. As an example that points to the need for change and also holds up in general when conversing anecdotally, the University of Arizona College of Medicine's 2000 Grace Project found the following.

- Women took longer to be promoted to associate professor.
- A greater proportion of women felt they did not know the requirements for being promoted.
- Women were more likely to have considered changing track.
- Yet there was no significant difference between the sexes in delaying the tenure clock—an important finding in terms of the argument that women don't succeed because they're too focused on family.

The summary conclusion: "Promotion to higher ranks takes longer for women, and the tenure track as currently structured seems to carry particular challenges for women."

Additionally, when it came to salary in the Grace Project, female full professors earned 11 percent less than their male colleagues and female assistant professors earned 9 percent less, with disparities evident among both the clinical and tenure-track faculty. The reality, the report notes: "Women in most departments at the UA College of Medicine are less likely to be rewarded for their terms of salary even after accounting for rank, track, years in rank, specialty, departmental leadership roles, clinical revenues, and research productivity."

Since the 1960s, America has seen some increase in women earning science degrees but still, the United States ranks below thirteen other countries in the percentage of twenty-four-year-olds with a math or science degree. Notes Maria Klawe, dean of Princeton University's engineering school, "We have to change our culture to one that believes that it's really important to have a population that is well educated in math and science."[11]

In France, all students are required to take math and physics, and there the number of women scientists is higher. Thirty-five percent of the advanced doctoral degrees in physics are earned by women in France. Compare that to women earning a quarter of physical sciences PhDs in this country and an estimated 7 percent of employed female American physicists and astronomers. Are there more Lawrence Summer thinkers out there discouraging women, even unconsciously, from trying to achieve their dream of a scientific career? Or is it, as we have seen in business and law and will soon read in higher education and nonprofit, that because women reach their career peak at the same time they reach their childbearing peak, the workplace structure and the old rules and ways of doing things are barriers that get in the way? It's time for a change of attitude. It's time to inspire another budding Marie Curie (Nobel Prize in Physics, 1903; Chemistry, 1911), Barbara McClintock (Nobel Prize in Medicine or Physiology, 1983), and Linda Buck (Nobel Prize in Physiology or Medicine, 2004) to dream what is possible and to discover the next cure and/or scientific advancement for (wo)mankind. Women have the education. Women have the aptitude. Women have the desire to heal and to explore the world of science and medicine. Women need release from the archaic attitudes that have left them on the sidelines for far too long in the scientific fields. Our health and future depend on it.

Just Imagine

Girls and young women are encouraged to be excited about math and science at an early age. Sciences of all types are viewed as cool and are encouraged for girls and boys in America—the only answer to America's ability to compete globally. Women have role models in engineering, technology, the life sciences, and medicine at the college level, and into the workplace. Our healthcare system has been restructured to encourage women to go into all medically related professions, including administration and public policy roles, and to institute better healthcare for all.

CHAPTER 9

Bias in Higher Education: The Firestorm

"To me, leadership is a culture, not a person. What a leader does is to encourage everyone to think creatively and even aggressively, to problem solve, to find the new paths, and then support that."

—Ruth Simmons

The tipping point for women in higher education arrived when Harvard's now ex-president Lawrence H. Summers not only casually commented in 2005 that innate differences between men and women might be one reason fewer women succeed in science and math careers than men, but then he also went on to question whether discrimination actually plays a role in the lack of female professors at universities. His remarks created a firestorm of attention that turned a white-hot spotlight on the bias against women at institutions of higher learning. Thank you, Lawrence Summers. It had previously taken a generation of women to insist that girls be given an opportunity to be heard and recognized in elementary schools and on through high school. Finally, there are now rumblings at the next level, higher education and its faculty, where women must be afforded the same recognition. After all, professors shape the intellect and social conscience of their students, "and, hence, of our society. Offering students a faculty as diverse as the world they live in and ensuring the fairness of the promotion process is thus of tremendous importance."[1]

But the rumblings are going to have to crank up to thunderous decibels because there is still much to overcome in academia for women's success in faculty and senior executive positions. While the American Association of University Women's (AAUW) "Tenure Denied" notes that women are graduating from colleges and universities in record numbers, their arrival at critical mass is not reflected in their professional status. Only one-third of associate professors and one-fifth of full professors are women. Instead, women mostly remain stuck in the lower-echelon positions in academia, where they represent more than half of instructors and lecturers, and nearly half of assistant professors. Compound the one-fifth full professor status with the trend of women PhDs opting out of academia and into other sectors that promise greater opportunity, and higher education is on the brink of major talent drain.

According to the American Council on Education (ACE), women tend to be less likely to pursue tenure-track faculty positions at research universities after earning their doctorates.[2] *Harvard Magazine* paraphrases Caroline M. Hoxby, professor of economics at Harvard University, this way: " . . . the future of scholarship depends on drawing from the largest possible pool of talented individuals. While women are at least equally represented in selective schools' student bodies, and so are being prepared for high-performing careers, they are being disproportionately attracted to nonacademic professions which have made far more progress in hiring: law, business, and medicine. That should lend urgency in the academy to more effective searches."[3]

In other words, the competition for qualified candidates is fierce and if universities are interested in drawing from the full pool of the best and brightest, they must be flexible on issues such as work/family balance and take a look at how they are attracting women to pursue tenure and promoting them to the president's chair. The ACE's "The American College President: 2007 Edition"[4] reports little change in the percentage of women among newly hired versus seasoned presidents since the organization began collecting data in 1986. Just as in other professions, there must be enough female role models at the highest level to provide women the ambition and the confidence that the top is attainable. Considering that, according to the ACE "Tenure-Track" report, women comprise 51 percent of earned PhDs, it behooves higher education to figure out how to attract and retain half of its potential workforce who today have myriad choices to work outside of academia's walls.

The good news is, women are increasingly focusing their attention on advanced degrees. Why? The answer is simple. Just as we've seen in other areas of our society in our history, when women see an obstacle to conquer, they do so. It may take years, decades, or centuries, but once the doors are opened, women don't walk but run to the head of the line. Education is one of the answers to leadership in this country and around the world. Education has always been the promise to higher wages. Education is the possibility, not a guarantee, to power, emphasis on "not a guarantee," particularly in the case of women PhDs. It's time that women in academia have a clear path to full professorships and top administrative roles so that higher learning institutions' faculty and administration better reflect their student populations.

Tenure Track or Tenure Off-Track?

It wasn't all that long ago that higher education was viewed as too taxing for women and that many schools of medicine, law, and business did not admit women. "Before Title IX of the Education Amendments of 1972 and Title VII of the Civil Rights Act of 1964, employers could, and did, refuse to hire women for occupations deemed 'unsuitable,'" says the president of AAUW, Ruth Sweetser. "They fired women when they became pregnant or limited their work schedule because they were female. Schools could, and did, set quotas for the number of women admitted or refused women's admission altogether."

Certainly, women have made great progress in attaining education, which makes the time now most critical in matching their leadership opportunities with their numbers. But if you look at the reasons behind the barriers to women's promotion in academia, the same gender-bias culprits exist as thirty to forty years ago.

Tenure is a promise of lifetime employment and can only be taken away for adequate cause. Those choosing the teaching profession have a right to assume that tenure is based on their academic excellence and service and is not biased. Here is where tenure can begin to go off track for women. Not only do standards and requirements for tenure vary institution to institution, but there is also no straightforward publication of what constitutes a tenure guarantee within an institution—another finding in AAUW's "Tenure Denied" report. Some reasons cited for refusing women tenure: "One department chair argued that a woman professor didn't need her job as much as a man did because she was married," a woman professor "did not seem sufficiently 'collegial,'" and another "was deemed 'too feminine.'" The married professor, it was assumed, would be supported by her husband. The less collegial woman did not conform to how her colleagues thought a woman should behave. Who can guess at what "too feminine" means?

Candida Brush, who holds the entrepreneurship chair at Babson College and has been in academia for more than twenty-five years, also finds danger in the promotion process. "In some schools, the process is where the faculty votes on the candidate and that can be a very messy process because people might vote for things that have nothing to do with the candidate, like: 'I didn't have this so why should I vote for this person?'" When the president, provost, and board of trustees have the veto power to reject a candidate, which is typically the case, "since they're so far removed and they may not know the candidate, that can set up situations where stereotypes or perceptions would be the basis for the decision rather than the merits for the case," Brush adds. "I'm not saying that this necessarily happens, but the potential is there."

Tenure is generally offered five to seven years after a candidate is hired, and here is another offsetting factor for women. Traditionally, the tenure clock has not stopped ticking—a key problem since many women are on the tenure track from ages thirty-three to forty, right in the midst of their childbearing and early childrearing years. Even though there are now approved maternity leaves and there is some movement in stopping the clock for childbirth, plenty of women are not choosing the tenure track at all. The ACE "Tenure-Track" report found that women with children under the age of six were half as likely as married men with same-age children to enter tenure-track posts. University of California, Berkeley, researchers call this the "leaking pipeline for women PhDs"—when women completing doctoral programs opt out of the tenure race in numbers that are highly disproportionate to their male peers or when women who do jump into the race are 20 percent less likely than their male counterparts to achieve tenure (see Figure 9.1)

Furthermore, an Alfred P. Sloan Foundation report notes that junior faculties working at schools that have established policies to help with work/family conflicts do not take advantage of them out of fear of discrimination in future promotion and tenure decisions. So we're back to the prehistoric worry over pregnancy and families getting in the way of promotion, not to mention acceptance. If women do step out of the professoriate to tend to personal issues, reentering a tenure-track position is no easy matter since a liner progression is still expected. As in previous chapters, the same solution exists in higher education—individuals' careers must be viewed from the lifelong perspective, not the immediate, here-and-now, what-can-you-give? (or more to the point, what-can-you-give-up?) framework—but it is a solution still awaiting implementation.

And then there is the dire result of not receiving tenure. Often the candidate who is denied tenure also loses his or her job with very little information as to how the decision was made. It is very difficult to prove gender discrimination when tenure is denied since so much of the

Figure 9.1
Leaks in the Academic Pipeline.

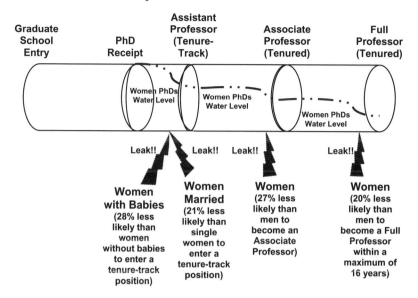

* Results are based on Survival Analysis of the *Survey of Doctorate Recipients* (a national biennial longitudinal data set funded by the National Science Foundation and others, 1979 to 1995). Percentages take into account disciplinary, age, ethnicity, PhD calendar year, time-to-PhD degree, and National Research Council academic reputation rankings of PhD program effects. For each event (PhD to TT job procurement, or Associate to Full Professor), data is limited to a maximum of sixteen years. The waterline is an artistic rendering of the statistical effects of family and gender. *Note:* The use of NSF data does not imply NSF endorsement of research methods or conclusions contained in this paper.

Source: From Mary Ann Mason, Marc Goulden, and Nick Wolfinger, "Leaks in the Academic Pipeline," University of California (used with permission).

process is subjective and ambiguous. As the AAUW "Tenure Denied" report notes, "Pinpointing sex discrimination amidst the tangled web of subjective judgments behind a tenure decision is a Herculean task."

For those women who do receive tenure, the statistics compiled in the ACE "Tenure-Track" overview aren't all that great, either. Women at all faculty ranks are significantly less happy than white males when it comes to work/life and career satisfaction. Women report feeling that they must compromise their values in order to fit into the academic culture. Twelve percent of associate professors are likely to leave academia within three years of their start, and women associate professors holding that rank for ten years or more are especially likely to feel that they're stagnating. Even tenured women report lower satisfaction than their male counterparts on colleague relationships, professional development, overall career experience, and the integration of their professional and personal lives.

Not surprisingly, there are fewer married women than men with tenure. The *Harvard Magazine* article notes that 44 percent of tenured women in its faculty of Arts and Sciences are married and have children, compared to 70 percent of the tenured men. A worse ratio was the number of tenure offers extended to women within the FAS in 2004: four out of thirty-two. Action was underway to improve the situation, particularly in the form of thorough searches for prospective professors and aggressive recruiting.

In their first "Do Babies Matter?" Mary Ann Mason and Marc Goulden[5] found that men having children within five years of receiving their PhDs were 38 percent more likely than their women counterparts to achieve tenure. In their "Do Babies Matter? (Part II) Closing the Baby Gap,"[6] they asked men and women who had secured their first assistant professor job before becoming a parent if they would still like to have a baby. "The short answer: Men do and women don't. 'Married with children' is the success formula for men, but the opposite is true for women, for whom there is a serious 'baby gap.'"

In "Part II," Mason and Goulden say, "Only one in three women who takes a fast-track university job before having a child ever becomes a mother. Women who achieve tenure are more than twice as likely as their male counterparts to be single twelve years after earning the PhD. ... [W]omen who are married when they begin their faculty careers are much more likely than men in the same position to divorce or separate from their spouses. Women, it seems, cannot have it all—tenure and a family— while men can. On the other hand, the 'second tier' of women PhDs— those who are not working or who are adjunct, part-time, or 'gypsy' scholars and teachers—looks very different. Second-tier women have children and experience marital stability much like men who become professors."

Their survey of the University of California faculty provided Mason and Goulden with the confirmation that the current structure of American research universities forces a fast track that, for women, results in choosing between work and family. "Many faculty members reported having sacri- ficed time with family to demonstrate they were committed to their work. One faculty member advised, 'Avoid having kids before getting tenure. I wish it wasn't so, but I had to learn it the hard way myself.' Another faculty member observed, 'You should know that female graduate students are telling us over and over again across the nation that they are not going to become faculty members because they do not see how they can combine work and family in a way that is reasonable.'"

Mason and Goulden advocate for "stopping the tenure clock for child- birth" as well as for providing "generous childbirth leaves, modified duties, and onsite child care." Any initiatives to help attract and promote women, they say, "depend on a collective will to change the campus culture. Passive and active resistance on the part of men (and even many women) poses a serious roadblock to cultural change."

The AAUW recommends that the tenure process be more consistent and better communicated. Institutions must take all the supposition out of the process and provide written tenure policies and procedures to all faculty and potential employees. If you are a female applicant, you must do everything you can to avoid the risk of discrimination in the tenure process. Simply asking for any written information that the university has on its tenure policies is the first step in protecting yourself. Learn everything you can about the department head you will be working under and ask what teaching and scholarship credentials are necessary for you to become tenured. Don't be afraid to ask. Your long-term career depends on it. Women have worked long and hard to reach the level of tenure at universities and colleges across the nation, but the struggle has just begun when it comes to attaining their rightful place in the highest ranks of academia. Every time another woman attains tenure, it is a win for all women. But there's a long way to go. As AAUW's Sweetser says, "The outstanding performance and investment that women are making in their educations today has yet to translate into full gender equity among tenured faculty—and into full gender equity in the workplace as a whole."

For the university administration, the ACE "Tenure-Track" report advocates for a lifetime view of faculty careers, more work/life balance policies, and a ten-year tenure track with reviews at set intervals. Institutions of higher education will also want to pay attention to Rensselaer Polytechnic Institute's (RPI) new initiative to increase women's representation in its higher-ranking positions universitywide. Announced on March 27, 2007, and funded by a $239,960 grant from the National Science Foundation (NSF), the RAMP-UP (Reforming Advancement Processes through University Professions) program is to be a national model for advancement reform. Noted RPI President Shirley Ann Jackson during the RAMP-UP kick-off celebration, "Understanding and unraveling the myriad twenty-first century challenges requires tapping the entire talent pool, including the 'new majority' [young women and ethnic minority youth who represent nearly two-thirds of the country's population]; engaging students early in science to excite the next generation of scientists, engineers, leaders, and decision makers; and reevaluating and reforming university advancement processes to ensure that all academics are extended an unbiased, equal opportunity to excel."

There are four key components to the RAMP-UP initiative: a designated faculty coach at each of RPI's five schools; a pipeline search for women in industry, national labs, and other nonacademic sources for tenured, full-professor positions; career campaigns in which senior faculty mentor junior women faculty as they begin the advancement process; and a faculty workshop offered each semester on a major issue around women's advancement. Under Jackson's leadership that began in 1999, Rensselaer has experienced 33 percent growth in women faculty, to 29-percent representation. Due to her many firsts as an African-American woman, including chair of the National Regulatory Commission and president of a major national research university, *Time* described Jackson in 2005 as "perhaps the ultimate role model for women in science."[7]

In truth, all of those in education are important role models for the next generation. When the message is sent loud and clear to young women exploring a career in higher education that women wanting to have children need not apply, the profession and all of society lose. We are all victims when a culture of a specific vocation does not advance with society. And, it is particularly puzzling that those in a profession who are often labeled "liberal" or "left of the center" have not figured out how to retain and promote half of the PhD holders. Today's tenure system must be reengineered before the women pursuing an academic career choose to follow other options with more opportunities. The sexism that exists in the tenure process affects everyone. Students benefit from a diverse faculty that has been treated equitably.

President Is Gender Neutral, Right?

If women are opting out of academia and, when they are opting in, are not making it on the tenure track, then who's left to lead an institution of higher learning? Forget the fact that, at this writing, Harvard just appointed Drew Gilpin Faust as its first woman president, putting women in charge of 50 percent of the Ivy League. In 2006, according to the ACE's "The American College President: 2007 Edition," only 13.8 percent of presidents leading doctorate-granting institutions nationwide were women. Women do comprise 29 percent of two-year, community college presidents—where, interestingly, the boards of trustees are more diverse, but more on that later. Overall, women represent 23 percent of presidents in higher education. As Donna Burns Phillips, director of ACE's Office of Women in Higher Education (OWHE), says, "The high-profile hires have the tendency to give the impression that equity has been accomplished—'See, the president of Harvard is a woman; women are just fine now'—and of course that is not born out by the facts."

It is true that the percentage of women presidents has doubled since the ACE began collecting data from more than two thousand colleges and universities across the country—from 9.5 percent in 1986 to 23 percent in 2006—but we're talking twenty years to getting less than a quarter of the country's higher education presidents to look like the majority of their student body. Remember, females outnumbered males in college attendance in 2000, according to the AAUW. And there is no continued momentum in filling higher education presidencies with women today. In 1998 and 2001, 19.3 percent and 21.1 percent of presidents, respectively, were women. At the doctorate-granting institution, women presidents' 13.8 percent today is up from 13.3 percent in 2001 and 13.2 percent in 1998.

Phillips worries about the pipeline to the presidency, and not just in terms of women. The typical president in 2006 was a white male with a doctorate degree, sixty years old, married, in office for eight-and-a-half years, and previously was a provost or chief academic officer. A massive turnover is expected over the course of the next decade, and the question ACE is beginning to ask now is: Who will be left? Is everyone in the pipeline for the presidency now in the same age group as the soon-to-be retiring presidents? Anecdotally, Phillips says, the answer is yes.

Apparently, there's no time like the present to prepare for becoming a college president. That is exactly what ACE does with OWHE—prepare people in higher education administration through its network system of state chapters and national forums and conferences for top leadership positions. "We do this because higher education, unlike corporate America, does not tend to grow its own," Phillips says. "Very few institutions work specifically at developing males or females within their own institutions with the idea of moving them up. This is not to say that internal candidates never get the position, but that's not the same as having a specific intent to develop people within your institution who can move on."

The paths to presidency for both sexes noted by participating presidents in the "2007 Edition" survey include (1) already serving as a president (21%) (2) serving as provost or chief academic officer (31%) and (3) coming from outside of academia (13%). It's odd that the provostship is still the usual path to presidency, Phillips points out, because provosts rarely do much fundraising—they're busy running the campus. What OWHE often helps women focus on is the finance piece: fundraising, budgeting, and negotiating—the areas in which women are deemed "weak" as a gender when considered for the presidency. Women must provide "visible proof" of their ability to handle money, Phillips says, whether inside the institution—"we recommend that they go to the development office and say, 'I want to learn how to do this' "—or outside through major fundraising as a member of a nonprofit board.

Adding finance to the resume is especially pertinent today: The surveyed presidents report spending most of their time on fundraising, followed by budgeting and financial management. Even with the finance credential, however, women face a tough time being considered during the search process. "One of the things to which I attribute the slow growth rate in terms of women in presidencies is that colleges and universities are on the whole financially strapped right now, and when money gets tight, boards of trustees tend to be even more conservative than they are at other times," Phillips says. "And when they're being conservative, there's still that old stereotype that women don't know how to handle money."

So, what does this all mean for women? *The New York Times* reported in 2007[8] how shaky the top position at most universities is due to the sometimes volatile relationship of the president and the faculty. After the no-confidence vote of the Harvard University faculty for former president Lawrence Summers, faculties across the country have felt the need to have their collective voices heard. The position of president at most universities has become similar to that of a CEO of a company. First and foremost, the pay scale of the position has increased to a point where it is dramatically out of scale with the rest of the faculty. Some university presidents receive more than $500,000 in compensation, putting them more in line with corporate America. Of course, with the high cost of education, the role of president has changed as well. Today's president must not only hire and fire faculty, but must also attract large donors and make sure to keep their institutions on the cutting edge and marketable.

Some women have made it to president and their success will help future generations. But where will women come from to fill the pipeline? The numbers of presidents brought in from outside of academia are dwindling. There are only so many university women presidents, so critical mass and comfort level aren't helping. And while adjunct and part-time professorships may be more attractive to women for their flexibility and to colleges and universities for the savings in salary, benefits, and longevity payouts, the situation does not get women in line for promotion to president.

The need for flexibility once again rears its head—63 percent of women presidents in the ACE's report[9] were married compared to 89 percent of male presidents, and 24 percent of women were either divorced or were never married, compared to only 7 percent for men. It can be argued that the choice is up to the woman, but as Phillips notes, "It's a forced choice as a result of pressures that perhaps don't need to be there." Universities and colleges must revamp their internal structures to support women and men, whether on the faculty side in attaining tenure, or on the administrative side by grooming administrator talent for promotion. If higher education is busy fundraising now, wait until the economics of failing to draw and retain faculty and administrators hit their bottom line.

On the bright side, women's visibility at the helm of some of the country's largest and most prestigious universities helps with role modeling. "If I were a twenty-one- or twenty-two-year-old woman contemplating what I might do and I thought I might want to go into academia, the landscape of opportunity for leadership looks very different from what it did thirty, forty years ago," says Ann W. Caldwell, chair of ACE's Commission on Women in Higher Education and, at the time of her interview, about to retire from her role as president of MGH Institute of Health Professions. Caldwell calls herself "an accidental president," invited to turn around a troubled institution. Then, she was vice president for development at Brown University, where she oversaw a five-year $534 million fundraising campaign, and, before that, she was a vice president at Wheaton College. Although she had turned down initial prodding to accept the president's job, she did finally say yes when told by the board chair, Matina Horner, herself a former college president, "They need a leader. If you know how to lead, you can do this job." Not knowing about healthcare and overseeing a graduate school without having a graduate degree herself, Caldwell relied on faculty to bring her along—and told them so. Mutual trust got them through.

"Women have to be willing to take a risk, to be willing to move away from their comfort zone of what they know and what they're good at," Caldwell says. "I think men are more comfortable doing that than we are. Women always feel as if they have to have every credential, every 't' crossed and every 'i' dotted and then maybe they'll be ready. The truth is, you're never completely ready and you learn while doing. And if you have enough confidence and curiosity and enough faith in the other people you're working with, you might as well take a shot."

So, what will women bring to a higher education presidency? In her first year leading Brown University, Ruth Simmons wasted no time in getting things moving: She restructured the administration for the right support by reshuffling positions and hiring a provost, a new vice president for finance and administration, a new vice president for development, and a first-time vice president for planning physical plant improvements. She secured consensus and approval for a $37 million commitment to increase faculty salaries, increase faculty numbers, and accept students without knowing their financial status. And she was closing in on completion of a complex review of the governance process to ensure all-inclusive, forward-moving decision making.[10]

Caldwell, who through collaboration with her faculty and staff during her tenure doubled enrollment, updated programming, and secured the school's largest gift ever to put toward a $20 million capital project, believes that a different perspective is a woman's greatest contribution to leadership. The diverse group of senior leaders that she worked with at Brown University brought a variety of perspectives to the table, regardless of the issue. "It was a much richer discourse from what I had ever experienced. It's not so much what women bring, but when everyone at the table is the same, I don't think you make as good decisions because you don't have as much input from different backgrounds and experiences to bring to complex and difficult issues."

Interestingly, Caldwell notes that if she had gone through a traditional search process for the Institute presidency, she never would have been chosen. Instead, she knew the board chair through previous work. Which brings us to what may be the greatest stumbling block for women in their aspirations to become president of a higher education institution—the board of governors. We've already mentioned the inclination to cling to stereotypes when times are tough. Couple that with the predominance of white males comprising boards of trustees and fewer women in the pipeline, and there is little ostensible chance for seeing more women leading institutions of higher education. Where women are most representative is in the community college presidency—the very schools with the most diverse boards. So this is something women anywhere can do to help get more women in the lead in higher education—serve on a college or university board and begin to make the changes that will match the faces in the classroom to the face in front of the class and at the head of the higher learning institution.

How does a university improve its recruitment, promotion, and retention of women? It must support an increased number of women in university administration and populate its recruitment committees with more women, as these actions reflect the desire to attract women as serious candidates for these positions. There is a need for greater flexibility in the path to president and, at the same time, for more formal mentoring and guidance structures for women who aspire to academic leadership. Too often, women are tapped only for administrative roles before finishing their tenure track and then no longer have the credential other faculty will find adequate.

There is no reason to wait the decades or centuries that it will take to reach parity in academia. Once again, observers see the collaborative style of women leaders as a plus in higher education and particularly at the college and university level. The need to work with faculty, alumnae, donors, and students is critical to every university's success. This trend will most certainly continue as the women now leading bring a style of consensus building to the table. It's time more women take the positions they have trained for and receive the prominence that accompanies those roles to hasten the change that is so desperately needed.

Just Imagine

More women reach full-professor status and lead universities and colleges across the country, thereby providing role models to the next generation and proving that anything with an education is possible.

CHAPTER 10

Women and Nonprofits: Wage and Donation Gaps

"Giving back is a part of participating. Helping others merely mirrors what so many have done to help us. And we are where we are today not just through our own efforts, but because of the path blazed by those who have gone before us."

—Cathleen Black

The business of nonprofits—and what a growing business it is! Called a growth industry by Action Without Borders, there were approximately a million-and-a-half nonprofits with combined revenues of more than $670 billion in 2006 employing approximately thirteen million Americans. The Bureau of Labor Statistics states that there will be a 10-percent increase in the number of nonprofits by 2010. The motivation behind the growth predictions is increasing layoffs in the private sector. There is also a correlation between the increasing number of nonprofits and the mood that lingered over the country after September 11, when the decision to "do well by doing good" became a mantra across the land in finding work that is meaningful. The response to this frame of mind has been an increase in certificate programs in nonprofit management offered by graduate schools nationwide. What's women's stake in all of this? Nearly half of all foundation CEOs and 70 percent of program officers are women, according to Women & Philanthropy, the nonprofit that promotes women's representation in social change and strives to increase resources allotted to women-and-girls' issues. But don't be fooled by these numbers. There are still plenty of problems to address when it comes to women and philanthropy.

Women have long been a force in the nonprofit world as volunteers, but are only recently moving into leadership positions in these organizations. As has already been noted in this book, during our history, women have done the work needed by society that either wasn't professionalized or didn't require pay. As we fast forward to the 1950s and 1960s, during times of economic growth, the majority of women's work became almost exclusively volunteer. If you had asked me when I was growing up what women did, I would have answered, "Help out at school, bake cookies and cakes for school and church bake sales, teach Sunday school, lead Boy Scout and Girl Scout troops, drive sick people to hospitals, and wrap presents at Christmas time for orphaned children." These are the things my mother did and this was my experience with women's work outside the home. Of course, all of the organizations that this volunteer work was provided to were nonprofits. I later learned that this work had monetary value, just as the work my dad did. The leaders of the nonprofit world were men and were, and are, paid very handsomely for their work. The nonprofit world has always depended on the work of volunteers, and those volunteers have generally been women. But as women have gained the education and experience necessary to lead nonprofits, the issue of equal pay for equal work is most relevant in this sector.

At the top positions of national associations, millions of dollars separate the pay of top male and top female earners. In the 2006 *National Journal* survey of salaries and compensation for national associations, professional societies, think tanks, and labor unions,[1] the highest-ranked woman, at Number Twenty-Four out of the Top Fifty, earned $1.24 million (total salary, benefits, and allowances). The Top Three: "[The late] Jack Valenti, formerly of the Motion Picture Association of America ($11.08 million); Thomas Donahue of the U.S. Chamber of Commerce ($6.78 million); and Craig Fuller, formerly of the National Association of Chain Drug Stores ($3.13 million)," writes Karla Taylor in an *Associations Now* article.[2] As she notes, compare the Number Three male ($3.13 million) to the Number Three female on the Top Ten best-paid women's list, who earned $667,161. Out of the forty-eight CEOs receiving salary, benefits, and allowances of more than $1 million, only two were women.

The same can be said for any career path—law, politics, healthcare and the sciences, nonprofit, and education. Women are perfectly capable of making important contributions but obstacles can either have them fleeing to more accommodating options or compromising their own values in order to make it as a round peg in a square hole.

The message for women today in the nonprofit world is clear: There are plenty of opportunities for you to fulfill your desire to give back and make the world a better place—but don't expect to have your work valued equally with the men who have sacrificed themselves by not going into (or staying in) the private sector where the real money is made. The *National Journal*'s survey confirms that 16 percent, or ninety-five of the five hundred and ninety-seven surveyed organizations, were headed by women. Another significant survey, conducted by the American Society of Association Executives and the Center for Association Leadership entitled the "2006 Association Executive Compensation and Benefits Study," shows that among nine hundred and twenty-five organizations, women held the top job at 38 percent of them, up from 33 percent in the smaller 2004 survey sample of six hundred and fifty-nine organizations. The survey also found that women earned just seventy-two cents for every dollar that her male counterpart received in the smaller associations. So nonprofits, like other professions, are promoting a wage gap. As Taylor writes, ". . . When it comes to running an association, the Y chromosome is worth a lot of money." Today's nonprofit must operate like any well-run business in order to survive, and, naturally, competitive salaries are a large part of that equation.

Why the divide? What we see in nonprofit is exactly what is holding women back in just about every sector. For one—women are holding themselves back. They haven't followed the "right" career path and so they're missing essentials for the top job, or they aren't negotiating their pay, or at least talking about their compensation so the numbers and the outrage can get out there. And then, once again, men have to take some of the blame. They have to get outside of their comfort zone and start giving women a leg up.

The problem, according to Leonard Pfeiffer, managing director of Leonard Pfeiffer & Co., is that women at the top aren't bringing in comparable dollars to their male counterparts because they never have. "Organizations will pay an increase over what you're earning now, but it won't be enormous," he told Taylor. Rather than bring a woman earning $225,000 up to the job's $350,000 salary, he imagines the board saying, "Let's give her a 25-percent bump; she'll be happy, and we'll save $70,000." It's time the men in charge start seeing the inequality they're perpetuating and start valuing the job and the gender fairly. Otherwise, they'll be quite sorry when the majority of nonprofit leaders finally wise up and find better opportunities elsewhere.

The "Daring to Lead 2006: A National Study of Nonprofit Executive Leadership" report[3] revealed that women, who are twice as likely as men to lead a nonprofit, lead less than 50 percent of nonprofits with budgets greater than $10 million. This study also found that women are paid less than their male counterparts in nonprofits of every size. (See Figure 10.1.)

The study surveyed two thousand executive directors in eight cities and learned that 75 percent of the executive directors planned to leave their current positions in less than five years. These executive directors reported frustrations with their boards, their funders, and the lack of support and

Figure 10.1
Nonprofit Executive Leadership

Executive Gender Overall

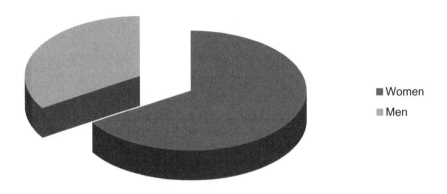

Executive Gender
Over $10 Million

Source: From "Daring to Lead 2006," published by CompassPoint Nonprofit Services (used with permission).

concern for their below-market compensation. Although 26 percent admitted to not having asked for a raise, they believed they could make more in the for-profit sector. Again, it's time women are equally valued before there's a mass exodus. To compound matters, the nonprofit sector must be concerned with the fact that the majority of its leadership is composed of baby boomers, in their fifties, thinking about retirement when there is no succession plan. Without a happy, willing pipeline, what will become of the nonprofit sector in the years to come?

Another study, sponsored by the United Way of Allegheny County and the Bayer Center for Nonprofit Management at Robert Morris University, looked at one hundred and eighty-one nonprofits in western Pennsylvania. It found that women leaders earned $27,861 less than their male counterparts. Studies such as these lead today's very educated, experienced woman to look more closely at the choices she has in both the for-profit and nonprofit worlds. She will need more than a "feel good" reason to pursue nonprofit, particularly if her compensation package does not equal that of her male competitor.

Women's Contribution

Why are women so important at the salaried levels of nonprofits? An interview with Marian Heard, former president and CEO of the United Way of Massachusetts Bay (UWMB), provides an example of how one woman turned around two nonprofits that were in crisis and continues to effect social change at the national level. After getting the Bridgeport, Connecticut, United Way chapter on the road to recovery, Heard moved on to the Massachusetts Bay chapter, which then served eighty communities in Greater Boston. At her start in 1992, UWMB was Number Eighty-Seven in fundraising efforts among United Way chapters across the country. By the time Heard left in 2004, the chapter was nationally ranked Number One among United Way chapters in fundraising, stature, and portfolio of youth and family programs.

The first woman at both United Ways, Heard says her gender never got in the way. "I think, quite frankly, it's been an advantage. I could kiss people without having second thoughts about it," she says with her trademark sense of humor. "I've been told that nobody kissed in Boston until I came, that until then people were all very formal and shook hands from three feet away." But don't think Heard is all good-fun and glad-handing. "I inherited United Ways that needed an extra measure of attention," she says. Whether that attention was restructuring around business principles or ensuring donor "euphoria" over giving, as she calls it, Heard's work drew attention outside of the national United Way. In 1992, then-President George H.W. Bush appointed Heard the founding president and CEO of the national Points of Light Foundation, of which she has been board chair twice and remains a board member today. Then-President Bill Clinton named her CEO of the steering committee of the President's Summit for America's Future, the largest gathering for a single domestic issue in the country's history. She's now involved in MENTOR, a national women's leadership initiative garnering support for the mentoring of more than seventeen million youth across the country.

Deeper empathy, greater quick-decision capacity, and an ability to juggle are some of the characteristics Heard believes women versus men bring to the nonprofit sector. Listening, asking the right questions, and coalescing people around the table are her strategies "that always result in a format, a formula, and a plan for implementation, whether it's fundraising or designing program initiatives." Her leadership style is "what I call the Clint Eastwood form of management: I want to know everything—the good, the bad, and the ugly—and I want to know it now, not necessarily in that order."

Here's another example of what women bring to the nonprofit sector. While national executive director of the American Red Cross from August 2002 to December 2005, Marsha J. "Marty" Evans rebuilt the reputation of the Red Cross during some of its toughest challenges: the hurricanes of 2004, the tsunami of 2004, and then Hurricanes Katrina and Wilma in 2005. Also, Evans was heir to the damage done by damning headlines over giving processes post-September 11 and a tainted-blood scandal.

"We rebuilt systems. We worked on some of the organizational management issues that had surfaced after 9/11, and we rebuilt our capability to respond," Evans says. "To be perfectly honest, I inherited an organization that was flat broken. Public trust was really low. Yet, at the height of Katrina, we had extraordinary public trust rebuilt. We had raised more than $2 billion in the Katrina disasters, and I think of all the large organizations performing in the extraordinary circumstances at Katrina, the Red Cross was the best of all."

Evans ultimately resigned due to differences with the board, but she outlasted her predecessors at an organization that was turning over CEOs, men and women, at the rate of five acting or permanent heads in seven years. She doesn't attribute the problems at the Red Cross or the news coverage surrounding its problems to her being a woman, however. "I don't think there was any media glare because of my gender. The media glare was because of all the extraordinary problems I inherited—all the controversy over 9/11 and the blood issues. It was a matter of how many alligators were trying to get in the boat."

Prior to the American Red Cross, Evans was national executive director of Girl Scouts of the USA. There, she says, "Gender was a real plus. There were men staff members in the Girl Scouts, and I was sensitive to any reverse sexism they might feel." The interesting gender piece of Evans' story is board governance and what women bring to the table when they are the primary representatives on the board. For years, the Girl Scouts had thoughtfully examined governance, Evans points out. "It really is extraordinary, as I think about it in hindsight—how much time and attention was spent on philosophy and concepts of governance. For example, many of the members had local Girl Scout experience but there was great attention paid when one joined the national board to the fact that you were now on the national board and you were responsible and accountable for the Girl Scout movement."

In contrast, Evans points out, a good number of the American Red Cross' board members during her tenure believed they represented their local chapters. "The Girl Scouts long ago started grappling with this issue of balancing local versus national, and they have some of the best publications and programs for local boards as well as new national board members to scope out the subtleties of the different levels of governance." Evans compares her dealings with the Girl Scouts and American Red Cross as "night and day," although she's quick to point out how passionate people were about their missions at both organizations. "We did a lot of management changes [at the American Red Cross], but at a certain point I didn't control the board," she says. "The board was fifty members and chaotic."

The Second Career

One more thing about Marty Evans. She represents a growing trend: Men and women making a second career out of the nonprofit sector. Evans was a rear admiral in the Navy when the Girl Scouts recruited her, and she signed on because she liked the fact that it was an organization about helping girls grow into confident, strong adults, and that she would be the national executive director, and that she could improve what she considered an underperforming organization. Even though fundraising was not part of her job at the beginning, Evans made it so during her tenure in order to leverage a budget beyond cookie sales and membership dues. As much as Evans sees a correlation between the military and the nonprofit—both are volunteer organizations, provide opportunities for leadership management, and have budget challenges that require getting more out of people than money allows—she sees a challenge in terms of getting women's numbers up in nonprofit leadership from this new recruitment pool.

"You see women getting to a certain point and they just go off the career track. They don't want to hang around to gut it out anymore, and I think that's unfortunate to the extent that the future leadership of nonprofits is drawn from the business community. When women opt out and go off the upward mobility track, they're really taking themselves out of the possibility of both the private sector as well as the public sector," Evans says. "On the other hand, I think as women come through the for-profit ranks and they get stopped at the top level C-jobs, there are opportunities to move over to the nonprofit and have as large a scale and scope of responsibility, and maybe it's a little more hospitable."

There is a strong trend of women in their fifties leaving corporate jobs or selling their own businesses to move into the nonprofit sector in order to fulfill a need and lend their business acumen to the business of running a nonprofit. Search firms are working with those whose skills can be transferred to help them succeed in the nonprofit world. As corporate leaders or business owners, these women understand budgets and they have made the connections necessary for fundraising, which is so often the most important qualification needed to lead today's nonprofits.

The important point here is to understand that it is because women have broken the barriers to running large businesses that they have built the reputation needed to make a go of running a large nonprofit. But for the nonprofit sector to fully engage all available talent, women need to win in other areas besides just business to swim in the recruitment pool. Across America, men have built reputations not only in business but also in politics. Across the country, men move easily from a political life with a small salary into a nonprofit life tripling their compensation. The success of many nonprofits is based on the ability of the executive director or president to lobby a particular constituency successfully, a talent the local politician knows well. Once again, most women take a backseat to men as they have yet to make their mark as strong lobbyists. Nonprofit success, like business success, is based on solid connections within the community it operates.

Negotiating the Nonprofit Way

Whether it's a man or woman who takes the job in the local nonprofit after a successful career in business or politics, compensation comes down to negotiating the best package possible. The "Daring to Lead" study confirmed that women lag behind men in negotiating their compensation and responsibilities. I've heard over and over again from nonprofit fundraisers and executive directors that women never, and I mean *never*, negotiate their time, their giving, or their salary. Yet, men do it all the time. Alexandra Friedman, development officer for individual giving at the AIDS Action Committee in Boston, says, "When we ask a man to be on our board or for a particular donation, he immediately maps out what he wants in return. He makes it very clear how his effort for the campaign can be a win-win. Women never do this. I believe this is why they get burnt out or feel that they are being bled dry." Very often, a board member becomes a staff member of a nonprofit. These negotiations must start at the moment of involvement.

Women, listen up! You have a right to negotiate your time, your money, and your work for nonprofits and for-profits. You can't expect to get even unless you do the negotiations work. The wage gap in the nonprofit arena has little chance of ending until women take it upon themselves to demand parity. And since nonprofits are required to make all their financials public, the homework assignment for women before signing on is simple. First, set up a meeting with the executive director and other management team leaders at the organization. Ask questions about the mission of the organization, turnover of staff, and participation of volunteers. Read several years' worth of annual reports so you can gauge the consistency of the leadership and the volunteer involvement. Make sure you don't lose sight of what your needs are because of your passion for the cause. Every nonprofit must run like a successful business to succeed, and part of that success comes from allowing its staff to feel fairly and adequately compensated. Never underestimate the power of negotiation. If you don't ask, you won't get.

Women-and-Girls Programming

It is no less important here—and perhaps in many ways more important as it is essential to have women in the nonprofit sector—for women to be valued equally if the money from the philanthropy spigot is to flow to programs for women and girls. The role of philanthropy in the nonprofit world and the lack of women leading nonprofits and writing the checks all have a dramatic effect on what gets funded. The depressing amount of philanthropy—about 7 percent of every dollar, according to Women & Philanthropy—currently going to programs focused on the needs of women and girls is spotlighted as one of the major reasons women must lead in America and support their sisters. Women's leadership can end the disparity of giving levels in the nonprofit world.

Or so one would hope. The correlation hasn't proved to be true if looking at the 7 percent of giving versus women's representation among foundation CEOs (50%) and program officers (70%). So, what's the disconnect? The characterization of "women and girls" as a task already checked off the to-do list, for one. "There's a feeling, to quote a phrase, that 'we did that,' 'we did women and girls,' 'that problem is solved, '" says Sara Gould, president and CEO of the Ms. Foundation for Women and vice chair of Women & Philanthropy. "And it's looked at as a problem to be solved when, in fact, women and girls are fully 50 percent of the population, so we're not talking about a special interest group or a problem to be solved. We're talking about 50 percent of humanity. Yet there is a feeling among institutions that women have attained equality, so that's the end of the conversation. But, in fact, women have not, first of all, attained equality, and even if we were farther along, I don't think that's the end of the conversation. I think that's the beginning of the conversation."

And then there's the familiar drumbeat heard throughout every chapter in this book: There are plenty of women worker bees but few who are in positions of authority. In the case of the philanthropic sector, the lack of representation shows up somewhat at the CEO level, but more significantly at the trustee-level boards, where women are 25 percent of those sitting around the giving-decision table. There is also a discrepancy when looking at the size of the foundations that women lead. "If you go up the chain of command, there are fewer women," points out Nicole Cozier, Women & Philanthropy's director of programs and planning. "But also, when you look at the breakdown of where these CEOs are located, you'll find that they tend to be in community foundations, family foundations, and smaller foundations. When you look at the assets of these foundations, there again is a drop-off in terms of the representation of women CEOs leading those more-moneyed foundations."

The women-and-girls' equation also gets lost in the diversity discussion, when attention generally shifts to race or ethnicity for donor decision makers. "When women's issues first came out in the 1970s, they were more 'straight forward.' One could say, 'Look, women are 50 percent of the population, but aren't getting their fair share; we need to increase resources,' and make that case," Cozier says. "The issues have become much more complex over the years. It's about more than being a woman, it's about being an African-American woman, it's about being a low-income woman, it's about any number of intersections of experiences. This complexity of issues isn't necessarily reflected in how the field generally goes about moving resources. That's going to continue to be a challenge."

What can be done so women-and-girls' issues see a greater chunk of the philanthropy dollar? Emphasize gender analysis in giving, Cozier suggests. "We have to stop looking at funding women and girls as the 'right thing to do,' even though it still is, and start recognizing that without factoring in how women are impacted by different issues and how women contribute to resolving issues, our efforts are just not going to be effective." In order to catapult more women to the board decision-making level, where, like we've seen on other boards, there's comfort in the old boys' homogeneity sitting around the table, "[t]hat's going to take a major intervention," Gould says. "We do not have the next two hundred to three hundred years that it would take for that to happen naturally, even if it would happen in that period of time. It takes an intervention to really motivate people and move people to do something different than what they would usually do."

Her Part

Because nonprofits must rely on the generosity and community involvement of companies in their region—once again the volunteers with time and money to give—women must succeed in this sector as well as in the for-profit sector. Without women's success, the commitments needed for the causes representing women and girls pay a heavy price.

Teresa Heinz Kerry, chairman of the Heinz Endowments and the Heinz Family Philanthropies, is an example of a woman as the decision maker who understands that she can change women's lives by focusing her foundation's attention on the issues that face them. Her spotlight on such concerns as women's environment-related health issues, women's economic opportunities, and children, youth, and family are making a difference across America. She sees her role as a catalyst in furthering thoughtful advancement. "I look for alternatives. I want to bring people together who might even view each other as enemies. Otherwise, too often, people don't talk. They don't have the whole conversation. This is the disservice I constantly see perpetrated on people's lives. If I can promote conversation and smart decision making that lead toward health and economic stability, that's what I do."[4]

Following are some examples of her action to benefit women.

- Heinz convened the first Conference on Women's Health and the Environment in Boston in 1995. Now an annual event attracting several thousand participants, the organizing themes have included "Women's Health and the Sexual Environment," "Women's Health as We Grow Older," and "Mind Over Media: Women's Health and the Cultural Environment." The 2007 theme, "Women's Health & the Environment: New Science, New Solutions," also went on the road to Pittsburgh for the first time.

- In 1998, the Heinz Family Philanthropies and *Good Housekeeping* magazine launched a collaborative effort to help educate around the importance of savings and retirement security. Heinz established the Women's Institute for a Secure Retirement and created a magazine supplement entitled, "What Every Woman Needs to Know about Money and Retirement." Today, it is available in Chinese, English, Portuguese, and Spanish, with millions of copies distributed nationwide. This same information was also used to create radio public service announcements.

- The Heinz Plan to Overcome Prescription Expenses (HOPE) has provided the basis of a number of states' adoption of plans that offer seniors choosing to participate sliding-scale premiums, deductibles, and co-pays.

"It's more a matter of ideas than work," Heinz says. "I see the ideas coming to fruition, and it's satisfying to know that an intelligent process does work."

To note other examples of women's impact, when they see a need in their community, they can call upon their education and their experiences, and go out and start a nonprofit. I personally have worked with others to form four nonprofits. All are still operating as 501c3s, bringing women together for the purpose of growing their businesses, accessing capital and resources for these businesses, and assisting the local government in identifying qualified women for appointed office.

Lynn Margherio started Cradles to Crayons while she was also negotiating, on behalf of the Clinton Foundation's HIV/AIDS Initiative, a first-ever reduced rate of 50 to 90 percent off the lowest market prices for drugs and tests by working with developing countries and pharmaceuticals and their suppliers. She had been home to visit family at Christmas and noticed all the toys, clothes, and supplies her nieces and nephews had quickly outgrown. The need that she saw to fill was two-fold: The haves needed to find a place for perfectly good items while plenty of have-not kids were going without. Researching her idea just like she would any business plan in her consultancy role, she found that social service agencies, homeless shelters, and hospitals needed help in acquiring donations. The larger organizations that collected clothing typically turned around and sold the items. And, in the cold calls she made, elementary schools, churches, synagogues, day care centers, and nursery schools told her they were ready, willing, and able to put donor and volunteer muscle behind a connecting organization if the needy received the items for free. Today, Cradles to Crayons makes sure that poor and homeless children have everyday basics, from cribs to underwear to books and toys, by filling out individual needs lists with volunteer help. Starting out in Boston, Cradles to Crayons launched in Philadelphia in 2007, the outgrowth spearheaded by a woman who had mobilized volunteers in that city during the Katrina effort. "I don't see why there can't be an organization like ours in every community," Margherio says.[5]

Launching and heading a nonprofit isn't the only role women can play in getting socially responsible efforts off the ground. Martha Crowninshield says she "backed into" her role in supporting the International Multiple Sclerosis Genetics Consortium, which was called "a landmark effort to search for the human genome for genes that put people at risk for multiple sclerosis" by *USA Today*. When we talked with Crowninshield in 2007, the consortium was preparing to submit its findings for peer review publication. General partner emerita of $2.5 billion venture capital investment partnership Boston Ventures, Crowninshield applied basic investment principles to helping secure $15 million for Phase One research. She also personally donated $1 million to the cause. Crowninshield, who has MS, learned about the genetics consortium from an MS physician and research scientist at Harvard Medical School who was involved with establishing the groundbreaking research collaboration.

"I was trying to figure out whether and how I could make a contribution because I'm not a scientist," she says. "And then I realized that many of the people who would make contributions to this kind of cause could benefit from having the proposal outlined in a manner in which they were familiar. It would be like a business proposal in language that they readily understood: What were the timelines, what would the governance be, who would be making the decisions about how the money would be spent, when would you get to go/no-go—what would be those markers? The content was the work of the scientists. My role was to help organize the material using the more traditional language of business so that it would be familiar to the people who would be able to make and be interested in making contributions to the project. At that point, time was of the essence. We needed meaningful donations quickly so that we could get this consortium funded."

The right kind of outreach was necessary to enlist a return on investment based on advancing science for an eventual cure of an illness. The governance piece was important, Crowninshield says, because six institutions are involved: Harvard; MIT; University of California, San Francisco; Cambridge in England; Duke; and Vanderbilt. Now Crowninshield is the founding cochair of the advisory council of the Harvard NeuroDiscovery Center, an innovative collaboration across diseases and laboratories connected with Harvard Medical School.

What women bring to the nonprofit leadership table is exactly what they bring to the other parts of their lives. As Gould says, "To overgeneralize, possibly, women bring a great deal of creativity, they bring the ability to put things together with few resources because that's often the situation they find themselves in, and they also bring a fairly wide view of how a problem can get solved and even what bears on a problem." Finally, it can't be said enough that women bring empathy to every situation and that that characteristic serves the nonprofit world best. The ability to transcend their own reality and for more than a moment understand the world of those they serve is a strength that the nonprofit world relishes.

Follow the Leaders

The nonprofit industry is in need of women role models at the highest level in order for current and future generations of women to see that they can "do well by doing good." Perhaps, Melinda Gates, cofounder of the Gates Foundation, can be just that. In a 2006 interview in *The Wall Street Journal*,[6] Gates speaks out about her role in a question-and-answer session.

WSJ: "How to you, as a woman who is viewed as being reserved, counter the impression that you have been living in Bill's shadow?"

Mrs. Gates: "Ha, ha! I think it's really important for people to understand Bill and I are behind the foundation and it's important for people to understand it's us as a couple ... [A]s our children get older, I decided to speak out more publicly ... [A]s our children start going to school for the first time, the time I have spent at the foundation has increased."

Melinda Gates is well aware of the impact she has on the visibility for women in nonprofits and in running foundations. Her visibility goes a long way to bring women into the forefront of history in leading foundations.

Barbara Lee, who started the Barbara Lee Family Foundation to promote women's political aspirations as well as the contemporary arts, sees herself as a role model for other women to follow as they become the majority of wealth holders in the future. "Role modeling is, in fact, why I decided to be public about my giving and my work, which was a very big thing for me. It would have been easier to be anonymous and quiet, but I believe so strongly that women need role models, that women need to be public about their giving in order to inspire other women to give."

To fill the pipeline, girls need role models, too. Marian Heard, who saw her mother collecting money for everything from the American Red Cross to UNICEF, learned a lesson in giving that didn't sit well at the time but certainly resonates now. "When I was a child, my mother made me baby-sit and not charge when neighbors didn't have the money. It was a concept that was foreign to a child who wanted to earn money."

According to a 2000 survey,[7] 27 percent of high school girls participate in service with volunteer groups through school compared to 18 percent of boys. From an early age, girls are encouraged to nurture, help out, and look out for others, either at home or in formal programming. During Marty Evans' tenure at the Girl Scouts, a Share Our Strength patch was initiated at five different age levels. "For the younger girls, it was the notion of giving and, then, for older girls it was organizing giving. I think people have to learn social responsibility at a young age," Evans says.

A surprise to Cradles to Crayons' Margherio was the community outpouring of volunteerism—particularly in terms of the numbers of families who volunteer together as a way to spend time together. Kids have even requested specific donations on invitations to their birthday parties in lieu of receiving presents themselves. Does role-modeling get any better than that?

Role-modeling also parlays inside the nonprofit, where it's critical to boost women up the chain of command. "I would bet that if you talk to any leader," Women & Philanthropy's Cozier says, "they will say they can identify key people over the course of their careers who took an interest in them and made a difference in how they progressed through their career, the choices that they made and the opportunities they had. We don't institutionalize that enough. It's often left to the individuals. In my own experience, I have been fortunate enough to have people tell me, 'I really want to help you because when I was your age, somebody helped me,' and that's a really important piece to this leadership puzzle. But we also have to recognize that people tend to connect with and support those like them, so this is only one strategy among many that we need."

Writing the Check

As women become more successful and have the means, they naturally turn to writing checks for nonprofits, or do they? Women & Philanthropy's Web site lists various gifts from women in an array of causes, which demonstrates the breadth of women's philanthropic interests. But Sara Gould, Women & Philanthropy's vice chair, questions whether women of wealth actually control their checkbooks. "Women of wealth who grow up with wealth often are told that the management of the wealth is taken care of, that it's in the hands of the advisors. The experience of women with wealth has been that they have been kept from the true control of that wealth and have often had to fight to get control." Adds Women & Philanthropy's Nicole Cozier, "Being a woman doesn't necessarily mean that top of mind is that experiential feeling of, 'I am passionate about women; I need to give to women.' On an institutional level, we have seen that even though there are significantly more women in the field, giving to women and girls has only moved very moderately. On an individual level, women give a lot to their universities, to their churches—things that move them as individuals. These issues aren't necessarily related to gender directly, and so it's important to try to find out how to reconnect these women donors to issues of relevance to women and girls—part of that is identifying and illustrating how the things that do have an impact on women and girls can have an experiential connection with the donor."

Martha Crowninshield believes that women will come around, and soon. As the baby boomers with business backgrounds begin to get involved, she says, they "start looking at these organizations as businesses, bringing transparency to the financials, bringing understanding to what kind of goals funders will want and what funders will want to see. They will begin transitioning their wealth into philanthropy and realize what they can do with their philanthropic efforts."

To help get to the connections that Cozier speaks about, Marian Heard has this advice for nonprofit leaders: "We need to listen and find out where women want to focus. We need to provide enough options and we need to then suggest the appropriate vehicle so they can then fulfill their dreams and wishes." In other words, women will and do write the checks when they see that their philanthropy has impact on something they have a particular interest in.

Finally, Marty Evans says, "If you look at trends in women wealth holders, their giving patterns are different from men's. If you talk to women, it will be this fear of giving away everything and then not being able to take care of themselves carried almost to an extreme. It all boils down to encouraging philanthropy at a young age, and then the other piece of it is designing gift structures like trusts and the legal structures that help take care of one's current needs while at the same time make sure that their requests are structured so that they can leave behind a legacy."

Just Imagine

As the majority of wealth holders in America in 2010 and beyond, women are changing the direction of philanthropy in this country. The programs for women and girls are given equal funding to those earmarked for boys and men. It is not just the money and resources that help raise women-and-girls' issues to parity but also the attention these programs attain that benefit the society at large. The legacy of our society, girls and boys, are the greatest benefactors of our generosity.

CHAPTER 11

When Women Rule: A Woman in the White House

"I guess they're called women's issues because if women did not focus on them, there really wouldn't be any chance of getting them done."

—Nancy Pelosi

It has been eighty-six years since women fought for and won the right to vote. And where are we now? For a gender that tips the balance in terms of numbers, we are nowhere near proportional representation in terms of holding elected offices. In 2007, women's representation in Congress—16 percent—hit an all-time high. That's up from 10 percent in 1992, the year the media declared "The Year of the Woman" because more women ran for and were elected to national office than ever before. Clearly, we have a long way to go to achieve women's constitutional right of equal representation in the political spectrum in America. Why is this? Do we all fall too easily for the media's trap of, "She isn't electable?" In contrast to one popular misconception, electing a woman to the nation's highest office will NOT put everyone at risk because of monthly hormonal changes, poor fashion choices, or delinquent parenting. And if you think I am being too glib here, just ask a group of women or men how they view a particular woman candidate. Unfortunately, the above biases are just some of the ridiculous comments you will hear as to why "she" can't be our next governor, representative, senator, or president.

An example of this is a study The White House Project conducted during the presidential campaign in 1999. The study compared the newspaper coverage of candidate Elizabeth Dole with that of then-Texas Governor George W. Bush, Arizona Senator John McCain, and publisher Steve Forbes, all Republicans running for the White House. Four hundred and sixty-two stories totaling thirty-nine hundred paragraphs were studied from August 1, 1999, through October 20, 1999, from the *Des Moines Register*, the *Los Angeles Times*, the *New York Times*, *USA Today*, and the *Washington Post*. Dole (19.9%) received less coverage than Bush (52.4%) but more than McCain (13.5%) and Forbes (9.7%). The quality of coverage on issues, however, is what is important. Dole received 17 percent of the paragraphs on issues, compared to 33 percent for Bush, 40 percent for Mc-Cain, and 22.5 percent for Forbes. Dole, however, received the majority of personal coverage—35 percent of all paragraphs that included descriptions of her clothes and personality. Interestingly, the research found that Dole was more often paraphrased than the other candidates, 55.5 percent of the time compared to Bush's 44 percent, McCain's 37 percent, and Forbes' 33 percent. The researcher believed that the discrepancy could be attributed to the fact that the gender ratio of the reporters was 65-percent male to 23-percent female.[1]

The point of looking at this research is to show how in politics the perspective of those reporting on the race and its participants has a direct affect on how we the public view the candidates. We cannot dismiss the gender stereotype that permeates our culture. If our attention is focused on some candidate's attire and personality more than it is on the issues, aren't we likely to believe that that candidate is not as serious on the issues? I am not just pointing a finger at the media here. We are all suspects when it comes to judging how a candidate will perform if we base our opinions on traditional stereotypes. So what are we afraid of? What's the worst that can happen if women rule? Can you honestly say that the men are doing such a bang-up job that we wouldn't want to even consider a change? Why is it that twelve (as of this writing) other countries around the world are led by women? What do they know that we in America don't know? Perhaps politics in America is in need of greater compassion and empathy.

Marie Wilson, founder and president of The White House Project, works daily to advance women's leadership in all sectors, including the goal of getting women elected up to the U.S. presidency. The nonprofit, nonpartisan organization provides groundbreaking research on female candidates who have successfully run for office. She thinks that once there are a number of women running for a particular political office, say three or four, then the spotlight will shine on issues and not on gender. Imagine an equal ratio of male-to-female candidates seeking a party's presidential nomination. Imagine no longer hoping for just one woman to run—and then no longer basing women's potential for success on just that one woman. What will convince more women to run for political office? The positive role modeling of more women. To that end, Wilson says, "We also have a special focus on getting female leaders and experts on the Sunday morning political shows. [Our] SheSource provides qualified women for the variety of topics covered by these shows so that other women can see themselves for future elected office."

Barbara Lee, the Barbara Lee Family Foundation's founder and principal, is leveraging the governorship in order to get more women onto the national scene through research and active support. "History teaches us that the pipeline to the presidency runs through the governor's office. Four of our last five presidents served as governors, and voters have shown again and again that they see gubernatorial experience as good training for the top job. Yet, in the entire history of our nation, only twenty-seven women have served as governor," she wrote in 2006.[2] Lee says that it was in 1998 that she began asking how to get more women "above the fold on the front page of the newspaper, and that's usually the president or the governor of your state." That year, ten women ran for governor. The two incumbents retained their seats but the other eight women lost. What she has seen since is that states that do elect a woman governor are doing better at electing women at every level. Also, several states, once a woman has been in its top job, have gone on to elect more than one woman governor. Connecticut (where Ella Grasso became the country's first woman governor in her own right in 1975), Washington, Kansas, and Texas have elected two women as their governors. Arizona has had three women governors.

Jeanne Shaheen, who was elected governor of New Hampshire for three terms until she ran for U.S. Senate in 2002, is now the director of the Harvard Institute of Politics. In her classes she routinely asks students to raise their hands if they want to pursue elective office. While most of the men want powerful positions, very few women raise their hands. "There is no doubt that women running for office face different challenges than men," Shaheen says. "We know that women candidates start by facing an electorate where male voters prefer a male candidate to a female candidate, while women voters are ambivalent about gender. Research also shows that senior citizens, who are the most likely to vote, are the least likely to vote for a woman."

Shaheen is hopeful, however, that with 2007's record number of women governors, record number of women serving in Congress, a woman running for president, and the U.S. House of Representatives being led by a woman speaker for the first time, "the road may be getting a little bit easier." She believes the confidence to run for elective office for her female students can come not only through the classroom but also through leadership in extracurricular organizations at school and on sports teams.

U.S. House Chief Deputy Whip Diana DeGette, a representative from Colorado, sees the same show of hands when she asks the same "running for office" question while talking to high school groups. "I think part of it is because politics has always been a really confrontational business," she says. "And then there are the scandals. I always have people say to me, 'Oh, I would never do that. That seems so dirty,' or, 'I would never want the public scrutiny.' I always say, 'I don't know what you do in your private life, but if you have a normal life, then that's not a problem.' I always try to remind them about the great accomplishments you can make with public policy if you're in elected office."

Making those accomplishments is exactly why DeGette transferred out of a law practice in impact litigation and into politics. While also volunteering on campaigns, she says, "I realized at some point that I could either do law cases and help one person at a time or I could run for office and help people on a much larger scale by passing legislation." In 1992, a twenty-seven-year veteran state senator announced his retirement. DeGette won the seat in a heavily targeted Statehouse race and then became a highly visible leader passing significant legislation. In 1996, when Pat Schroeder, the first woman elected to Congress from Colorado, announced that she was retiring from the U.S. House of Representatives, DeGette was her state's assistant minority leader—additional visibility that helped her overcome a difficult election and win a seat in Washington, where she is now in her sixth term.

What DeGette sees as a key difficulty in getting more women to run for top offices is the age at which they begin their political careers. As noted earlier, when DeGette first ran for Congress, her daughters were two and six. "When I got to Congress, I was one of only a handful of female members who had young kids and, even to this day, ten years later, we still only have a handful of young women with kids. We need to get a bench at the highest levels of Congress and in governorships because we need to have more than just one or two women at that level, and, in order to do that, women have to start running for office when they are younger," DeGette says. "When I came to Congress in 1996, I was thirty-nine years old. I was one of the two youngest women in my class. The youngest man in my class was twelve years younger than I was. A lot of women wait until they raise their families and then they start running for office, and what that means is, by the time they get the seniority and the clout, they're already too old to run on a national ticket."

Wilson also knows that getting women involved also means starting young, and so The White House Project works closely with the *Girls' Leadership Project*, *CosmoGIRL!* and the *Girl Scouts of the USA*. The Project's "Pipeline to the Future: Young Women, Motivation and Success in Political Leadership" survey was conducted by Lake Snell Perry & Associates in April 2000 to gauge young women's interest in running for political office. The study showed that 43 percent of young women say yes to the idea of running even though they admit to viewing politics as rich, old white guy territory. The main turnoff for young women (75%) in getting into politics was that they believed they couldn't make a difference or accomplish their goals. Their perception of local politics was much more positive than that of national politics. Wanting to make an impact on their local community was far more interesting and motivating than effecting change at a national level.

All and all, the findings of the study showed that young women want to help to make their communities a better place to live and will run for office if they are shown that they can make a difference. So the message to young women is to get involved in extracurricular activities leadership, which can be practice for future leadership, and local politics, which can be the stepping stone for a larger campaign. And then it's important to continue following through with the right supports. "It's not just about making the case for why a woman should get your vote," Wilson says. "In the United States, it's also about raising money and knowing the right people to build a campaign."

Show Me the Money

Ah, one of the pieces to the "she isn't electable" conundrum: money. MONEY = INFLUENCE = POWER. The Allianz "Women, Money and Power Study"[3] presents a serious picture of where the wealth lies in America. Women control 48 percent of estates over $5 million and, as noted earlier, by the year 2010 will control 60 percent of the wealth in the United States. So if women have the money, why don't they have the influence that will get them the power? Because they aren't ready to put that money toward women political candidates. Swanee Hunt, Hunt Alternatives president, says, "Like it or not, money talks in political campaigns, and it has become a barrier that has kept many women out of politics. Historically, women have not had the kinds of professional and social networks that men have, although that's starting to change."

In the United States, a political action committee, or PAC, is the name given to a group organized to elect government representatives. The Federal Election Campaign Act states that an organization becomes a PAC by receiving contributions or making expenditures in excess of $1,000 for the purpose of influencing a federal election. The Center for American Women and Politics (CAWP) at Rutgers University reports thirty-six PACs in 2005 that either gave principally to women candidates or boasted a largely female donor base. You can compare that to more than four thousand federally registered PACs with various other focuses and you can easily do the math and comprehend that less than 1 percent of federally registered PACs are vigilant about getting women elected. These donor networks provide the power, money, and influence that are necessary to get the job done.

EMILY's List (Early Money Is Like Yeast) is the nation's largest political network. Its Web site declares that more than one hundred thousand Americans from across the country are committed to their objective of recruiting and funding viable women candidates. Before its founding in 1985, "no Democratic woman had been elected to the United States Senate in her own right." EMILY's List was the nation's largest PAC in the 2006 election cycle, raising more than $34 million, with an average contribution of less than $100. Since its founding, EMILY'S List "has raised over $240 million to elect sixty-seven pro-choice Democrat women to the United States House, thirteen to the United States Senate and eight governors."

Other women PACs focus their attention on Republican women, women in specific states, women minorities, and more. The message from the success of these networks of female donors is that we have only begun the work that must be done to get women elected to national office. As long as money is the answer to getting elected, women of all ages, all backgrounds, and all economic means must participate to ensure women their place in the political structure.

Funding, DeGette concurs, is a tremendous problem for women running for office. "I see that even to this day, where, Number One, women as donors tend to give a lot less money, so a wealthy woman, if I go to her and say I need a campaign contribution, would give me $100 whereas a wealthy man would give me $1,000. And then, particularly, the business community has traditionally not been as supportive of female candidates and that, I think, is just part of the gender issues in our society in general. I remember when I first ran for Congress and I was first elected to Congress, I had a very difficult time getting the business community to even meet with me even though I had been appointed to the Energy & Commerce Committee, which is one of the most important committees to business in the House. I think I've overcome that now, but it took me ten years."

Too often my experience, particularly with businesswomen, has been that they believe that politics is a dirty business—just like DeGette's hearing that it's "so dirty." My answer to this is women have begun to change what they didn't like about the business world by taking the reins and starting their own. It's time we did the same with politics. The longer women allow themselves to stand on the sidelines complaining about our nation's politics, the longer it will take to see change. Getting involved means running yourself, backing a woman candidate, or writing a check. Barbara Lee is one of the women who has put her money to work to make sure more women nationally have the chance to run for public office. Supporting women in politics is as much a part of her philanthropy as is supporting the contemporary arts. "Women need to be thinking about giving and actively devoting their time to politics the way they devote their time to volunteerism and community service," she says.

Too often women don't see the connection between their lives and those that serve them in public office. Perhaps—no, definitely—this will change when women lead the way in public service in state and federal offices. As Nancy Pelosi is quoted at the beginning of this chapter, "They are called women's issues because if women didn't focus on them, they wouldn't get done."

Too Silent a Majority

The organization, Women's Voices. Women Vote (WVWV), conceived of and founded by Page Gardner, who serves as president, provides the research that assists women in reaching out to constituencies too often forgotten. Its February 2006 study[4] provides groundbreaking information particularly regarding married and unmarried women and the dramatic differences in their involvement in the nation's political process. As with everything else in life, knowledge is power, and the research of WVWV is critical to determining how women can affect the outcome of elections in the future.

For example, in the 2004 election, although there was a high turnout in many segments of the population, the study found that five million registered unmarried women did not vote and another fifteen million unmarried women were not even registered. The reason this information is important is that together with unmarried men, who are also less politically active, unmarried people will make up the majority of the heads of households by the 2008 election. In 2004, 65 percent of eligible women voted compared to 62 percent of men, according to the U.S. Census Bureau. Just think what power women will have if all women register! What does this have to do with getting women elected? Everything! This brings us back to networks.

DeGette says, "Women need to start understanding the importance of getting involved in campaigns, and that means taking out their checkbooks and writing the checks but it also means volunteering and helping in other ways. Women need to understand that politics is a necessary way to effect social change and to pass laws that they care about for their families and their communities."

By joining the network, women not only get themselves connected but they also serve as role models for the other women who aren't involved or even registered to vote, and in the process create the momentum necessary for overcoming disinterest and distaste, thereby changing the perception of politics from "dirty" to white-glove clean. The political structure in America goes back to the days before women had the vote and, since then, change has been slow. The current political structure has continued to disenfranchise a majority of our people—whether on purpose or not is not really important. Too many people feel they have no real choice by the time the candidates are whittled down to the party favorites. The political parties themselves are too often reactive rather than proactive and therefore turn the voter off before she or he has an opportunity to get involved.

The nastiness of the campaigns and the media coverage is a clear reason many have chosen not to seek elective office. Massachusetts' only woman governor, Jane Swift, can attest to how difficult it was to be in the media's glare. Elected lieutenant governor in 1998, Swift later became the first and only U.S. governor, albeit acting governor, to give birth while in office. Announcing in December 2000 that she was pregnant with twins, Swift continued with her duties while the media attention swirled. With the support of then-Governor Paul Cellucci, she did what any expectant mother does—she did her job.

The twins were born by the time Swift was acting governor due to Cellucci's appointment to a U.S. ambassadorship. Even though she chaired a meeting of the Massachusetts Governor's Council by teleconference from her hospital bed before even going home with the twins following their birth, the media was relentless in its negative portrayal of a new mother at the helm. Work/family balance became the front-page story regularly in Massachusetts, and every working mother was put on trial. How interesting it is that even women began to question Swift's ability to do her job. Women who work and know plenty of other women who do their jobs admirably with one, two, three, four, and more children allowed the media to question working women in general.

So where was the media attention in June 1994, when John Engler, running for governor of Michigan, announced that his wife was due to give birth to triplets in December of that year? The suggestion that his focus should be on his wife, and home, and family as they prepared for their family to arrive was nonexistent—and dramatically different from the concern that Jane Swift's mind would be off the job before and after the birth of her twins. Certainly we know that giving birth and preparing for birth are two very different jobs. But "pregnant" is not "sick" and "giving birth" does not mean "losing one's ability to work." We deserve the best leaders possible, and leadership qualities cannot be stereotyped.

The qualities that women, and particularly mothers, can bring to the job, and particularly politics, is the understanding that the legislation that is enacted and our diplomacy with others must be in the best interest for future generations. "According to psychologists Felicia Pratto and Jim Sidanius, women are more supportive than men when it comes to people-oriented policies such as government-sponsored healthcare, guaranteed jobs for all, and greater aid to poor children."[5] We cannot live in a vacuum nor can we lead only for the moment.

Breaking the Mold: The Candidate of the Twenty-First Century

First, more women need to come to grips with wanting and being comfortable with power. "One of the big issues is that men jump into a job thinking they can do the job whether or not they have the experience," Barbara Lee says. "Very often, women censor themselves and think that they don't have enough experience when they actually do. One thing we need is to have women promote other women, so when women see a woman who has the drive to make a difference and is ready to commit to public service, women actually need to ask her to run. It's surprising how few women get asked to run compared to men."

Women can get their feet wet by starting from the beginning in politics. Too few women seek local office such as selectman and mayor. The public needs to know their leaders well in order to support them in the long-term. Every state in the union has chapters of organizations like National Women's Political Caucus, National Organization for Women (NOW), League of Women Voters, EMILY's List, WISH List, and more. These multicultural, intergenerational, and multi-issue grassroots organizations were created to increase women's participation in the political process. Chapters of the National Women's Political Caucus work locally to recruit, train, and support pro-choice women in every level of government in the respective state. So if you are someone who has been thinking about political office and, while reading these pages, you're finally fired up to take a step—here are some places where you can find support.

Jeanne Shaheen got her start in politics by volunteering on several Democratic campaigns before running for the New Hampshire state senate in 1990. Politics is open to all walks of life and provides an accessible proving ground within its structure. As such, Barbara Lee believes a very successful businesswoman could run for state treasurer or secretary of state as a way to develop her base of support. Martha Coakley, in preparation for running for district attorney one day, ran for state representative first. Although she lost that race, she says, "I don't regret it for one minute. I learned a lot about politics and how to shake hands and walk into a room of people I didn't know."[6] Coakley, by the way, was elected a district attorney after that trial run and, during her eight-year tenure, established high regard among voters for her tough but fair, thoughtful, and inclusive approach during some of the state's most publicized and troubling cases. The visibility and her skill at handling difficult situations gave voters the confidence to elect her Massachusetts' first woman attorney general in November 2006.

And then, when women are comfortable with seeking power, they have to figure out how to project themselves in a way that is true to their values while still resonating with the voters. "People still perceive women as having one set of qualities and men as having others," Lee says. Women are relegated to the nurturing side of government like education and healthcare— and they do care about these things. Men are seen as the ones who can deal with the hard topics: economics and security. Case in point: Shaheen attributes her 2002 loss and the losses of other women candidates in the Senate and House of Representative races to the prominence of national security, homeland security, and foreign policy post-9/11. "The voters' perception that women are not as tough as men is the most difficult stereotype for women candidates to overcome," Shaheen says. She recommends that women play their strengths and emphasize what they do better than men: build consensus in solving problems and be task oriented in a collaborative and democratic way. "In today's often partisan and polarized environment," she says, "being able to build bridges and reach consensus in solving problems is a critically important skill to have."

Lee believes key qualities for women candidates are dignity, toughness, and authority. Toughness and authority go hand in hand, and dignity is what she calls "grace and grit." The balancing act for women is to overlay a traditional feminine style with being competent, strong, and decisive. The male versus female approach to power was a subject broached during Diane Sawyer's interview of the "Sweet Sixteen" women senators during a January 2007 series on ABC's *Good Morning America.*[7] "I want to point out this is a tough, tough group of women," said Senator Claire McCaskill, a Democrat from Missouri. "Don't [cross] these women if you want to mess with America, if you want to do something that harms our country. I think that, at the same time, we talk about how we are good at finding common ground and we care very much about collegiality."

The Women Who Have Been There

The Sweet Sixteen are exactly what we are in dire need of—more women who can instill the confidence and drive in other women to run for political office, who can do the same for the next group of women until women's numbers exponentially increase at all levels of elected government. Nancy Pelosi, the first woman to lead a major party in the U.S. Congress, couldn't be any more front and center as a role model. Coming from a family of public servants—her father was the mayor of Baltimore for twelve years after representing the city in Congress for five terms and her brother also served as Baltimore's mayor—she has represented California's Eighth District in the House of Representatives since 1987.

Capturing as much attention as Pelosi is now back in 1981 was Sandra Day O'Connor, a former Arizona State Republican legislator who was appointed by then-President Ronald Reagan as the first woman to sit on the U.S. Supreme Court. During her twenty-four years in the country's highest court, she approached cases as narrowly as possible in order to avoid the generalizations that could provide fodder for future cases. Retiring from the Supreme Court in 2006, she continues her involvement in the highest level of government as a member of the Iraq Study Group of the United States Institute of Peace.

Here are other, recent women to emulate. Janet Reno served as the first U.S. Attorney General in 1993. Madeleine K. Albright was the first woman to serve as U.S. Secretary of State when she was appointed by then-President Bill Clinton. She was the highest-ranking woman in the U.S. government, but since she was not born in the United States, she was not eligible to serve as president. Geraldine Ferraro was the vice president on Walter Mondale's 1984 presidential run. Gender was the talk then, just like gender is the talk now. Elizabeth Dole ran for her party's presidential candidate in 2000 to the earlier mentioned sorry press coverage.

Just as important are diverse role models, as America is a melting pot of cultures and does best when young people can see themselves reflected in their leaders. Shirley Chisholm, a New York Democrat, was the first black woman to serve in Congress and she remained in the House of Representatives from 1968 to 1982. In 1972, Chisholm also ran for president, again the first black woman to do so. She died in 2005, leaving a legacy of working to improve opportunities in the inner city and to increase spending on education, healthcare, and other social services. Carol Mosley Braun, an Illinois Democrat, was the first African-American elected to the U.S. Senate and, a senator and an ambassador, she also ran for president in 2004. Condoleezza Rice became the first woman to hold the office of National Security Advisor when she was appointed by President George W. Bush. Elaine Chao became the first Asian-American woman to serve in a presidential cabinet when she was appointed Secretary of Labor.

In a speech given at Brown University on April 8, 2006, Senator Hillary Clinton spoke about leadership, and specifically women's leadership, in America and around the world. She said, "It means standing for what you believe and inspiring others to do the same. Even when people do not agree with you, it is important to decide what you think is right, and you decide how you will pursue the particular perspective that you agree with. Now I know that leadership sometimes carries a cost. It requires standing up for your views even when they are not popular.... I think that as we talk about leadership, particularly at the beginning of this century in our country, there are many challenges that are not easily addressed. There are no easy answers when we think about our position in the world, when we think about some of the problems we have here at home."

Clinton is one more woman who understands that when it comes to leadership, both genders must be prepared and willing for the commitment, and that it will take all of us working together to keep America strong. Speaking to male and female students in this speech, she is quick to point out the importance of standing strong by one's convictions and the importance of one's passion.

She continues, "But I'm very proud of the fact that women are assuming positions of responsibility increasingly here at home and around the world. We are a steady and growing presence. I'm very proud of the fact that women are now earning more than half of the bachelor's degrees awarded in our country, that women own nearly half of all privately held businesses, that in every sphere of life here in America, women are stepping up and being willing to take responsibility for their decisions and their views. And,

I deeply respect the fact that not only in our country, but more importantly around the world, women are exercising leadership at great personal cost. Women are breaking new ground in their efforts to not only articulate but obtain the rights of humanity and citizenship."

Clinton understands better than most women the importance of the delicate balance necessary when women assert themselves and their ideas. For women, confidence is too often seen as arrogance, and assertiveness is too easily viewed as aggression. But she realizes the significance of having women's voices as part of the important conversation that will take place in our country going forward.

So, women have the money, the numbers, their own political structure, and the role models. When are we going to have a woman in the White House? Hunt muses, "Particularly in these times of war and uncertainty, America needs women in leadership positions. In a country as diverse as the United States, a leader's ability to unite is critical. A woman leader will move beyond religious, cultural, racial, and regional differences to find common ground. I feel sure our country is ready for a woman now."

Other countries have successfully elected women to their highest offices: Michelle Bachelet, president, Chile, since March 2006; Ellen Johnson Sirleaf, president, Liberia, since January 2006; Angela Merkel, chancellor, Germany, since November 2005; Maira Das Neves, prime minister, Sao Tome and Principe, since June 2002; Luisa Dias Diogo, prime minister, Mozambique, since 2004; Gloria Macapagal-Arroyo, president, The Philippines since 2001; Tarja Halonen, president, Finland since 2000; Helen Clark, prime minister, New Zealand since 1999; Vaira Vike-Freiberga, president, the Republic of Latvia, since 1999; Mary McAleese, president, Ireland since 1997 (the country's second female president); Chandrika Kumaratunga, president, Sri Lanka, since 1994; and Portia Simpson Miller, prime minster, Jamaica since 2006.[8]

All of these women and thirty-six more are members of The Council of Women World Leaders, an organization of current and former women presidents and prime ministers. Launched in 1998, the council's mission is "to mobilize the highest-level women leaders globally for collective action on issues of critical importance to women and equitable development." Five ministerial networks have been organized: Environment; Finance, Economics, and Development; Women's Affairs; Health; and Culture. Former U.S. Secretary of State Madeleine K. Albright serves as chair of the Women's Ministerial Initiative.

When we speak of women's networking organizations, it doesn't get any more powerful than this group. If you want a visible example of what women can and will do when they rule the world, you'll want to follow the

Figure 11.1

Percentage of Women in Parliament by Country.

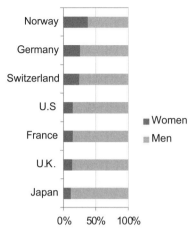

Norway 37.9 percent, Germany 25.3 percent, Switzerland 24.5 percent, United States 14.6 percent, France 14.5 percent, United Kingdom 13.6 percent, and Japan 11.5 percent.

Source: From "The 40-Percent Rule," *Ms.* Magazine (Summer 2006). Used with the permission of *Ms.* Magazine, © 2006.

council and their collective voice on world issues. Their successes individually, nonetheless, remain under scrutiny from our country's perspective as to whether women can truly lead a nation. Irene Natividad, president of the Global Summit of Women, in a *Pink Magazine* article says, "If these women fail, there will be a subliminal perception that women can't cut it, even though their male predecessors couldn't do it either. When it comes to women in politics, the U.S. is not progressive. In the Interparliamentary Union's ranking of countries by the percentage of women in electoral bodies, we're in the middle of the list."[9] (See Figure 11.1.)

It's up to women to unite to make women's political leadership in this country happen. Women must understand what their power is, how to work together to use it, and why it's time to stop whining and take control. Yes, I said it, "whining." First, women must do more to support women candidates with their money. We are fortunate that raising money has not been a problem for Hillary Clinton as she is well entrenched in the political structure that could well make her our first woman president. Second, women must stop holding other women to a higher standard than the men running against them. We are all guilty of this, and you know it. Too often I hear women complain about the woman running for office as someone who is not likeable. We rarely hear the same thing about men. Men know that business and politics are not about "like" but about "getting the job done."

Marcia Angell, in a 2007 *Boston Globe* editorial,[10] pondered how "in polite company, people often insist with a virtuous air that the right thing to do is to vote for the best candidate without regard to gender. But that this is a limited view of what's at stake." We have had forty-three presidents—all have been men. The rest of the world has moved forward with women at the helm, why not the United States? Angell writes, "Here comes Clinton—well qualified, talented, and smart. Why the unease about her? To hear people talk it has nothing to do about gender. What we hear is she is polarizing, opportunistic, too tough (or not tough enough), and finally, that most self-fulfilling of all prophecies, not electable." There it is. She said it. She is not electable. Why? Angell goes on, "All of the parsing of Clinton's personality and policies ignores the elephant in the living room: She *is* a woman, and the first woman with a serious shot at the presidency." Again I ask you, what are we so afraid of?

Having a beer or a glass of wine with a candidate is not nearly as important as making sure that that person represents, and follows through on, your issues. It is a fact that when women are elected, they bring a different perspective and emphasis to the issues that are important to all Americans. For example, in 1999, all U.S. legislators (male and female) agreed that education was the priority issue, yet men named taxes as the second priority whereas women named healthcare. When asked about their priorities in foreign policy in 2000, women legislators were more likely than men to include social concerns such as health, education, fair labor practices, and birth control.[11]

Once again, diverse voices at the table representing a broad spectrum of grassroots interests and concerns are needed to maintain America as the global leader. Throughout the world, women's labor is a key ingredient to the global economy. Women's continued focus on human rights is critical to international alliances in the twenty-first century. If women are to reach a political majority, we must work together and understand that, as former *CNN* reporter Gail Evans says, "Women will have a female president when they want one." Why? Because, according to the Center for American Women and Politics, and as noted earlier, more women vote than men.

I believe that 2008 will be the real year for women, not only because I believe we have the best chance to have a woman president but also because women will work together to make it happen. A 2006 *CBS News* poll[12] showed that 92 percent of American adults would vote for a qualified woman from their political party for president, while a February 2007 *USA Today*/Gallup poll[13] found 88 percent would vote for a "generally well-qualified" woman for president. The results show a continuing increase of support for a woman president from similar polls: 52 percent (1955), to 73 percent (1975), to 82 percent (1987), to the current 90-percent range.[14] So-called women's issues will be on the forefront of the debate, including healthcare, education, and security and safety at home and aboard, whether a woman runs for president or not. Descriptive words such as "compassionate," "empathetic," and "nurturing" will be words that candidates won't want to shy away from. For the first time, women will be proud to be seen as feminine. They will follow the lead of women like the German Chancellor Angela Merkel who, although she did not deliberately call attention to herself as a woman, ran in sharp contrast to her "macho, cigar-chomping predecessor, Gerhard Schroder."[15] Or perhaps, more specifically, women will run on a platform similar to Segolene Royal, France's Socialist party's 2007 candidate for president. She brought attention to her femininity by introducing herself to audiences as the mother of a family of four and announcing that "I want to do for the children of this country what I was able to do for my own children." In her book, *The Truth of a Woman*, Royal argued that a world run by women would be "a less violent place."[16] Or our first woman president could follow the example of Chile's first woman president, Michelle Bachelet, and appoint for gender balance. Bachelet appointed ten women and ten men to her Cabinet and required gender parity in all government appointments.

America is more than ready for a woman. And, I continue to ask you, if not now, when? What will it take to make every woman and man understand that the issues confronting America's future can be artfully addressed by a woman? Women's issues are America's issues: healthcare, education, the environment, and global diplomacy. The question is: What will you do to help?

Just Imagine

More women are in political office, locally and nationally. A woman becomes president. Our daughters, granddaughters, sisters, aunts, and friends finally believe that anything is possible for a woman in America. America's image around the world changes in an instant.

CHAPTER 12

What's in It for Men and Women?

"Women are not going to be equal outside the home until men are equal in it."

—Gloria Steinem

The women's movement has benefited men as well as women since its inception. Each time a door has been opened for women, the men in their lives have joined in their greater satisfaction as complete human beings. More education for women has meant better partners, colleagues, and associates for men. Better working conditions, more attention to equality, and greater focus on outside activities create a more balanced work environment for men and women.

Pride

Men have missed out on the joys of parenting, community involvement, volunteer work, and downtime long enough. It's time for a change in our attitudes toward the sexes. We must each define who we are and who we want to be without allowing the media, our employers, our parents, or the world to do it for us. Society works best when individuals are given their God-given right to the pursuit of happiness and to be all that they can be.

With women ready to assume true partnership at work and at home, quality of life becomes an issue that applies equally to men and women.

By sharing leadership, both benefit. The dream of a better life for our children is as important to men as it is to women. Men have daughters, granddaughters, nieces, aunts, wives, mothers, and female associates, and they wish for every advantage for those they care about. A *CBS News* poll[1] found that the majority (65%) of women today consider themselves feminists and, perhaps more startling, 58 percent of men are comfortable with the title. These men and women responded affirmatively upon hearing this description of a feminist: "Someone who believes in the social, political, and economic equality of the sexes." From my experience, this is not at all surprising. We have reached a time in our history when men and women want what's best for each other. We do not want gender to stand in the way of what we desire as human beings.

My experience has shown me time and time again that men who have daughters really care about the future of women. When I launched *Women's Business* in 1998, one of our first advertisers was a father whose daughter had just opened her own law practice. He bought her a year's worth of advertising. He cared about her success and wanted her to be visible in her industry and among her potential clientele. To this day, ten years later, she is still a regular advertiser. I can't count the number of subscriptions men have bought for their wives and daughters, or how often a husband has nominated his wife for an honor that the newspaper awards. These are true examples of the importance of women's success to the men in their lives. In other instances, I am often asked by fathers to consult with their daughters on getting a new business off the ground or to help their daughters get networked into the community. These men get it. They know that it isn't easy to be successful and that being a woman is one more obstacle to face. They care enough to reach out and ask for help for their daughters, wives, sisters, and female friends. They understand that there are different tracks to success and that the traditional career path is not yet available to most women. So they look for the alternative. They look to those women who have access to the networks they want for the women in their lives to belong to.

On her first interview with Diane Sawyer after becoming the first woman speaker of the house, Nancy Pelosi shared the outpouring of support she had received from men with daughters. They understood that this moment in history meant that their daughters could believe in their dreams and ambitions and relate. It is difficult for men to understand this as they have always had role models. When I grew up in the 1950s and 1960s, father-and-son businesses were everywhere. It was assumed that, if a man had a business of his own and a son, the son had a career path to follow. You rarely heard a story of a dad bringing his daughter into the business. Although,

Christie Hefner, daughter of Hugh Hefner, has not only been successful at Playboy Enterprises but she was also selected by *Forbes Magazine* as one of the "100 Most Powerful Women in the World." Of course, there are many other famous and not-so-famous women who have taken over from a father or a husband in the past, often after a death, and today more likely due to careful planning, and they have been successful at taking the company to the next level. But the majority of family business stories is still one of men bringing their sons into the business and then turning it over to them. They become the role models for others to follow.

With women owning nearly half of all businesses, however, the scenario is about to have a dramatic change. A 2006 Center for Business Women's Research study[2] found that while 91.4 percent of women and men business owners planned to pass their businesses on to their children, women thought of their daughters in their succession plans nearly twice as often as men (37% vs. 19.2%). Men overwhelmingly considered their sons (75.6%), and women thought of their sons slightly more often than their daughters (46.6% of women). Interestingly enough, in companies with revenues of $4 million or more, women are as likely as men to pass the business to a daughter (23.9% overall). (See Figure 12.1.)

The complexity of the mother-and-daughter relationship can be an obstacle but with the current trend of successful women-owned businesses growing, these are obstacles that will be met and conquered. I've personally worked with mother-and-daughter companies to help them talk through the issues that are not typical of other employer/employee firms. My experience revealed the biggest challenge was the "letting go" by the mother. Having worked with other companies with sons and fathers and sons and mothers, this struggle is fairly typical of family-run businesses. Mothers and daughters just tend to have a bit more of an emotional bond that is inclined to get in the way of advancing the agenda. An outside mediator is beneficial for every family-run business. As more and more daughters take the helm at firms, whether from their mothers or their fathers, they will be able to learn from each other the tricks to making it work. The key to achieving a successful transition is about giving children the opportunity at an early age to get a feel for what the work is about.

I remember being involved in the first Take Your Daughter to Work Day in 1993. Not having a daughter, I contacted the Girl Scouts and suggested that we collaborate on a special program in connecting women without daughters to daughters of women who didn't work. In 1993, fifty Girl Scouts came to a meeting of the South Shore Women's Business Network and met with their role models for the day—women who had businesses but no daughters. We listened to a presentation on business

Figure 12.1
Family Members Chosen to Inherit the Business: Percentage Planning to Pass the Business on to a Family Member.

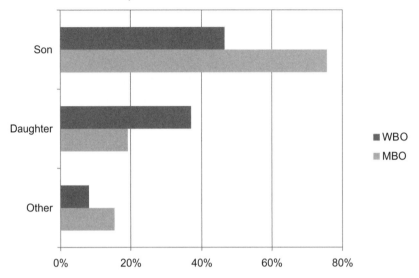

WBO = Women Business Owners; MBO = Men Business Owners.

Source: From "Exit Strategies of Women and Men Business Owners," Center for Women's Business Research (2006), (used with permission).

and then each girl went to work with a member of the group. It was a fabulous opportunity to expose girls to what business is all about and their potential place in it. The Take Your Daughter to Work concept quickly evolved into taking your daughter or son to work so as to be politically correct and inclusive. The opportunity for young children to understand the nature of work is as important today as it was in 1993, or in the 1950s when my dad took me to work with him without the urging of a dedicated day. I learned at an early age what a real estate developer did and what fun it was to watch my dad wheeling and dealing. He inspired me then to think big and always look at the big picture. And, he taught me to believe in myself. That confidence has brought me through every difficulty, every time.

The Simmons School of Management and Committee of 200 study referenced in Chapter 5 proved that the more exposure teens have to business, the more interested they become in pursuing it as a career. The entrepreneurs I have known in my life, both male and female, have often been people who had at least one entrepreneurial parent. Again, role models are critical to how we choose to map out our lives. Surgeon Barbara Rockett, introduced in Chapter 8, and her surgeon husband's five children are an example: Two are doctors (one of whom is married to a doctor), one is considering premed, and one uses his MBA in working with medical groups of doctors; only one is out of the medical field altogether.

I am often asked why it is that women are not forthright at asking for help. Whatever profession they choose, they tend to hold back and think they have to do it all on their own. Men instinctively ask for help and delegate responsibilities from the start. The debate on whether this difference is the result of men having played more team sports than women should be coming full circle since girls have played more team sports since the passage of Title IX in June 1972. It reads, "No person in the United States shall, on the basis of sex, be excluded from participation in, be denied the benefits of, or be subjected to discrimination under any education program or activity receiving federal financial assistance." Girls today have the advantage of learning early on about teamwork. The dramatic success of women on college campuses today may partially be a result of their greater involvement in teams early in life. We are what we learn and what we are inspired by. The important point is that both men and women have daughters and want to believe that they will have equal opportunity to pursue their dreams. Our pride in our children is what keeps us working for a better tomorrow.

Women as Boss

The next generation is already different in many ways from this generation. They are women and men for whom "change is constant, communication is instant. They are more comfortable with globalization and working in different ways, anywhere and anytime," says Catalyst's president, Ilene Lang. The question is: What advice can we give them? Lang relates a story about giving her son some career advice upon his college graduation and realizing something for herself. Remembering the 1967 movie, *The Graduate*, and the significance of the one-word answer to Dustin Hoffman's what-to-go-into dilemma—"plastics"—Lang wanted a similarly catchy answer for her son. This is what she told him, and what she discovered for herself as well: "When I was in business school, people said 'computers,' and they said computers because that was an industry that was desperate for talent in the 1960s and 1970s and they would hire women—and that was really important. But, I don't have a pithy little one-word answer for you. I will tell you to go find a company with a great reputation, where there is integrity in the leadership, where they will train you and invest in your future."

And here is Lang's epiphany: "Lo and behold, my son chose a company with a woman CEO. When I thought about that, I figured out the one word: The one word is 'women.' If you want to find companies that are going to be around forty years from now, the word of advice to the future is 'women'—that's where the competitive advantage comes from, not because women are better, but because companies that develop and advance women are working toward sustainability, because they can include differences, and they can see a world in the future that is different from the past and seek meritocracy comparable with representation, and that's the true measure of a company that is reinventing itself."

Yes, there are advantages for both men and women as they have the opportunity to work for and report to women. It breaks the stereotyping of bosses of the past and provides a new meaning to who sits in the corner office. It can't be said often enough that these gender role reversals, as they may be seen by this generation, will prepare the next generation for gender parity in all situations—paving the way for what needs to be a respect for men in the home. Mr. Mom, Madame President, Ms., Mrs., and Mr. should all be titles of respect. Let's reach beyond the glass ceiling at the office and the linoleum floor at home by envisioning men and women in both places. For the first time in our history we may have the occasion to watch a new role model evolve—that of First Gentlemen. Every first has the opportunity of designing the role for others to follow. I look forward to watching the next generation of men respond to this important role traditionally held by a woman, and making history around the world utilizing the power that this new positioning represents. An ambassador to other countries, the First Gentlemen will speak volumes about equality of the sexes in America.

Family Time

As I speak on college campuses, I find that most young women do not see the challenges that face them as career women. They see themselves able to compete directly with men as they are confident about their education and abilities. They are unfamiliar with the struggles of their sisters from past generations and believe that their performance will speak for itself and get them to where they want to go. They have heard of glass ceilings and old boys' networks but they see only opportunity ahead. Today's young women also know that they have options—the ability to choose what profession to pursue and how high to reach. They feel equally prepared as their male counterparts for the future.

Several years ago I spoke to a group of Boston College undergraduates. They were the elite at the school and had to be selected to be a member of this particular group that invited in business leaders to talk about different areas of business and the opportunities that awaited them upon graduation. As I often do when I speak to students, I told the story of why I started *Women's Business* and how important visibility is for both men and women. As usual, during the question-and-answer period, I was asked many questions about starting a business, getting funding, knowing my market, and balancing it all with a husband and child.

What was most interesting about the session was that the questions about balance came from the young men in the room and not the young women. These young men wanted to know how they could have a business and a family all at the same time. It was clear that their concerns were based on the fact that family meant that someone had to work all hours and someone had to stay home with children. From their experience, the young women in their lives had every intention of having a career. How interesting it is to see life from a different perspective. These young men wanted to know if I believed that they could take paternity leave without it affecting their long-term careers and salaries. Many wanted to know what I thought about stay-at-home dads.

Clearly, the questions on today's students' minds are quite different than when I was in school in the late 1960s. Having a long-range plan of when to get your education, get married, start a family, buy a house, start a business, plan for your children's education, and save for retirement is something both young men and women are thinking about. There is no playbook on just how to do it right, however. When I am asked these questions by young women, and it happens every time I visit a college campus, I generally give my flip answer: "Don't get married if you don't have a boyfriend. Don't have a baby if you aren't pregnant. And if you want to start a business, you better get a day job because that's what will pay the bills." This usually snaps them back to realizing that all of this planning just isn't going to work. Life happens and we must do our best to be prepared to make the most of it.

My point is that, for male or female, the rules have changed and each must go after life with all the vitality he or she can muster. It is interesting to note that right now on college campuses across the country, women are excelling more than ever. From valedictorian to leaders in campus groups, women have found their calling. As their numbers on college campuses have increased, women's power has increased, once again proving there is power in numbers. There is currently an outcry to get males back on track with their education and their outlook for the future. If only this trend taking place on the college campus will catapult itself into the world of work and politics that we have been discussing, then we will see true gender parity with this generation.

I adore watching young fathers with their children and know that today's children will have a better opportunity to see themselves for the future when no boundaries have been placed on what they can or cannot be. And yes, I know as well as you that not all families are made up of a man and a woman. How wonderful it is for a gay couple to have the opportunity to choose between who will have the joy of staying home, or the shared responsibility of juggling child care as they both head out to work.

It is clear that nothing in our society is as simple as it was decades ago, but this is not a reason not to see the bright light ahead. By standing up for equality of the sexes in everything we do, we have the opportunity to do what is best for our children while doing the best for ourselves, whether that means one parent stays home or parents rely on workplaces and government to participate in providing healthy, child-safe environments. Studies show that women-owned firms are more accommodating to parents when it comes to child care or elder care. Women understand better than anybody the demands that are placed on women for the care of loved ones.

With more women running companies, more women in the boardroom providing guidance for human resource departments, more women in politics to focus on social concerns here and abroad, more women leading hospitals or sharing responsibilities in medical groups, more women standing at the front of the college classroom, and more women allocating a nonprofit's funding equally to women-and-girls' to that of men-and-boys' issues, America can strengthen its image in the world and reclaim its leadership status. Men win when their choices are respected and they become positive role models as father, caretaker, homemaker, and cheerleader for their children and others. There are many things we can "do over" in our lives, but reliving our children's childhood is not one of them.

Family Leave/Parental Leave

The question is: why? Why, in the richest country in the world, has so little attention been given to what is best for families? Why, when it is clear that the family structure is in trouble, does the United States and the companies and the organizations in it increase working hours rather than look for greater productivity and effectiveness as other countries have done? So much rhetoric is espoused by politicians about the importance of family values, yet little if anything is done to protect employees from being exploited during the most critical moments in their family's lives. As was mentioned earlier, the United States is embarrassingly far behind other countries around the world, and women and men have been penalized long enough for our leaders not making family life the first priority. In countries such as China and Russia, state-run nurseries have been established, and women have paid maternity leave and a guaranteed job when they return. In Sweden, men and women have a parental leave law in which men are encouraged to participate in order to become more involved in the family—and they are—70 percent of men take advantage of Sweden's parental leave.

Closer to the United States, the Canadian Labor Code entitles female employees a standard seventeen weeks of mostly paid, job-protected maternity leave. The law also grants both male and female employees up to thirty-seven weeks of job-protected parental leave, so there is additional leave, though unpaid, for women, and generous time for men with some pay. Maternity and parental leaves are compensated by unemployment insurance, which consists of fifteen weeks of benefits at 60 percent of the employee's regular wage. All leave benefits are taxable income. This is the federal standard regarding maternity and parental leave laws, but each province can vary. There are conditions of employment, such as six consecutive months of continuous employment with the same employer, before a female can receive the seventeen weeks of absence. The law also demands that when the employee returns to work, he or she is reinstated back to his or her former position with the same wages and benefits. If the position is no longer available, a comparable position must be offered. "Parental leave may be taken any time during the fifty-two-week period starting the day the child is born or, if adopted, the day the child comes into the employee's care," according to the Canadian Labor Code. These are just more examples of countries that put families first.

Limited women's involvement in the decision making at the legislative level has kept America back in this policymaking arena. Recommendations for paid leave were part of both the 1963 President's Commission on the Status of Women report and the 1967 NOW Bill of Rights. As more women reach the highest levels of government, more attention will be placed on what's best for families—men, women, and children. It's time to focus our national attention on what is best for families in America. Clearly, the present course we are on is not working. Work/family balance is a win for men and women. That's why the time for a woman to lead is now.

Equal Pay

The United States continues to have the strongest protections in terms of guarantees for equality. But legislation against discrimination, as we know, does not mean discrimination doesn't exist. The Equal Pay Act of 1963 was passed when women were making an average fifty-nine cents for every dollar a man was earning. Today, that number averages in at seventy-seven cents for every dollar a man makes. Equality is too often in the eye of the beholder, and we now know that this pay gap begins within the first year after graduation from college.[3]

Regardless of hours worked, occupation, parenthood, and other factors typically affecting pay, 25 percent of this early gap was unexplained—and determined likely to be "due to sex discrimination." As we have discussed, the wage gap affects men as well as women. Jobs should not be gender specific, and compensation should relate to the talents and skills needed, not the sex of the participant. Period. The newest census figures show that women earn less than men in every state. The narrowest gap was in Washington, DC, where women earn ninety-one cents for every dollar that a man earns. Women in the finance and insurance industries earn just fifty-five cents for each dollar a man earns. The hope is that as these two industries focus their attention on the women consumer, women in these professions will become more valuable.

The legal profession as well is riddled with inequities. Within all areas of the legal profession, men's median income is $102,272, with women earning slightly less than half that.[4] This disparity puts the legal profession at the head of the class for wage gaps. In a country where every available worker is needed—and more so when the Baby Boomers retire—a wage gap is not just illegal, it is counterproductive. Women supporting families and women without families deserve equitable pay for equitable work. We know well that women generally outlive men and that, although they hold the majority of wealth in the country, they also are the majority of the poor. As our government struggles with how to fund the future of social security and Medicare, the first order of business must be to guarantee an end to the wage gap.

Give Peace a Chance

What do I see with more women at the helm in political positions? Legislation that benefits families, including the enactment of universal healthcare and education rather than incarceration becoming the norm, along with a more humanitarian approach to our country's social problems to transform our inner cities. Globally, women's power would be seen as strength, not because of harsh words or harsh sanctions, but because of a strong middle class and a commitment to peace. The greatest difference between men and women may just be the most important reason why we need more women in government: the ability and desire to build relationships rather than control those around us—diplomacy over tyranny. Anyone who has ever worked for a woman knows well her style is about bringing about consensus and working toward a common goal.

Women nonetheless are very capable of aggression and will fight mightily for what they believe in and when they feel they or those around them have been wronged. But they also understand the importance of peace. Men and women benefit when peace is the major objective. Former ambassador Swanee Hunt says, "Women are adept at bridging ethnic, religious, political, and cultural divides. Through my work as chair of The Initiative for Inclusive Security, I've interviewed women around the world. Particularly in conflict regions, women have proven adept at cutting across international borders and internal divides. Ironically, women's status as second-class citizens has been a source of empowerment, since it has forced women to find innovative ways to address problems."

America's current relationship with many world leaders is tenuous at best. Our longtime standing as the strongest nation on earth and a land of the free where anyone can realize a dream is loosing ground. Hunt says, "Global anti-Americanism is on the rise. America and its leaders need to understand why the world loves and hates us. Bringing more women into decision making could fundamentally change the way America does business. Rather than dealing with North Korea or Iran by severing diplomatic relations, I expect a woman would engage all players at the negotiating table. She can empathize with the experience of being ignored, and thus she'll reach out to others." I respond with: The alternative—the severing of diplomatic relations—is unacceptable and foolhardy.

When women lead in America, the world will take notice and be prepared to work with us on issues common to us all. We Americans have been role models for the world. It's time we make ourselves *better* role models. We live and work in a global economy and therefore, as our planet becomes smaller, every woman and man must consider what is best for all nations and people on the earth. Our humanitarianism and actions toward peace are at a critical juncture in history. We must have inclusive leadership and social responsibility as our mission at home and abroad.

CHAPTER 13

Getting a Place at the Table

"One can never consent to creep, when one feels an impulse to soar."
—Helen Keller

Ten Recommendations

It's time for women and men to take action. But how? What can we do to change the power structure that exists today? I have ten recommendations.

First, every woman must become less judgmental about the other women in her life. We have more in common with each other than with the other gender, and it is our responsibility to educate ourselves to this fact. Every woman knows what I mean when I say this. Every time we criticize another woman for any reason, we lose. We particularly lose if we share our criticism with someone else. Women—be honest. You know that this is true. When you find fault with other women, you present the case that women are faulty—and that includes you. Too often, women criticize other women in the workplace and men view this as the greatest form of disloyalty—a stab in the back. Men know and understand the importance of backing each other up in the workplace in the spirit of being supportive. Women have yet to learn this.

A 2006 *Psychology Today* article makes the case that a woman's worst workplace enemy is another woman. The perception that this is true is just as, if not more, dangerous for women because "it reinforces some inchoate portrait of the woman executive as insecure bitch, easily threatened, overly emotional, less able to focus on achievement because she is preoccupied with squelching young talent."[1] Whether or not this is true, we know that there are fewer women at the top in every profession and every industry, and therefore it seems as though we must compete among each other to get there. The article suggests that perhaps women are disappointed as they have expectations of sisterly cooperation.

The truth is that studies show women at the top are less likely to mentor young women than the men at the same firm. This may be because, once at the top, women feel as though they must spend as much time as possible relating to those in the same position in order to keep what they've fought to earn. I've heard this over the years from senior executive women who felt "playing the game" was more important to their career than bringing in others to watch their backs or join their ranks.

Men very rarely, if ever, criticize another man to others. They keep their thoughts to themselves and let the chips fall where they may. You may think I am being insincere with this opinion, but I promise you, degrading other women will never put you in a good light or help other women succeed. It is true that when she wins, you win. We need more women winning than women losing, as my earlier story regarding Carly Fiorina illustrates. One woman's fall—if it can in truth be called that—must not bring us all down.

Second, career women and women who choose to stay home must find common ground. When books such as *Get to Work*[2] chastise women who choose to stay home to raise a family, they only further the gap that exists between these two groups. Author Linda Hirshman declares that women who choose to stay home have made a meaningless choice. She believes value can only be found in a flourishing life—defined as one that includes a love of work. I believe that a flourishing life can be found at home or at work by both men and women. The fact that our society continues to accept only women in the role at home is what is meaningless. The homemaker role is as important as any other occupation this country has to offer. I've been there. Shame on those who want to find fault with those who find value in creating a home for spouse and children and providing the foundation for a healthy life. There is plenty of tedious work done in so-called work environments that causes the average woman or man to go nuts. Making a bed, cleaning a house, and crafting a meal are not nearly as tedious as some of the tasks one might perform in corporate America—and love of that work, most likely, will not be the motivator.

In other words, it is time we value the work that is done at home—the shaping of the next generation—and accept that there are many ways of doing it. Women and men are capable of nurturing the next generation, and when we as a society demean the chore of raising children, we demean the role itself. Is there a performance review for this job? Ask yourself this—what, if any, performance reviews have you been accustomed to that really took into account the long-term importance of the job? Most performance reviews only take a look at the goals and objectives of the months previous to the review process. The review criteria are generally based on short-term rather than long-term goals. No one can disagree with the fact that parenting is a long-term job, and no performance review early in the process can determine the long-term affect of being present in a child's life. The youngest generation, as I have said time and time again in this book, is everyone's responsibility, and until we really become accountable to this fact, we as a country are hurting ourselves as a world leader. Think about the fact that in the past twenty years, our technology has substantially changed the way we work. Computers, cell phones, PDAs, teleconferencing, and more have allowed work to be done 24/7 anywhere on the planet. Yet, our idea of parenting hasn't changed much. The work/life balance that is so desired just doesn't add into the equation. Women who want to have it all find that they can't do it all at the same time. So what is the answer to this dilemma?

The answer is in my third call to action: Men and women: Don't allow the media, or anybody else for that matter, to define who you are. Hunter, gatherer, assertive, aggressive, CEO, assistant, and on and on. You and only you should decide who you are and what you bring to the table. Leaders are people who know themselves well and go about expressing themselves to anybody and everybody they come across. Leaders are not afraid to stand out in a crowd, to be different, to take risks, or to make mistakes. It's the nonconforming that allows leaders to advance their ideas and be seen separately from others. Women are the perfect nonconforming leaders with their intuitive leadership style.

Remember grammar school, when the teacher picked on the boys time and time again because they were louder and out of their seats repeatedly? (Yes, I once was a teacher). Life isn't grammar school. We no longer have to kowtow to the boys just because they spend so much time out of their seats and in our faces. The true leaders may just be those who are able to restrain themselves and are ready to get the job done. The hip and hollerin' that goes on in movies such as *The Boiler Room* or *Two for the Money* may be fun to watch, but it clearly shows the juvenile side of business at its worst. Are all men really risk takers? It's time you looked behind the curtain to see that the one you think is the all-knowing, all-powerful ruler is just like the little man in *The Wizard of Oz*—a simple man using his tricks to appear great and powerful. Or, in other words, not that different from you and me.

The smoke and mirrors used by too many leaders keep the potential next group of leaders (women and some men) at bay—or have them leaving in droves to make their mark elsewhere. The time is now for men and women to stand up and scream, "I'm as mad as hell and I'm not going to take it anymore!" (Thank you, actor Peter Finch, in the movie, *Network*). We are the richest country in the world and have the greatest resources at our disposal, yet we haven't been able to figure out how to utilize the talents of 100 percent of our population.

Fourth, it is time to demand equality. That means, as a start, quotas for female representation in the boardrooms across America. It is not enough to report annually on the progress that corporations are making in recruiting, interviewing, and selecting women to join them in the boardroom. It is not enough to measure annually the number of women earning their rightful place in the top senior executive positions at America's corporations. It doesn't make sense for us to expect that the next generation of women will watch as this generation of talented women is rejected for these positions and will still want to pursue the dream that ends in disappointment.

So, if we don't change this now, when? As has been pointed out, women are losing ground in the race to the top, and this loss has, and will continue to have, a dramatic affect on how young women perceive their opportunity for corporate success. When Norway boasts 28.8 percent of women on board seats, Sweden 22.8 percent, Finland 20 percent, and Demark 17.9 percent, versus our 14.6 percent, we in America must demand change.[3]

Improving the statistics is not just about performance. It is also about changing the comfort zone's definition. Quotas are the way to show intelligent people year after year that diversity is beneficial, not only for the company's bottom line but also for the shareholders. That will be the tipping point. Without quotas, there will be no urgency and no change. Like water, comfort seeks its own level.

And then we must demand that there be equal gender representation with appointees to state and federal government offices. These are the people who make the laws that govern us all, and women are the majority. Just as our ancestors demanded no taxation without representation, women must demand representation now. We must not allow the press to characterize women as ignorant regarding foreign policy as they did with Geraldine Ferraro. What she told *CBS News* about her 1984 vice-presidency run has every chance of being repeated today, but in a different year, and with a different face: "I had been in Congress not a tremendously long period of time, but I certainly had more knowledge about foreign affairs and other things than Ronald Reagan did when he became president of the United States. So, I was secure. I didn't have a problem with how I would deal with the Soviet Union. But the press did. Ted Koppel did. I mean, I was taking a test every time I went in for an interview."[4]

We have qualified women to fill the positions locally and nationally. We have the vote and the money and now we must use it to put women in power. Yes, I'm asking you, no, begging you, to vote for women. It is the only way women will truly have equal representation in government. You have seen how the dialogue changes when women have a voice in government. A focus on education, healthcare, national security, and equal wage is in the best interest of every American. If not now, when?

We must demand that the White House Women's Office of Initiatives and Outreach be reopened to continue the work it began in the early 1990s. The office, launched by then-President Clinton and directed by Betsy Myers, was established, as Myers said "to provide women a seat at the policymaking table."[5] The office coordinated federal agencies' programs that addressed the interests of women with the women they were designed to assist. Most important, the office provided women a voice and a chair at the table of government. Until true gender equality is reached in American government, women have the right and the need to be heard through a separate office when necessary. Women are the consumers and the voters and the most educated, so they should not have to wait another forty-seven years, or seventy-three years, or two hundred years, or however many more years it will take for the current structures to catch up with what is needed now.

My fifth point: We, men and women, must take it personally that there is a wage gap. If you find that you are not being paid fairly, bring it to the attention of your boss. Often, this is all it takes to have the matter rectified. If you are not taken seriously, you must do the work in your organization to find out if the problem is gender based. You can log on to the WAGE Project, http://www.wageproject.org, and get information to see if you have a case. Or check this site just to read about what other women are doing about wage discrimination. If you are in a leadership position, you can follow Fidelity Investments' Ellyn McColgan's example and ferret out the wage inconsistencies: "I don't know if people look for it like I do. I go to the women's names on the list and I look to see whether or not they are being paid equitably. I have found unconscious inequities in compensation and when I do, I go back and fix them. You look at two people—a man and a woman side by side—and say, they've been here the same amount of time, done basically the same work, so why isn't she making as much as he is? That's not right, it has to be fixed."

Evelyn Murphy, founder and president of the WAGE Project Inc., says she has learned two things since starting the project: "First, I underestimated how hard it is for women to talk about this [their wage]. They need their job and they are afraid of losing it. They have a great fear. They need the paycheck. Second, the dialogue must get started. Women won't act until they talk about it." So I ask you, if not now, when? There is no excuse for a wage gap in our country based on gender. As we have discussed earlier, the wage gap hurts both men and women and must be rectified. Unless we address the discrepancies in pay scale across all industries for gender and race, we, as a society, are not doing the best we can for all our people.

The next generation, Murphy says, are already benchmarking salary and learning to negotiate: "Those already on the job need to get informed about ways to get promoted. Those in mid-career need to gather their allies, talk about what their pay is and how to rectify it. And, finally, professional women, high-earning professional women, have to believe that they have been affected." Take a look. Take a stand. It's never too late. Men and women must stand up when they believe wage discrimination is at work. Getting a place at the table means more than just getting a seat. It means security in knowing that every chair has equal clout.

Sixth, we must understand the importance of women's organizations, supporting them every chance we get, not only with our involvement but also with our checkbooks. Almost every industry has a trade organization devoted to the issues of women in the trade. If you are not a member of your respective women's trade organization, ask yourself why. Too often, I hear from women that they just want to be treated equally by their peers, not as a woman and particularly not as a representative of a women's organization in the industry. Unfortunately, these women do a major disservice to the women who put all their energies into securing a place in history for them in their respective industries—not to mention a great disservice to themselves.

Think about the difference women make in your life every day. Think about the difference a women's organization makes in empowering women to keep at it and fight for every opportunity they can to achieve success. Here's an example of how you can make a difference. TV station owner Diane Sutter, president and CEO of Shooting Star Broadcasting, started a ten-month executive MBA-style broadcast leadership program for the National Association of Broadcasters because so few women and minorities are owners, 5 percent and 3 percent respectively, in contrast to their 50-percent sales staff representation. "It's designed so the people who teach the course are the bankers, the brokers, the venture capitalists. The participants get the relationships that they frequently haven't had access to and, secondarily, they learn. So it's relationships and information that have not been available to them," she says.

I know that once you "get there" it is difficult to reach back and bring others along. Evelyn Murphy told me this six years after she was out of the Massachusetts Lieutenant Governor's Office: "I was so busy watching what was coming at me, I never realized how important it was that I watch my back. I wish I had brought more women up behind me to assist me going forward." Women may get to the top but without the pipeline of women behind them, they are isolated and need to rely solely on their own resources. It's time that the pipeline is filled with women, and that women at the top can depend on those around them to support them. It's time they be part of The Club. It's time for women, instead of fearing that they will be seen as a peculiarity by the shareholders, the market, the customer, the media, and their peers, take their place among the leadership in whatever field they choose to pursue.

Too often, I hear from women that once they get into the male-dominated arena, they fear that bringing other women in will label them as biased. Can you imagine—one woman in a sea of men suggesting that another woman be brought in is seen as bias? If you believe in the power and intellect of women and the importance of diversity, you, woman or man, will want to bring more women to the table. This is the world I want to live in and this is the precedent that America must embrace in order to continue as the world's most powerful country.

Women's trade organizations give credence and visibility to the important roles women play in an industry, particularly in the industries viewed as male territory. The Women's Transportation Seminar (WTS) was founded in 1977 to provide professional and personal advancement and develop industry and government recognition for the increasing involvement of women in the transportation industry. Today, the international organization has more than thirty-nine chapters and forty-five hundred members successfully connecting with women and men and helping to shape a diverse workforce. How many Americans know that Jane Garvey, appointed by then-President Bill Clinton in 1997 to head the United States Federal Aviation Administration for a five-year term, ran the $13 billion organization with fifty thousand employees during one of the most critical chapters in American history, the horrific tragedy of September 11?

Since that day, America has relied on the people involved in the transportation industry to provide the highest level of security and safety. Garvey restored America's faith in air travel after the terrorist attack on our nation and she did it by building consensus and collaboration. Senator John

McCain said, "She's reached out to a lot of segments of the industry and she's done a good job listening to them." Garvey is not only a role model, she has also provided visible recognition that women do succeed in the transportation industry and therefore she has made it easier for others to follow.

President George W. Bush appointed Mary E. Peters the fifteenth secretary of transportation in September 2006. Peters, like Garvey, rose through the ranks of the private and public sectors of the transportation industry for more than twenty years. These are just two of the thousands of women in an industry that is all too often thought of as male-only—all the more reason a trade organization like WTS is so necessary. You see, the pictures in your head about who does what are based on years of media influence, family background, and basic environment. Women have been at the forefront of many arenas—even industries in safety and security. Just because we don't see them reflected often in the media or come into contact with them in our everyday lives doesn't mean they don't exist. This is just one of the many women's trade and/or professional organizations that have been launched to support the advancement of women. It is an example of a women's organization whose mission has helped advance women. Its members span across the country, Great Britain, and Canada and are in charge of roads, bridges, airports, subways, railroads, and all other forms of transportation. Its meetings are attended by women and men, and the networking fosters a comfort factor important to the trade.

Seventh is the visibility factor. I have been asked many times during my ten years in the newspaper business: "If there are so many high-powered, influential women in the region, why don't we see them?" Even my lawyer, when I started *Women's Business*, asked, "What will you do when you run out of successful women to write about?" There is no chance of that. Women are achieving success in every industry every day in this country regardless of the lack of media coverage and despite the obstacles in their way. Your job is to go out and support them. You must hire them, promote them, buy from them, and vote for them. You must, men and women, realize that America is better when we make the most of the talent we have available.

This is especially important for women running for elective office. Statistically, in contrast to the way things used to be, when women run for office—they do win! The Center for American Women and Politics and the National Women's Political Caucus both report that the percentage of women in federal, state, and municipal legislatures has been rising steadily for the past decade. I've given the example of more women holding U.S. Senate seats than ever before in U.S. history. So to "get even," that is, to compete on a level playing field and get the visibility they need, women candidates must be supported with your energy, time, money, and, of course, a check mark next to their name in the voting booth!

And eight, here's a charge for my opposite sex: Men must become more aware of the subtle discrimination that hovers in most office environments. They must then demand that it stop. Men must also mentor more women and help them move upward on the management ladder and the path to leadership. Men and women working together as equals at all levels is the goal.

Management thought leader Tom Peters saw the light after meeting with a group of high-powered women in 1996. "I thought I was as thoughtful as a male can be thoughtful," he says. "I thought I was with the program. I walked out of that meeting a changed man. There was nothing fundamentally emotional about the meeting. They spent three hours telling me tale after tale about the way women were treated as brainless, ignored, on and on by lawyers, bankers, automobile dealers, and everyone in between. I decided to take them at their word and so I started to talk about this stuff within a week. At the end of an hour-and-a-half presentation, I'd be surrounded by two guys and twenty-five women regaling me with more stories of the same sort."

Sexual harassment training must be accepted as a primer on how to work with the opposite sex. There are still many obstacles in the workplace for women and men to work through successfully together. These obstacles cannot stand in the way of having equality as the benchmark for success. Whether it's working together or living together, men and women can and must find conduct that succeeds.

Nine, the push for gender equality must start as early in life as possible. The education of the next generation, both boys and girls, is critical to the success of women's leadership. Gender stereotyping is as harmful for girls as it is for boys, reports Carol Gilligan, author of *In a Different Voice: Psychological Theory and Women's Development.*[6] Walk through any baby department and you'll see onsies stamped with "Princess" in pink and "Stud" in blue. Am I suggesting swapping out these newborn-sized outfits? No. I'm saying, don't buy them at all. Acceptance and encouragement of the innate skills and talents of both sexes is the answer to raising healthy children.

This doesn't discount the value of single-sex activities such as the Girl Scouts or the Boy Scouts, which provide early opportunities to develop leadership skills. Leadership, however, should be a value that's also taught and realized in mixed company, since it is only in the mixed company of women and men that true leadership will advance. Women must get into the mainstream of what has been male-dominated up to now and act with clarity, strength, and vision. In this way, both women and men can work together to ensure that the next generation of women will have an equal and powerful place at the leadership table.

And ten, whether or not we see a woman president soon, the task is clear. We must spring into action. We must recognize talent at all levels and not discount someone because of gender. Men have the right to take care of their children and women have the right to bring home the bacon. Stereotypes from the past will not move us forward. All of the elements are in place for change. We are ready to surpass the political progress of so many of our European and global neighbors and share leadership at every level, not by putting children at risk but by elevating them to our collectively achieved first priority. It's time there be a true balance of power. Yes, I want women to have their 52 percent of power. America is ready for the challenge of new leadership—shared leadership. America is ready for women to lead.

CHAPTER 14

Finally: Woman to Woman

"If particular care and attention is not paid to the ladies, we are determined to foment a rebellion, and will not hold ourselves bound by any laws in which we have no voice or representation."

—Abigail Adams

"If society will not admit of woman's free development, then society must be remodeled."

—Elizabeth Blackwell

"Men are not the enemy, but the fellow victims. The real enemy is women's denigration of themselves."

—Betty Freidan

"You gain strength, courage, and confidence by every experience in which you really stop to look fear in the face. You must do the thing which you think you cannot do."

—Eleanor Roosevelt

"There cannot be true democracy unless women's voices are heard. There cannot be true democracy unless women are given the opportunity to take responsibility for their own lives. There cannot be true democracy unless all citizens are able to participate fully in the lives of their country."

—Hillary Rodham Clinton

It's time to speak directly to the women reading this book. It's time to beg you to take everything you've read and will read to heart—to understand completely that it is up to you and you alone to turn the tide for women in America. What I'm asking you to do is not easy, as you have been conditioned to put yourself and other women second. You have been brought up to be fair and just and to make sure that you never show a sense of bias—until it comes to you and other women. How do I know this? Because you've told me over and over again. When you have an opportunity to make a decision to bring another woman on board, you tell me, "I can't just pick a woman because she is a woman. I have to view the candidate's skills and abilities and choose the best one for the job."

Really? If I asked you to select the best fitting dress you could find, you wouldn't go to the store and try on every single size. You'd go directly to the rack with your size and start from there. In other words, you would automatically narrow your search and in the end you would have successfully chosen the best fitting dress. That's what I'm asking you to do with women. If women aren't selecting women to get ahead, then who will? You know as well as I do that you support women every chance you get when it comes to community service projects, breast cancer awareness organizations, and much more. Why is it so difficult to support the women who aspire to leading roles in our universities, hospitals, foundations, government, law firms, C-suites, and boardrooms? These are the areas where women can and are ready to make a difference. Yes, I know the men you know tell you that there is equal opportunity at the top. The best candidate will be chosen to move forward. So where are the women at the top? Is it your assumption that there really are so few qualified women to lead? You know better.

Deloitte & Touche's Sharon Allen says just the opposite regarding the numbers of candidates for corporate boards, and really, you can substitute just about any leadership position for the business version in her discussion. She says, "Many times you hear, 'Well, there aren't enough qualified women available' and I think that they are just not looking far enough and not throwing the broader net to find them. We've undertaken a series of workshops within our corporate governance service line that we call 'Diversifying the American Board,' designed for external participants. We've had great groups, and they're just a small sampling of people who are interested in participating on corporate boards and don't otherwise have the connections to get into the process. In part, it's a matter of matching up capabilities with opportunities."

It is natural for people to work with people they know, like, and trust. Men are more comfortable with men. Their wives are more comfortable when they work with men. It is up to women to bring more women onto the golf course, into the clubhouse, anywhere where men congregate to ensure they feel comfortable. If you are a woman who enjoys being the token woman in the room, pay attention right now because this is for you. You may think you are being heard. You may think you've broken down barriers but you haven't because you can't change the dialogue or the perspective alone. I've heard too many times from men that when a token woman is asked to suggest someone to join the group, she often chooses another man. Is it competition she fears? Is it jealousy? Is it only seeing what's in it for her and not seeing what can be in it for someone else? I don't have the answer. I only know that the attitude must change. Until we have an equal number of men and women in leadership positions, things will not change. Women will continue to earn the majority of college degrees and stay right where they are—somewhere in the middle—unless you are ready to effect change.

The Number One cry across America in the past decade from career women is that they want to be taken seriously. It tops every survey list of what women want. Go into any bookstore and look at the magazine section. Seek out the Women's Interest section. Is this all you are interested in? How is it possible this section hasn't changed but added more of the same in the past thirty years while you and I have been expanding our horizons? Magazines on fitness, weight control, glamour, celebrities, food, make-up, clothes, gossip, television, and homemaking: Have women no interest in business, politics, education, medicine, law, and more?

Take a moment to talk with the bookstore staff about a new book on leadership for women. They will tell you to look in the Women's Studies section. You'll be told the same thing at the library. "What? No Men's Studies section?" I have asked. The librarian was not amused. Neither was the bookstore manager. Think about how truly seriously women are treated in every aspect of our lives. Think about what you can do about it. Think about what we can collectively do about it.

Ten years ago, my eyes were opened by a minister preaching on the importance of women supporting other women. He compared our journey with that of other immigrant groups in America. But, he stated, "The difference is women do not work to elevate each other. Instead, they put their gender aside and choose to elevate the men in their lives." For a moment, I was indignant. Who did this guy think he was, telling me that I wasn't doing my best to help other women? I continued to listen as he described beautifully the Irish immigration to America during and after the Potato Famine. The anti-Irish, anti-Catholic sentiment at the time pushed the new settlers to form tight communities in major cities and eventually to learn that change could only be made through the ballot box. They focused their attention and work toward government and law enforcement. By the

1850s, they were a major force in police departments in all the larger cities and held ranks all the way up to police chief. Their successful organization placed them at the head of labor unions and politics, and they voted 80 to 95 percent together as Democrats. The election of our thirty-fifth president, and first Catholic president, John Fitzgerald Kennedy, can be attributed to the hard work and determination of this immigrant population. This is an example, the minister explained, of what a group can do to elevate itself to power in this country. The light went on in my head. Of course, women must put women first if we expect to attain true equality. Again, if not women, then who?

Women have been struggling for equality in America since the day they arrived. What has changed is that women can have it now if they would just take it. So what's stopping women? Perhaps this story will help shed some light on how easy it is to gain power. You don't have to be a resident of Boston to know the strength of being a Boston College graduate, known as an Eagle. If you are lucky enough to have gone to Boston College High School (male-only), Boston College, and Boston College graduate school, Triple Eagle status, your future is secure. Don't get me wrong; There is nothing wrong with this. The number of BC alums in the Boston area is staggering, and the networks are therefore very powerful, as they should be. But where are the powerful networks for women? Women have built networks, but none that compare with this example. Do you see how the search is narrowed when one of your own applies? I am not suggesting there is bias here. Just the contrary. These networks exist to provide a leg up for those in them. Every college and university emulates the examples mentioned. Women must create networks that not only support them but also put them in places of power.

When we look at politics, a similar story appears. Many, no, too many people vote the party line out of the assumption that the candidates of one's party are more closely in line with one's values and interests. Of course, in recent years, party lines have blurred and voting for the party doesn't guarantee you anything. Nonetheless, many do it, particularly if they are not aware of a candidate's platform. So where am I leading with this? My survey of one thousand women on the question, "Would you vote for a woman for president in 2008?" gathered the following representative responses.

"I always do my best to vote for the best candidate, regardless of political party or other variable such as gender or race. I would certainly give a woman presidential candidate serious consideration and would vote for her if I felt she was the best qualified among those running, but I wouldn't vote for someone solely based on gender, particularly for president since that office is so very, very important."

"I will vote for a woman president in 2008 only if I think she is the best candidate to deal with the issues that are important to me. I won't vote for a woman president just because she is a female."

"I will if she is a candidate who can articulate a vision, a plan, and take a stand on issues that I believe are important. In other words, I won't vote for her just because she's a woman, but because she is speaking the language of leadership I can support and buy into."

"That depends. I would like to say I will vote for a woman regardless, but in good conscience I cannot just vote for a woman simply because women have been left out of the political leadership. I will need to evaluate the candidates to determine who I believe will cause the least harm to the world."

"I'd vote for the right woman, but not just any woman. I'd love to see a strong female candidate run and win. I've always believed that our only true chance for peace in the world is if we could get the leading women from the war zones and troubled areas around the table and have them create the terms for moving forward. If the mothers, daughters, wives, and sisters put their efforts together, I am confident they would find a creative solution to keep their sons, brothers, husbands, and friends alive and living in peace. We know where the men have gotten us—it is time to give the women a chance."

These are just a few of the responses received. Can you hear the dilemma in the comments above? Women want women to lead, but only the right ones. Do we hold men to this same litmus test? Don't we compromise on our values when we're in the voting booth and are faced with two men candidates, neither of whom fully shares our views? Will the right woman meet my test and your test? Has any woman been able to meet the test of all women? This is exactly what is holding us back! Do you honestly believe that any woman who makes it onto the ballot for president of the United States hasn't proven herself along the way?

It's time for women to lead in America, and only women can truly make it happen. I've said it before and I'll say it again: Women must hire women, promote women, and vote for women. Do it for your daughter, your granddaughter, and the next generation of women. Do it for your son, your grandson, and the next generation of men. Do it for yourself. America deserves the best leadership in the world, and women have struggled far too long and far too hard not to be considered worthy of the task. The decision for women to lead in America is in your hands. The time is now.

Notes

Introduction

1. Catalyst, "2006 Census of Women Corporate Officers, Top Earners and Directors of the *Fortune* 500," (2006).
2. The White House Project, www.thewhitehouseproject.org.

Chapter 1: The New "Problem That Has No Name"

1. Sam Roberts, "51% of Women Are Now Living without Spouse," *The New York Times* (January 16, 2007).
2. Stephanie Coontz, "Marriage, Poverty, and Public Policy," prepared for the fifth annual conference of the Council on Contemporary Families at Fordham University (2003).
3. Diane Sawyer, *Good Morning America* (January 18, 2007).
4. Jennifer Millman, "Why So Few Senior People of Color and Women on Wall Street?" *DiversityInc,* DiversityInc.com (2007).

Chapter 2: Vive La Difference

1. Stephanie Goldberg, "When the Chief Justice Is a Woman," *Perspectives Magazine* (Spring 2005) 13(4).
2. Carol Hymowitz, "Raising Women to Be Leaders," *The Wall Street Journal* (February 12, 2007).
3. "The Importance of Sex—Forget China, India and the Internet: Economic Growth Is Driven by Women," *The Economist* (April 2006).

4. Mickey Meece, "What Do Women Want? Just Ask," *The New York Times* (October 29, 2006).

5. Carol Hymowitz, "High Power and High Heels," *The Wall Street Journal* (March 26, 2007).

Chapter 3: A Look Back to Look Ahead

1. Estelle B. Freedman, *No Turning Back: The History of Feminism and the Future of Women* (Ballantine Books, 2002).

2. Jennifer A. Hurley, editor, *Women's Rights, Great Speeches in History* (Greenhaven Inc., 2002).

3. Corona Brezina, adapted from *Sojourner Truth's "Ain't I a Woman?" Speech: A Primary Source Investigation* (The Rosen Publishing Group Inc., 2005).

4. Stuart A. Kallen, *Women of the 1960s* (Lucent Books, 2003).

5. *Women in the Labor Force: A Databook*, U.S. Department of Labor Bureau of Labor Statistics (September 2006, edition).

6. *CNN News* (January 4, 2007).

Chapter 4: The Time Is Now

1. Allianz Life Insurance Company of North America, "The Allianz Women, Money and Power Study" (August 2006).

2. Elizabeth Woyke, "A Tale of Two Inflations," *BusinessWeek* (March 12, 2007).

3. Warren Bennis, *On Becoming a Leader* (Addison-Wesley Publishing Company Inc., 1989), 113.

4. Dawn-Marie Driscoll and Carol R. Goldberg, *Members of the Club, the Coming of Age of Executive Women* (The Free Press, 1993).

5. Warren Bennis, *On Becoming a Leader* (Addison-Wesley Publishing Company, Inc., 1989), 13.

6. Penelope Patsuris, "The Corporate Scandal Sheet," *Forbes* (August 26, 2002).

7. Leslie M. Dawson, "Women and Men, Morality and Ethics—Sexual Differences in Moral Reasoning," *Business Horizons* (July–August 1995).

8. Martha Burk, "The 40-Percent Rule," *Ms. Magazine* (Summer 2006): 57.

9. Helen Graves, "Digging Deep is DBA for Mother-Daughter Mary O'Donnell-Keon Duggan," *Women's Business* (July 2003).

10. Helen Graves, "Judith Nitsch Sets Groundwork for Big Plans in Construction," *Women's Business* (October 2001).

11. Evelyn Murphy, *Getting Even: Why Women Don't Get Paid Like Men—and What to Do About It* (Simon & Schuster, 2005).

12. Hunt Alternatives, Cambridge, Massachusetts, and Washington, DC.

13. Swanee Hunt, "Let Women Rule," *Foreign Affairs* (May/June 2007).

Chapter 5: "Business as Usual?"

1. Public Accounting Report, "2006 Survey of Women in Public Accounting" (December 2006).

2. Catalyst, "2006 Census of Women Corporate Officers, Top Earners and Directors of the *Fortune* 500" (February 2007).

3. "Forget China, India and the Internet: Economic Growth Is Driven by Women," *The Economist* (April 2006).

4. Jody Heymann and researched by the Institute for Health and Social Policy at McGill University, Montreal, Quebec, Canada, "The Work, Family, and Equity Index," the Project on Global Working Families (January 2007).

5. JacTyne Badal, "To Retain Valued Women Employees, Companies Pitch Flextime as Macho," Theory & Practice column, *The Wall Street Journal* (December 11, 2006).

6. Ellyn Spragins, "Love & Money: I Adore You But Not Your Portfolio," *The New York Sunday Times* (July 7, 2002).

7. Graham Bowley, "Soul Survivor," *Financial Times* (November 11/12, 2006).

8. Julie Creswell, "How Suite It Isn't: A Dearth of Female Bosses," *The New York Times* (December 17, 2006).

9. Patricia Sellers, "It's Good to Be the Boss," *Fortune* (October 16, 2006).

10. *Business Women's Network*, "WOW! 2004 U.S. Women's Market" (2004).

11. Toni Wolfman, "The Face of Corporate Leadership: Finally Poised for Major Change?" *New England Journal of Public Policy* (Spring 2007).

12. Sumru Erkut, Vicki W. Kramer, and Alison M. Konrad, "Critical Mass on Corporate Boards: Why Three or More Women Enhance Governance," Wellesley Centers for Women (2007).

13. Mindy Fetterman, "Best Buy Gets in Touch with its Feminine Side," *USA Today* (December 20, 2006).

Chapter 6: Women Entrepreneurs

1. Center for Women's Business Research, National Numbers, http://www.nfwbo.org.

2. Helen Graves, "There's No Horsing around for Becky Minard and Smart-Pak," *Women's Business* (December 2006).

3. Helen Graves, "Building Community Is Lois Silverman's Dream Come True," *Women's Business* (March 2007).

4. *Fortune* Small Business, "2005 List of Best Bosses" (September 21 2005).

5. Helen Graves, "Circling in on Lifestyle Target," *Women's Business* (November 2006).

6. Hope Williams, "Multiple Careers Can Be Double, Triple (and More!) the Reward," *Women's Business* (August 2003).

7. Helen Graves, "Sue Welch Supplies Sourcing's Next Level Time and Time Again," *Women's Business* (September 2005).

8. Helen Graves, "Spiriting Control, Empowerment," *Women's Business* (November 2006).

9. Center for Women's Business Research, Top Facts, http://www.cfwbr.org/facts/index.php.

10. Deborah Marlino and Fiona Wilson, "Teen Girls on Business: Are They Being Empowered?" Simmons School of Management and the Committee of 200 (Spring 2002).

11. From 2006 FY Women in Management VC Data (Venture One) and 1Q 2007 Quarterly U.S. Financing Report from Venture One and Ernst & Young (used with permission).

12. Helen Graves, "The Battery Gets a Big Boost from Christina Lampe-Onnerud," *Women's Business* (April 2007).

13. Amy Barrett, "This Time It's Mine," *BusinessWeek* (February 16, 2007).

14. Center for Women's Business Research, Top Facts, http://www.cfwbr.org/facts/index.php.

Chapter 7: Legally Blonde

1. Commission on Women in the Profession, "A Current Glance at Women in the Law 2006," American Bar Association (2006).

2. National Association for Law Placement (November 2005).

3. Commission on Women in the Profession, "A Current Glance at Women in the Law," American Bar Association (2006).

4. Lauren Stiller Rikleen, *Ending the Gauntlet: Removing Barriers to Women's Success in the Law* (Thomson Legal Works, 2006).

5. Ibid., 18.

6. National Association of Women Lawyers, "National Survey on Retention and Promotion of Women in Law Firms," Chicago, IL.

7. Ibid.

8. Ibid., 7.

9. Jonathan D. Glater, "Women Are Close to Being Majority of Law Students," http://lawschool.com (posted March 21, 2001).

10. Valerie A. Yarashus and Denise Squillante, "Transition In by Working Out Supports through a Task Force," *Women's Business* (February 2007).

11. Lisa Eckelbecker, "Rikleen Book Details Law Firms' Failure in Helping Women Succeed," *Worcester Telegram & Gazette News* (July 23, 2006).

12. Melissa McClenaghan Martin, "The Gender Gap: Breaking through the Glass Ceiling?" *New York Law Journal* (December 29, 2006).

13. Helen Graves, "Regina Pisa Manages Law Firm with Charge for Change," *Women's Business* (May 2000).

14. Meredith Hobbs, "Wal-Mart Demands Diversity in Law Firms," *Fulton County Daily Report* (July 6, 2005).

15. Ibid.

16. Sue Reisinger, "Female GCs: Short-Term Gains, Long-Term Hope," *Corporate Counsel* (June 21, 2006).

17. Helen Graves, "Katherine O'Hara Perfects Science of Applying Broad Expertise," *Women's Business* (November 2006).

18. Stephanie Goldberg, "When the Chief Justice Is a Woman," *Perspectives Magazine* (Spring 2005) 13(4).

19. Ibid.

20. Ibid.

Chapter 8: Women in Healthcare and the Sciences

1. Estelle B. Freedman, *No Turning Back, The History of Feminism and the Future of Women* (Ballantine Books, 2002).

2. American College of Healthcare Executives, North Franklin, Suite 1700, Chicago, Illinois.

3. Catherine Arnst, "Getting Girls to the Lab Bench," *BusinessWeek* (February 7, 2007).

4. News Office, Massachusetts Institute of Technology, "Leaders of 9 Universities and 25 Women Faculty Meet at MIT, Agree to Equity Reviews," http://web.mit.edu/newsoffice/2001/gender.html (posted January 30, 2001).

5. Paul Basken, "Women Scientists Lag Far Behind Men in Patents, Study Says," *The Boston Globe* (August 4, 2006).

6. News & Information, "Percentage of Women Leading Medical Research Studies Rises, but Still Lags Behind Men," Massachusetts General Hospital, http://www.massgeneral.org/news/releases/071906jagsi.html (July 19, 2006).

7. Susan Youdovin, Helen Eldridge, Anne Camille Maher, and Robin Madell, "The Power Study, Pharmaceutical Company Climate for Women," *Healthcare Businesswomen's Association* (May 1999).

8. Helen Graves, "Deborah Dunsire Moves Cure Impact, Boundaries Forward," *Women's Business* (October 2006).

9. Crispin Littlehales, "Missing: Entrepreneurial Women in Biotech," *Bioentrepreneur* (January 2006).

10. Helen Graves, "Building a Business on Sense of Purpose," *Women's Business* (November 2005).

11. Catherine Arnst, "Getting Girls to the Lab Bench," *BusinessWeek* (February 7, 2005).

Chapter 9: Bias in Higher Education

1. Susan K. Dyer, editor, "Tenure Denied: Cases of Sex Discrimination in Academia," American Association of University Women Educational Foundation and American Association of University Women Legal Advisory Fund (October 2004).

2. Michael A. Baer and Claire Van Ummersen, principal investigators, American Council on Education's "An Agenda for Excellence: Creating Flexibility in Tenure-Track Faculty Careers," *American Council on Education* (February 2005).

3. John Harvard's Journal, "Women and Tenure," *Harvard Magazine* (March–April 2005).

4. "The American College President: 2007 Edition," *American Council on Education* (February 2007).

5. Mary Ann Mason and Marc Goulden, "Do Babies Matter? The Effect of Family Formation on the Lifelong Careers of Academic Men and Women," University of California (2002).

6. Mary Ann Mason and Marc Goulden, "Do Babies Matter? (Part II) Closing the Baby Gap," University of California (2004).

7. Julie Rawe, "Steering Girls into Science," *Time* (February 23, 2005).

8. Karen W. Arenson, "At Universities, Plum Post at Top Is Now Shaky," *The New York Times* (January 9, 2007).

9. "The American College President: 2007 Edition," *American Council on Education* (February 2007).

10. Helen Graves, "Ruth Simmons Positions Change around View of Education's Role," *Women's Business* (November 2002).

Chapter 10: Women and Nonprofits

1. Bara Vaida, "Pots of Gold," *National Journal* (February 10, 2006).

2. Karla Taylor, "Let's Talk about Sex," *Associations Now* (September 2006).

3. Jeanne Bell and Timothy Wolfred (CompassPoint Nonprofit Services), and Richard Meyers (The Meyer Foundation), "Daring to Lead 2006: A National Study of Nonprofit Executive Leadership," CompassPoint Nonprofit Services and the Meyer Foundation (2006).

4. Helen Graves, "Teresa Heinz Sets Foundation for Health, Economic Well-Being, and Choice," *Women's Business* (June 2001).

5. Helen Graves, "Supplying the Everyday Is Essential to Lynn Margherio," *Women's Business* (March 2007).

6. Marilyn Chase, "Melinda Gates, Unbound After Shunning the Limelight She Assumes a More Public Role at Her Global Health Foundation," *The Wall Street Journal* (December 11, 2006).

7. Frances A. Karnes and Kristen R. Stephens, *Empowered Girls. A Girl's Guide to Positive Activism, Volunteering, and Philanthropy* (Waco, TX: Prufrock Press, 2005).

Chapter 11: When Women Rule

1. Sean Aday and James Devitt, "Style over Substance, Newspaper Coverage of Female Candidates: Spotlight on Elizabeth Dole," The White House Project Educational Fund Series: Framing Gender on the Campaign Trail (September 2000).

2. Barbara Lee, "A Woman's Place in the White House," *Albany Times Union* (March 19, 2006).

3. Allianz Life Insurance Company of North America, "The Allianz Women, Money, and Power Study" (August 2006).

4. Women's Voices. Women Vote, "The State of Unmarried America—A Demographic, Lifestyle, and Attitudinal Overview of America's Emerging Majority" (February 2006).

5. Swanee Hunt, "Where Quotas Work," *Los Angeles Times* (October 15, 2005).

6. Helen Graves, "Responsive Representation Is Martha Coakley's Goal," *Women's Business* (January 2007).

7. Diane Sawyer, "'Sweet 16' Women Senators Talk Defense, Obama," *Good Morning America* (January 17, 2007).

8. Hunt Alternatives Fund, Cambridge, Massachusetts, and Washington, DC.

9. Taylor Mallory, "Eleven Female World Leaders," *Pink Magazine* (August/September 2006): 96.

10. Marcia Angell, "Hillary Clinton and the Glass Ceiling," *The Boston Globe* (February 19, 2007).

11. Estelle B. Freedman, *No Turning Back: The History of Feminism and the Future of Women* (New York: Ballantine Books, 2002).

12. "Ready for a Woman President?" *CBS News* poll (January 20–25, 2006).

13. Jeffrey M. Jones, "Some Americans Reluctant to Vote for Mormon, 72-Year-Old Presidential Candidates," *The Gallup Poll* (February 20, 2007). www.galluppoll.com

14. Gallup poll, noted in "Ready for a Woman President?" *CBS News* poll (January 20-25, 2006).

15. Gideon Rachman, "Why Royal Is a Sign of the Feminisation of Western Politics," *Financial Times* (November 18/19, 2006).

16. Ibid.

Chapter 12: What's in It for Men and Women?

1. Poll: Women's Movement Worthwhile, *CBS News* (October 23, 2005).

2. "Exit Strategies of Women and Men Business Owners," The Center for Business Women's Research (2006).

3. "Beyond the Pay Gap," American Association of University Women (April 2007).

4. Christopher Conkey, "Snapshot of America: Who's Richest, Poorest, Where Single Men Are," *The Wall Street Journal* (August 30, 2006).

Chapter 13: Getting a Place at the Table

1. Judith Sills, "Workwise: Catfight in the Boardroom," *Psychology Today* (December 2006).

2. Linda R. Hirshman, *Get to Work: A Manifesto for Women of the World* (Viking Penguin, 2006).

3. Toni G. Wolfman, "The Face of Corporate Leadership: Finally Poised for Major Change?" Women's Leadership Institute, Bentley College (2007).

4. "The Quest to Become Ms. President," *CBS News* (February 5, 2006).

5. Betsy Myers, "A Shortsighted President Shortchanges Women," *The Boston Globe* (April 10, 2002).

6. Carol Gilligan, *In a Different Voice: Psychological Theory and Women's Development* (Harvard University Press, 1982).

Women's Organizations and Resources

American Association of University Women
111 Sixteenth St., NW
Washington, DC, 20036
Telephone: (800) 326-AAUW
http://www.aauw.org

American Council on Education Commission on Women in Higher
  Education
American Council on Education
One Dupont Circle NW
Washington, DC, 20036-1193
Telephone: (202) 939-9300
http://www.acenet.edu

American Medical Women's Association
211 N. Union Street, Suite 100
Alexandria, VA, 22314
Telephone: (703) 838-0500
Fax: 703 549-1205
http://www.amwa-doc.org

American Society of Association Executives
1575 I Street NW

Washington, DC, 20005
Telephone: (888) 950-2723
http://www.asaecenter.org

Catalyst
New York
120 Wall Street, 5th floor
New York, NY, 10005
Telephone: (212) 514-7600
http://www.catalyst.org
San Jose
2825 North First Street
Suite 200
San Jose, CA 95134
Telephone: (408) 435-1300

Center for Women's Business Research
1411 K Street NW, Suite 1350
Washington, DC, 20005
Telephone: (202) 638-3060
http://www.womensbusinessresarch.org

InterOrganization Network (ION) and its Member Organizations
ION: http://www.IONWomen.org
The Boston Club: http://www.thebostonclub.com
The Board of Directors Network (Atlanta):
    http://www.boarddirectorsnetwork.org
The Chicago Network: http://www.thechicagonetwork.org
The Forum of Executive Women (Philadelphia): http://www.foew.com
*Forum for Women Entrepreneurs and Executives/Graduate School of
    Management, University of California-Davis*: http://www.fwe.org:
    www.gsm.ucdavis.edu/census
Inforum Center for Leadership (Detroit): http://www.inforummichigan.org
Milwaukee Women Inc. (inclusive):
    http://www.milwaukeewomeninc.com
Women Executive Leadership (Miami):
    http://www.womenexecutiveleadership.com

Ms. Foundation for Women
120 Wall Street, 33rd Floor, New York, NY, 10005
Telephone: (212) 742-2300

Fax: (212) 742-1653
http://ms.foundation.org

National Association of Women Lawyers
American Bar Center, MS 15.2
321 North Clark Street
Chicago, IL, 60610
Telephone: (312) 988-6186
Fax: (312) 988-5491
http://www.abanet.org

The Committee of 200
9080 North Michigan Avenue, Suite 1575
Chicago, IL, 60611-7540
Telephone: (312) 255-0296
http://www.c200.org

The White House Project
434 West 33rd Street, 8th floor
New York, NY, 10001
Telephone: (212) 785-6001
http://www.thewhitehouseproject.org

Women's Business Enterprise National Council Headquarters
1120 Connecticut Avenue, NW
Suite 1000
Washington, DC, 20036
Telephone: (202) 872-5515
Fax: (202) 872-5505

Certification & Affiliate Relations Office
1506 N. Greenville, Suite 230
Allen, TX, 75002
Telephone: (972) 359-0697
Fax: (972) 678-4689
http://www.wbenc.org

Women & Philanthropy
c/o Council on Foundations
1828 L Street, NW, Suite 300
Washington, DC, 20036

Telephone: (877) 293-8809
Fax: (202) 887-6240
http://www.womenphil.org

Women Presidents' Organization
155 East 55th Street, Suite 4-H
New York, NY, 10022
Telephone: (212) 688-4114
Fax: (212) 688-4766
http://www.womenpresidentsorg.com

Women's Transportation Seminar
1701 K Street, NW, Suite 800
Washington, DC, 20006
Telephone: (202) 955-5085
Fax: (202) 955-5088
http://www.wtsinternational.org

Bibliography

Barnett, Rosalind and Rivers, Caryl. *Same Difference: How Gender Myths Are Hurting Our Relationships, Our Children, and Our Jobs.* New York: Basic Books, 2004.

Bates, Suzanne. *Speak Like A CEO.* New York: McGraw-Hill, 2005.

Bennis, Warren. *On Becoming a Leader.* Addison-Wesley Publishing Company, Inc., 1989.

Boyd, Julia. *The Excellent Doctor Blackwell: The Life of the First Woman Physician.* Sutton Publishing, 2005.

Brezina, Corona. *Sojourner Truth's "Ain't I A Woman?" Speech. A Primary Source Investigation.* The Rosen Publishing Group, Inc., 2005.

Burns, Jennifer Bobrow. *Career Opportunities in the Nonprofit Sector.* Ferguson, an imprint of Infobase Publishing, 2006.

Driscoll, Dawn-Marie and Goldberg, Carol R. *Members of the Club, the Coming of Age of Executive Women.* The Free Press, 1993.

Evans, Sara M. *Tidal Wave. How Women Changed America at Century's End.* The Free Press, 2003.

Fiorina, Carly. *Tough Choices, A Memoir.* Penguin Group, 2006.

Freedman, Estelle B. *No Turning Back, the History of Feminism and the Future of Women.* Ballantine Books, 2002.

Friedan, Betty. *The Feminine Mystique.* W.W. Norton & Company, Inc., New York, 1963.

Heffernan, Margaret. *The Naked Truth, a Working Woman's Manifesto on Business and What Really Matters.* Josesey-Bass, a Wiley Imprint, San Francisco, CA, 2004.

Hirshman, Linda R. *Get to Work, A Manifesto for Women of the World.* Viking Penguin, 2006.

Hurley, Jennifer A., ed. *Women's Rights, Great Speeches in History.* Greenhaven Inc., 2002.

Kallen, Stuart A. *Women of the 1960s.* Lucent Books, 2003.

Karnes, Frances A. and Stephens, Kristen R. *Empowered Girls. A Girl's Guide to Positive Activism, Volunteering and Philanthropy.* Prufrock Press, 2005.

Kipnis, Aaron and Herron, Elizabeth. *Gender War: The Quest for Love and Justice between Men and Women.* William and Morrow Co., New York, 1994.

Mattern, Joanne. *Elizabeth Cady Stanton and Susan B. Anthony: Fighting Together for Women's Rights.* The Rosen Publishing Group Inc., 2003.

McGrayne, Sharon Bertsch. *Nobel Prize Women in Science: Their Lives, Struggles, and Momentous Discoveries* (Revised edition). A Citadel Press Book, published by Carol Publishing Group, 1998.

Miller, Page Putnam. *Landmarks of American Women's History.* Oxford University Press, 2003.

Murphy, Evelyn. *Getting Even: Why Women Don't Get Paid Like Men—and What to Do About It.* A Touchstone Book published by Simon & Schuster, 2005.

O'Beirne, Kate. *Women Who Make the World Worse and How Their Radical Feminist Assault Is Ruining Our Schools, Families, Military and Sports.* Sentinel, 2006.

Petersen, Christine. *Rosie the Riveter.* Children's Press, 2005.

Rhoads, Steven E. *Taking Sex Differences Seriously.* Encounter Books, San Francisco, 2004.

Rhode, Deborah L. *Speaking of Sex: The Denial of Gender Inequality.* Harvard University Press, 1997.

Rikleen, Lauren Stiller. *Ending the Gauntlet: Removing Barriers to Women's Success in the Law.* Thomson Legal Works, 2006.

Ross, Mandy. *The Changing Role of Women.* Reed Educational & Professional Publishing, 2002.

Schafly, Phyllis. *Feminist Fantasies.* Spence Publishing Co., Dallas, TX, 2003.

———. *The Power of the Positive Woman.* Arlington House Publishers, 1977.

Wilson, Marie A. *Closing the Leadership Gap, Why Women Can and Must Help Run the World.* Harvard University Press, 2004.

Index

About the Authors

VICKI DONLAN is Publisher and Founder of *Women's Business* as well as its Web site, www.womensbiz.com, that reaches over 500,000 readers. A regular guest on New England Cable News and a popular speaker at businesses and business networking organizations, Donlan is a founder of the Alliance of Women's Business and Professional Organizations.

HELEN FRENCH GRAVES is the Founding Editor of *Women's Business*. An award-winning journalist, she has written for the *Boston Globe, BostonHerald.com, Community Newspaper Co.*, and the *Brockton Enterprise*.